WHEN JUSTICE FAILS

WHEN JUSTICE FAILS

The David Milgaard Story

Carl Karp and Cecil Rosner

M&S

Canadian Cataloguing in Publication Data
   Karp, Carl, 1954–
     When justice fails

   ISBN 0–7710–4551–4

   1. Milgaard, David.   2. Murder – Saskatchewan – Saskatoon.   3. Trials (Murder) – Saskatchewan – Saskatoon.   4. Judicial error – Canada. I. Rosner, Cecil, 1952–   .   II. Title.

   HV6535.C33S35 1991   364.1'523'092   C91–095391–0

Printed and bound in Canada.

McClelland & Stewart Inc.
The Canadian Publishers
481 University Avenue
Toronto, Ontario
M5G 2E9

Contents

Maps

Preface

Working journalists are often encouraged by their superiors not to express their views in public. By voicing opinions on the news they cover, so the argument goes, journalists exhibit a bias and endanger their objectivity. It follows that the best place for a journalist to sit is on the sidelines, listening to what everyone has to say but never uttering a word.

The problem with this logic is that it overlooks the essential ingredient of objectivity. Objective journalism is more than merely interviewing people and then printing or broadcasting their views. It involves investigating and analyzing a given situation, trying to uncover the truth about it, and drawing the appropriate conclusions. Journalists who begin their investigations with the aim of proving a predetermined thesis, and then express their opinions in support of that thesis, are indeed betraying objectivity and exhibiting bias. But those who set aside preconceived notions and seek out the facts, then arrive at conclusions based on those facts, have no reason to be afraid of expressing opinions in support of their research.

When we first began investigating David Milgaard's case, we had no idea whether his claims of innocence had any validity. If anything, we were sceptical. Many inmates insist they aren't guilty, and it isn't surprising to find a convict's mother standing up for her son, as Joyce Milgaard was. But enough questions had already been raised about Milgaard's conviction to warrant a thorough investigation, and we began our work. Our aim was not to prove his guilt or innocence, but to find out as much as possible.

With each interview and piece of research we carried out, our understanding of the case grew. When we looked at the nature of the police investigation, the prosecution's original case, and the credibility of the Crown witnesses, a pattern

vii

began to emerge. Then, when we examined the facts surrounding another likely suspect for the murder, the picture
came clearly into focus.

The results of all our research are in this book, and we
believe the facts speak for themselves. Even so, we have no
reluctance to state that we think David Milgaard is innocent
and should never have spent the better part of his life in prison
for a crime he didn't commit. It's a conclusion based not on
sentimentality, but on the facts of the case.

If justice has failed David Milgaard, he is by no means alone.
A recent inquiry in Manitoba found that aboriginal people are
routinely discriminated against and victimized by Canada's
criminal justice system. In varying degrees, the situation is
the same for many young people, the poor, and others who are
dispossessed in our society. Milgaard himself was young, poor,
and had a history of defying authority when the Saskatoon
police decided to target him as the main suspect for a murder
they couldn't solve. Throughout his ordeal, money was a significant issue. While he relied on Legal Aid to defend himself,
all the resources of the state were used to prosecute him. And
during his long fight for freedom, he was denied any form of
government assistance to prove that his conviction was
unjust.

There are aspects of Milgaard's case that raise questions
about a wide spectrum of issues in the criminal justice system. How often are innocent people convicted of crimes in
Canada? How often do police pressure witnesses to change
their stories in order to secure a conviction? Is it routine for
police and prosecutors to ignore evidence that raises doubt
about the guilt of someone who has already been convicted? Is
it normal for prison officials to suggest inmates continue to be
incarcerated, even if they suspect those inmates are innocent?
Should admitting guilt be a prerequisite for getting parole?
Should the process of reviewing applications to reopen wrongful convictions be done in secrecy, with no accountability?

It would be wrong to consider David Milgaard's case an
aberration. Rather, it can be seen as an example of a system
that has inherent defects. Barring some fundamental changes

in the near future, there will be many more cases of failed justice in Canada.

We would like to thank all those people who helped make this book possible, primarily those who granted interviews and provided information so that the story could be told. The encouragement and assistance some people offered is especially appreciated. We extend our thanks to Marv Terhoch, James Adams, Dinah Forbes, Gord McFarlane, Bruce Rapinchuk, and David Wolinsky, among others. Most of all, we thank David Milgaard himself, for having the courage to persist in telling his story until people finally listened.

1

The Murder

The sun was beginning to edge its way over the Saskatoon skyline as Mary Alice Marcoux stepped from her front door and started walking to school. It was a Friday, the last day of January 1969. And it was bitterly cold. Radio weathermen were advising people to take precautions if they went outside. The temperature was hovering at minus forty, and a thick ice fog was straddling much of the city. Human skin could freeze in a matter of seconds if exposed, the weathermen warned.

For eleven-year-old Mary, there wasn't much choice about being outside. Her Grade 6 teacher at St. Mary's School didn't expect a little cold weather to deter students from attending class. A blizzard was one thing, but freezing cold was no excuse, especially for the hardy kids of Saskatoon, who seemed to relish every second of winter. Besides, Mary was a patrol. The other kids were counting on her to be at her post. So Mary bundled up and headed out the door. It was 8:25 a.m.

Nothing seemed out of place in Mary's older west Saskatoon neighbourhood that morning. Lights were on in nearly all the homes as the large, working class families readied themselves for the day. While kids scurried to school, their parents – many of them descendants of East European immigrants who had populated the prairies after 1900 – struggled to

11

get their cars moving so they could drive to work. Others rushed to the bus stops on 20th Street for the trip downtown. There was the usual buzz of activity in the area's run-down rooming houses as well, a favourite residence for young working people and students who were attracted there by the cheap rent.

Mary lived about four blocks from school and could take a number of different routes to get there. In a hurry to get to her patrol duties, she decided on an unusual path that day. Mary walked down the block from her house on Avenue N to 21st Street and cut through a T-shaped alley, not far from a funeral home. She tried to keep up a brisk pace as the cold penetrated her clothing. Visibility was poor on account of the fog, but Mary could see about half a block ahead of her as she made her way up the alley.

From the corner of her eye, Mary spotted a black cloth coat at the side of the alley. As she moved closer, she saw there was more than just a coat lying in the snow. It was a woman's body, stiff and motionless, face down. The woman's auburn hair was mussed and matted with snow. Her arms were bent at the elbow, her hands under her body. The snow all around the body had been trampled, and red spots were clearly visible in several areas.

As she surveyed the body and silently wondered what to do, another neighbourhood child appeared on the scene – nine-year-old Matthew Hnatiuk. Mary quickly dispatched him back home to tell his mother what they had discovered. Matthew did as he was told. The boy's mother walked through her backyard into the lane and glanced at the body. Fearing the worst, she sent Mary to the nearby Westwood Funeral Home, while she rushed back inside her house and called police. Terry Michayliuk, the funeral home's assistant manager, came out and inspected the body. He tugged at the woman's shoulder and tried speaking to her, but there were no signs of life. Racing back to his apartment on the lower floor of the funeral home, he called for an ambulance. That task accomplished, he returned to the scene and covered the woman's body with a blue blanket.

At 8:40 a.m., an urgent message came crackling over the Saskatoon police radio. A woman's body had been found in the alley behind the 200 block of Avenue N, in the Pleasant Hill district of the city. Detectives John Parker and George Reid picked up the call on their car radio and were at the scene within ten minutes. Parker, a seventeen-year veteran with the police force, removed the blanket covering the body. He picked up the woman's right hand and found that it was frozen. He checked the pulse. She was dead.

"It appeared that a scuffle had taken place there," Parker said afterwards. "There was an indication that the body had fallen in the snow, and also there were patches of blood."

Within the next hour a platoon of city police officers arrived at the scene. The entire area was secured, and bystanders were prevented from disturbing any of the physical evidence. With painstaking detail, the police recorded every fact that seemed relevant in and around the lane. While a police photographer struggled to operate his equipment in the freezing cold, the woman's body was turned over. Only then did the grisly nature of what had happened to her become clear to everyone present.

It was obvious there had been a vicious attack on the young woman. Her three-quarter-length cloth coat, with its fur-trimmed cuffs and collar, was unbuttoned. The clothes underneath were crumpled at the waist. Her dress and under-clothes had been forcibly pulled down. Her right boot was missing, but her right foot was still in a white mesh stocking. Bloody cuts and wounds were evident on her throat and stomach.

It was also clear the attack had met with a measure of resistance. The woman's fists were still tightly clenched.

Police made another observation in those first few moments. The victim's dress was actually a white uniform. Attached to the uniform was a nursing assistant's button from Saskatoon's Institute of Applied Arts and Science. And just below that was a name badge reading "Miss G. Miller."

Before noon, police had a positive identification of the victim. She was Gail Olena Miller, a twenty-year-old nursing assistant at City Hospital. Her body had been found a block from her home, a rooming house at 130 Avenue O.

Gail Miller's friends remember her as a very pleasant, basic small-town girl. She was originally from Laura, a farming village southwest of Saskatoon. With nine children in the family, the Millers constantly struggled to make ends meet. For many of the kids growing up in Laura, especially the girls, there wasn't much to look forward to after high school. Most got married, settled down in the countryside, and began raising families themselves. As Gail was finishing her schooling, she wondered if there wasn't something more to life.

Gail was extremely close to her grandmother. She shared all her private moments with her. With high school drawing to a close, her grandmother took Gail aside and offered to pay her way through a nursing assistant's course at the technical institute in Saskatoon. Gail jumped at the opportunity. It was her dream to work in a hospital and help care for people, especially children and babies. She enrolled in the one-year class at the institute's Kelsey campus, and rented a room in Saskatoon. In September 1967, Gail was on her own in the city.

Living alone in Saskatoon was a novelty for her, but she enjoyed it. The course was intensive, and she had little time for social life, but her friends said she didn't mind. She had a shy, quiet personality and was never much for going to parties and socializing. It's not that she wouldn't have attracted her share of boyfriends, friends said. She was petite, with soft blue eyes and attractive features, and was meticulous in maintaining her appearance. She would often get up an hour early to make sure her makeup was just right.

Besides, Gail already had a boyfriend from her area back home. His name was Les, and she had had a crush on him for a long time. Gail's friends never could determine how much that affection was reciprocated. Les would occasionally visit her in Saskatoon, and sometimes they would meet when she went home on the weekends.

In January, Gail was one of a dozen students sent to Swift

Current Union Hospital for the practical segment of the course. She lived in residence with the other girls, hardly ever going out. Her roommate there, Orlee Lehne, remembers that they hardly ever had spending money. On the rare weekend when they stayed in Swift Current, their most adventurous outings involved going downtown and buying groceries to take back to the residence – an infraction of residence regulations. Most weekends, though, Gail would go to Orlee's aunt's place near Swift Current or return to Laura. She would go to church whenever she returned home on the weekends, Orlee recalls.

Gail remained intensely devoted to her family and talked about them constantly. At Christmas and on other special occasions, she made sure she bought presents for her five sisters and three brothers. It was a financial burden, but it was something she had to do.

The nursing residence in Swift Current was a target for some of the young male students in the area. Boys were always calling up and asking the nursing assistants for dates, usually to be rebuffed. There were also a number of peeping Tom incidents. Most of the girls took it in stride, but friends remember that it unnerved Gail. One day she looked up to see a man peering through her dormitory window. She became hysterical, and was upset by it for a long time. It led to a discussion among all the girls about protecting themselves. Some made sure they carried nail files or other home-made weapons just in case. Orlee remembers how Gail reacted to the inevitable question of what they would do if they were ever seriously attacked. "She said she would die first before she was ever raped."

With the fall approaching, the students began looking for permanent positions in area hospitals. There was an opening on the children's ward at Saskatoon City Hospital, and Gail applied. She was thrilled when she got the job. It meant she could spend all day doing what she loved – caring for babies, taking their temperatures, giving them baths, and helping the registered nurses on the ward.

Each evening Gail returned to her dingy one-room apartment in the boarding house. She told friends she didn't really like the place and intended to move at the first opportunity. What she disliked most of all was having to take the bus to work each morning, especially in the winter months when it was still dark outside.

Vicky-Lynne Fontaine was one of Gail's fellow students who also landed a job at the City Hospital's children's ward. She remembers a conversation they had on January 30, 1969, a day before the fatal morning. "There was a murder the day before in Buffalo Narrows, an axe murder, and we were talking about that at work. It was on the news. We were talking about going to work in pitch dark. She commented that she didn't like going in the dark. She was nervous about it."

The murder Fontaine remembered was actually a series of seven axe murders – one of the most vicious and infamous incidents in Saskatchewan history. It happened early in the morning on January 30 in Buffalo Narrows, about three hundred miles northwest of Saskatoon. A nineteen-year-old man went on a rampage with a long-handled fire axe, slaughtering six members of a family and a house guest. The children, aged nine, six, five, and three, were killed as they lay in their beds.

Everyone in Saskatoon was talking about the incident later in the day, and Gail was no exception. She thought back to the peeping Tom incident and started to worry more than usual about walking to the bus stop alone. One of her friends recalled Gail saying that if there were deranged attackers on the street, they might be attracted by the white panty hose the nursing assistants wore as part of their uniforms. Though she was small, Gail was sturdily built and strong. She was sure she could defend herself if she had to.

The next morning, Vicky-Lynne Fontaine reported to work at the normal 7:30 a.m. starting time. Gail was scheduled to work the same shift, and Fontaine expected to see her at any moment. An hour went by, then two. Gail was not there and hadn't reported in sick. Fontaine started to feel uncomfortable.

"It was unusual because you don't just not show up and not phone," she said. "Some time went by and then I was called to the personnel office. There were two men there, asking me all these questions. I remember thinking: Boy, do they ever make a fuss about someone who doesn't phone in. I knew nothing of what was happening. Then they asked all about her boyfriend and anybody she had contact with. I thought this was hospital policy. They were detectives, but I didn't actually realize it at the time. They didn't tell me till we were on the way to St. Paul's Hospital what we were going for. I was so naïve I didn't dare even ask any questions. Then on the way over they told me there had been a body discovered. I didn't even think it could be her."

Police detective Parker took Fontaine to Room 3 of the emergency ward at St. Paul's Hospital. That's where she saw her friend Gail Miller for the last time.

"I couldn't believe it. I remember thinking: No, how could anybody sneak up on her, just after her mentioning the day before that she didn't feel comfortable walking to the bus in the morning? How could this happen?"

While police continued to scour the scene, a pathologist performed an autopsy on Gail Miller. His findings confirmed that she had been the victim of an uncommonly brutal attack.

Dr. Harry Emson counted fifteen wounds to the front of her neck and upper chest. Some were just superficial cuts, while others exposed her underlying muscle tissue. The attacker must have held a knife to his victim, slashing her with the sharp edge. If that had been the extent of the injuries, Gail Miller would have survived.

But Emson found twelve more wounds, the result of a knife being plunged into her body. Miller had been stabbed four times in the front, four times in the back, three times around the collar bone, and once in the side. Each of the wounds was about three inches deep, and just over half an inch in width. At least two of the wounds had penetrated the chest cavity and injured the right lung, leading directly to her death.

The state of Miller's clothing strongly suggested she had been raped. Emson analyzed the sperm in the body and concluded that intercourse must have occurred within the twelve-hour period before his examination – in other words, sometime after 5:00 a.m. that day. But the pathologist was unable to find any physical evidence of forced intercourse. This anomaly only fuelled speculation among the investigators. Perhaps she was attacked by a rapist, put up fierce resistance, and was stabbed in a frenzy. Others suspected it might be the work of a jilted boyfriend. There was an even more macabre theory, one which the Crown would later hint was an explanation for how a sex act could occur in forty-below weather. The attacker, it was suggested, might have killed his victim first and only then embarked on the sexual attack.

For his part, Emson wouldn't speculate on why there was no evidence of forcible intercourse. But he noted that the attacker was clearly threatening her with a knife, and that this would have had an effect on what had happened. "It depends on the degree of resistance the girl would have put up," he said. "She was a young healthy girl. If she had wished she could have resisted very strongly."

As to the theory that Miller was unconscious or already dead when the sexual attack occurred, Emson was blunt. "It is a possibility. There is no anatomical evidence to prove or disprove it."

Back at the scene of the murder, police were collecting more evidence. The spot where Miller's body was found was saturated with blood to a depth of about a foot. Once her body was removed, a careful inspection of the site was made. It didn't take long for the apparent murder weapon to be found – a blood-stained knife blade. It was a paring knife type of blade, sharpened on one side, about three and a half inches long and five-eighths of an inch wide. All of the wounds on Gail Miller's body could easily have been made by just such a blade.

A few steps away, another officer spotted an indentation in the snow. He took a shovel and pushed it in, quickly uncovering Miller's other boot and a woman's sweater that had been turned inside out.

As the officers swarmed around the area, their frustration grew. They had a body and what looked like the murder weapon, but little more. In the likely event that the attacker wore gloves, there would be no fingerprints. It would be some time before they could determine whether any useful physical evidence would be available. Because of the extremely cold weather the snow was much like sand, making it impossible to discern footprints. Nor was there evidence of tire marks in the alley. No one in the neighbourhood had seen or heard the attack take place.

One aspect of the case ultimately became crucial – the timing of the murder.

Police determined that Miller likely left her second-floor apartment around seven that morning. A university student who lived on the third floor of the same rooming house told them she had seen Miller between 6:35 and 6:45 a.m. "I was on my way back up to the third floor to my suite and she had just come out of her door," the student said. Miller was dressed, and her hair was combed. All that remained was for her to put on her boots and coat. The student said Miller started work at 7:30 a.m. and generally left the house at 7:00 a.m. to catch her bus, about a block and a half away at the corner of 20th Street and Avenue O.

The autopsy revealed that Miller had been dead for about an hour before being discovered, putting her death sometime around 7:30. From all the evidence at hand, it appeared Gail Miller was attacked and killed between 6:45 and 7:30 that morning.

By the end of the day, police had a great deal of information about Gail Miller's death. They knew the exact location of each cut and the approximate time she had suffered the fatal wound. They had a good idea of the time she had left her apartment, and the route she would have travelled to get to her bus stop. What they did not know, and were anxious to learn as fast as possible, was the reason she had been killed, and who had murdered her. No effort would be spared in their search.

2

The Investigation Begins

Gail Miller's murder caused a sensation in Saskatoon. In a city that had seen just one homicide in the last two years, it was front page news. It's questionable whether the Saskatoon police department was fully prepared to handle a case that didn't lend itself to a straightforward solution. The department didn't even have a separate homicide division, so the case was turned over to the special investigations section. But it soon became the concern of every senior officer, including the chief.

The killing struck a sensitive spot in the public's consciousness. With a population of about 125,000, Saskatoon had long since shed its small-town mentality and was striving to take its place alongside other major Canadian cities. But the brutality of the slaying generated the kind of fear that's unleashed when a killer is on the loose in a small village.

Within hours of the news reports, rumours began to fly that the streets weren't safe to walk and that similar incidents were happening all over town. Those rumours became so intense that after a few days police had to deny them publicly. Superintendent Jack Wood, head of the department's detective division, told reporters that all such rumours were fictitious. At the same time, he said a number of women who had recently been indecently assaulted and had not pressed charges or reported the incidents were now coming forward. For many women in Saskatoon, the reluctance to report a rape or sexual assault had been overridden by the fear that a crazed attacker could strike again.

Police took other measures, which they believed would avoid spreading further panic in the community. Even though they issued a prompt release regarding the murder, with details of how Miller had been stabbed, they insisted she had not been raped. Memories were still fresh of a case years earlier in Saskatoon when a nurse was killed and her body dumped by the riverbank. That brutal murder had never been solved.

There was another important fact that police weren't eager to publicize – a fact that would have spread further alarm in the community. Two women who lived in the same area as Miller had been sexually attacked just months before she was murdered. In both cases, the attacker wielded a knife and dragged his victims to a nearby alley or yard. The similarities between the attacks and the Miller murder were obvious.

Hunting for physical evidence in the dead of a Saskatchewan winter has its own dynamics. Police brought gas-powered snow melters to the scene in an effort to uncover more clues. Over the next few days, neighbours began assisting in the search as well. Scattered about the area, in backyards and near trash cans, they found a pair of surgical scissors, a comb, the keys to Miller's apartment, and a maroon-coloured knife handle. Laboratory tests later confirmed that the handle and the blade found under the body were from the same knife. But on none of the articles could fingerprints be discerned.

It appeared the attacker had rummaged through Miller's purse looking for money, randomly throwing away objects that were of no value to him. It would seem logical that he would then have discarded the purse itself, whether he found money or not. Yet there was no sign of it in the immediate area.

In an attempt to solve that puzzle, one of the detectives assigned to the case decided to follow a city garbage truck on its route through the neighborhood three days after the murder. Sure enough, at the back of a house on 20th Street, close to the murder scene, a purse tumbled out of the garbage can before it was unloaded onto the truck. The detective seized it and found that it belonged to Gail Miller. Again, no fingerprints.

The snow-melting operation turned up another knife not far from the body. It was a double-edged, bone-handled hunting knife. Police took the knife to residents in the immediate vicinity to determine if it belonged to anyone. No one claimed it. Then, in a mysterious twist, the knife was lost. It was never produced at the preliminary inquiry or at the trial.

Police began interviewing everyone who might have known something about the murder. They learned that Gail Miller was well-liked and had no real enemies. Her friends and acquaintances, including her boyfriend back home, were rapidly eliminated as suspects, as were a variety of other people she might have met in the neighbourhood.

A local newspaper summed up the situation at the time: "Police said they were up against a stone wall as to clues or a motive."

In desperation, the police made an unusual move. Just three days after the body was found, the city's board of police commissioners offered a $2,000 reward to anyone providing information leading to the arrest and conviction of the murderer. Accompanying that offer was a public plea to all citizens for any information that might help the investigation.

In terms of volume, the response was overwhelming. In terms of quality, the leads that came pouring in were more arid than a prairie drought. Hundreds of people came forward with all manner of fantastic stories. Each one was meticulously checked out, and each one led to another frustrating dead end.

Eddie Karst was one of the detectives assigned full-time to the Miller investigation. He remembers many of the bizarre letters and phone calls that came in following the reward offer. "There were reports of people who were allegedly going around town committing rapes. We had lots of calls about queer people getting on the bus early in the morning, things like that. We had a lot of information coming in. Most of it didn't amount to anything, but you've got to investigate every one, because you don't know which is the right one."

Karst, who served thirty-five years on the police force before retiring in 1989, remembers the sense of urgency in the Miller investigation. The offer of a reward, the intense public scrutiny, the baffling lack of a motive all added up to pressure on the officers charged with finding the murderer.

"I think there's pressure on an investigator, like I was in the department, to solve any damn murder. I know I felt obligated to get to the bottom of it. That was the same with several others here. It was a gruesome type where you really felt you want to get whoever was responsible, so it can't happen again."

The pressure showed up in different ways. The department itself set up a round-the-clock investigation to assure police commissioners and the public alike that they were serious about solving the case. Joe Penkala was one officer who felt this pressure. A key investigator in the Miller murder, he had uncovered the knife blade in the snow under Miller's body.

Penkala was one of the first officers to arrive on the scene of Miller's murder. A lieutenant at the time, he headed the department's identification section and was in charge of collecting any physical evidence that might prove pertinent to the case. In the early hours of the investigation, when a number of articles relating to the murder were unearthed, it seemed Penkala's work would yield fruitful results. But as all the evidence was put under the microscope and examined, and nothing to indicate who the assailant might be was found, Penkala felt sure that something crucial had been missed.

On February 4, four days after Miller's body was first discovered, Penkala went to the Westwood Funeral Home, near the scene of the murder. He wanted to take a sample of the blue blanket that had been used to cover Gail Miller's body. Anything that had been in contact with the victim's body could yield potential clues. While in the area, Penkala couldn't resist the temptation to return to the original scene. No single spot in Saskatoon had ever been subjected to such intense scrutiny. A procession of policemen had trampled through the area, shovelling and melting snow in an effort to find clues. Under the circumstances, it was most unlikely that anything of significance would still be there. Still, Penkala wanted to search again.

For the lanky thirty-eight-year-old officer, this was a major case. He had spent fifteen years on the force, but this was his first homicide since being appointed lieutenant in 1968. It would also be an important case in his career with the department. Four years later he would be made an inspector, followed by promotion to superintendent and ultimately to chief. Penkala, one of fourteen kids from an immigrant Polish family in Melfort, about a hundred miles northeast of Saskatoon, realized very early that a successful prosecution in the Miller murder could only benefit his career.

Amazingly, Penkala made a discovery that was to form an important part of the case for the prosecution. Close to where he had found the knife blade, Penkala spotted two frozen yellowish lumps of snow, each about an inch in diameter. He carefully scooped them up and took them back to the police station. They were later analyzed by forensic experts and found to contain human semen. Further tests suggested the semen might have originated from a man with a particular blood group.

It was a triumphant discovery for the lieutenant. After all, it was the first piece of physical evidence that might eventually point to the murderer. At the time, no one raised any questions about the integrity of the evidence. It seems no one wondered whether material found four days after the murder was in its original and uncontaminated state, or indeed if it had been there at the time. Only twenty years later would the first serious doubts be raised – doubts that suggested the yellowish lumps were not human semen at all, but dog urine.

3

Hoppy

David Milgaard was a typical kid growing up at a time when the whole concept of being typical was in disrepute. He was in Grade 8 when his family moved from Winnipeg to the small eastern Saskatchewan town of Langenburg in the mid-sixties. It was one of many relocations for Joyce and Lorne Milgaard, who did everything in their power to make a living and provide for their four children. The family's care and attention was often focussed on David's younger brother, Christopher, who had undergone brain surgery. But David, a gregarious and good-looking young man, was never short of attention from a wide variety of friends. Many of them, like him, yearned to leave behind small-town life and travel to the big city.

It was the sixties, and young people across the world were in ferment. Youth and students everywhere were challenging existing values, questioning the status quo, and speaking out against injustice. The U.S. intervention in Vietnam served as a symbol to young people of everything that was wrong with the current state of affairs. But the protests and demonstrations were not confined to what the United States was doing overseas. There was an upsurge of concern on domestic issues as well. Young people were quick to protest any government action that they felt would perpetuate poverty, discrimination, and other iniquities.

Saskatchewan was not immune to this world-wide phenomenon. In fact, it boasted more than the average number of activists in the student movement. Around the same time that the Milgaards were moving to the province, some hundred and fifty activists from across the country were gathering in Regina to map a strategy for the Canadian student movement. By 1967, university students in Regina were holding mass meetings to protest government attempts at controlling budgetary decisions on the campus. A year later, twelve hundred students in Regina besieged newly elected Prime Minister Pierre Trudeau and demanded that student loans be made available to all academically qualified students. And shortly after that, a similar number of students boycotted classes and held a teach-in at the University of Regina. One of their demands was the abolition of tuition fees.

The sixties was not just a time for political dissent and activism, it was also a time of choices. It seemed young people were finding a variety of courses to follow. While some rebelled against their governments and social systems, others confined their protests to the social values their parents were espousing. Young people were in motion, and the desire to break away from the old ways was great.

For David Milgaard, coming of age in the sixties offered him a variety of choices. He developed a passion for cars and for the freedom that cars could offer. He also began to experiment with drugs and became involved in relationships with young women. David developed an urge to travel and to escape the obscurity of the small town he was in. At the same time, he recognized the necessity of working to earn a living. One of his mother's many pursuits at the time was selling Amway products, and David would sometimes join her in the door-to-door canvassing. He genuinely enjoyed the work, feeling it was a perfect way to put his outgoing personality to a useful purpose.

The financial burden that perpetually plagued his family had a profound effect on David in his developmental years.

Because the family constantly relocated in search of work, David was always forging new relationships and leaving old ones behind. He grew to hate the feeling of not being accepted, of being an outsider.

David was the oldest of the Milgaards' two boys and two girls, born in July 1952, in Winnipeg. He quickly developed a penchant for showing off in order to impress other kids. The goal was to be liked. Sometimes it took the form of pranks – childish games that occasionally got out of hand. He remembers the time, at age seven, when he and his gang set fire to a rival gang's fort – a fire that spread to some nearby trees. He also remembers putting hot tar from the roads on people's cars. Those kinds of activities got him into trouble with his parents, but they won howls of approval from his friends.

Between Grade 5 and Grade 8 David attended four different schools as his parents moved from house to house. In Langenburg, Joyce and Lorne tried running a restaurant for a while. Later, Lorne found work in Esterhazy, but the family finances were still worrisome. In fact, the economic pressures would eventually have an effect on all the relationships inside the Milgaard home. For David, the shackles of family life began to interfere with his desire to experience everything life had to offer.

"As a teenager I was just flying around, having a good time," David says. "I was just kind of happy to get away from home at some point, because it felt funny for me with my family. I wanted to be free and running around."

That running around led to a brush with the law when David, then fourteen, and a friend went joy-riding in a truck. His pranks could no longer be tolerated as childish games. He was becoming a young adult, and he had to face up to responsibilities. His parents were worried that his behavioural problems might be more deep-seated. David was admitted to a psychiatric centre in Yorkton in November 1966, where he spent three months. The doctor who examined him would be the first to explore how his mind worked, but by no means the last.

It soon became obvious David didn't belong in the Yorkton

centre. He was judged to have "no overt signs of psychotic or affective behaviour," nor did he exhibit any hint of violence or sexual deviance. He seemed to be a normal kid, albeit a rebellious one. While in Yorkton he refused to heed the centre's regulations, and he was eventually placed in a boys' school.

The boys' school felt like a prison to David. He disliked everything connected with the school and put no effort into his classes. His grades reflected it, and he recorded a failing mark in almost every subject. He ran away a number of times, eventually leaving for good after he turned fifteen. David had already experimented with marijuana and LSD by then, and he drifted into a lifestyle of travelling and meeting new people. He occasionally went back home for visits, but never stayed long. The last thing he wanted to do was live in Langenburg. He gave up on school for good in Grade 9 and began hitchhiking, first to Regina, then beyond.

"When I was sixteen it was just a matter of honest exploration. I just hippied it. I went around to the parks and all the girls would kind of chase you. Today everybody seems to hold too much guilt in their minds about sex and stuff. Back then everything was very real and very nice and very carefree."

It didn't take long before David had a steady girlfriend by the name of Sharon Williams. They hitch-hiked from one end of the country to the other. Sometimes they would get in trouble with authorities, but the penalty was never more than being put on a bus back home. While passing through Ottawa, Sharon found a job in a boutique and David started selling a newspaper called the *Canadian Free Press* on the Sparks Street mall. It was a newspaper that featured articles on the youth movement, drugs, student politics, and various aspects of popular culture, and the idea of disseminating it appealed to David. After work, they crashed in a basement apartment that friends were providing for them free. But this, like his other adventures, didn't last long. Eventually he drifted back to Saskatchewan and back into the routine of cruising through the parks, hippying it.

David's boyish good looks attracted as many girls as he wanted. He quickly gained a reputation as someone who hopped in and out of bed with as many girls as possible. "I was Hoppy," he explains, referring to the nickname most of his friends knew him by. "All the girls wanted Hoppy. The nickname is self-explanatory, I guess."

One of the girls who knew David at the time remembers a personable and smooth-talking young man who seemed to be straddling two worlds – the world of a salesman who sought to impress people and get ahead, and that of a hippie who was satisfied with smoking marijuana and just going with the flow.

"I first met David at Victoria Park," says Deborah Hall, now a hair stylist in Regina. "It was kind of a hangout at the time in downtown Regina. He was just there, with a whole group of people. I didn't even know his real name at the time. It was just Hoppy. Lots of people had nicknames back then. Nobody was really into alcohol in those days. It was just whatever drugs you could get your hands on. Sit around and smoke cigarettes and hang around the park.

"David had dark, wavy hair and had pretty blue eyes. He was boyish looking. At that time he was so clean-cut looking compared to most. He had a really short haircut. He used to wear jeans and sometimes a white T-shirt or a white dress shirt, open a couple of buttons. I got the impression that he was different from everybody. He was kind of an odd boy out."

Whenever David came to Regina he would rent a room at a hotel or motel. He would tell friends that he was earning money as a salesman, initially for Amway and later in commissioned magazine sales. He admitted that he also earned survival money through the small-scale buying and selling of drugs. Nor was he above engaging in petty theft. Still, his friends looked on him as a gentle person who was destined to make something of himself.

As the summer of '68 came to a close and the cold weather started creeping in, David Milgaard began to assess his future. He realized he had a gift for talking and persuasion, and decided to put it to good use. There was an opportunity for some work with Maclean-Hunter selling magazine subscriptions, and he delved into it wholeheartedly. Before he could make it a full-time occupation, however, he had to apply for a sales licence, and that meant a period of waiting – a period when his mind began turning to more carefree pursuits.

Towards the end of January 1969, David came to Regina once again. He booked into the Kitchener Hotel and began to visit some of his cold-weather hangouts. The kids who frequented Victoria and Wascana parks in the summer had moved indoors, hanging around restaurants and shopping malls. At Smitty's Pancake House, David bumped into his buddy Ron Wilson. Two months earlier, Wilson, aged seventeen, had dropped out of Balfour Technical School, finding that he had no interest in continuing past Grade 9. But that wasn't the subject of conversation between the two young men that day. Wilson was excitedly telling David about the new car he had been given for Christmas, a light green '58 Pontiac with a white top and grey hood. He was anxious to try it out, but he didn't have enough money to get it licensed.

David had known Ron Wilson for about a year and a half. Both shared an interest in cars, and both used to frequent the impromptu quarter-mile drag races that were held on the outskirts of Regina. Whenever he could get access to the family's '57 Ford, with its 390 engine, David would take part in the races. Otherwise, he was content to be a spectator.

·"I think that's where I first met Ron, at that quarter-mile thing," Milgaard recalls. "I think he was kind of going by and, how you say, mooning it – he was hanging his rear end out. But I mean he was going for the quarter-mile! And I said, 'Here's a weird character.'"

The two became fast friends, getting together whenever David visited Regina and travelling in the same circles. As Ron was extolling the virtues of his new car at Smitty's, an idea came to both young men at the same time. Why not take a trip out west and see just how good this new car was?

"It was just a kind of take-off-and-see-what-happens trip," David recalls. "It was even better than hitch-hiking. You didn't have to find a car."

It was also a trip that was to land David Milgaard in jail for the next two decades.

David and Ron decided to ask Nichol John to accompany them on the trip. She had been a friend of Ron for about two years and of David since the previous spring. Nicky, who was the same age as David, had dropped out of school in Grade 10. The boys persuaded her to quit her job as a waitress at Champ's Cafe and join in the adventure. It didn't take much persuasion. She cashed her last paycheque on January 30 and made quick preparations to leave town, taking her maroon parka and not much else. David gave Ron the money to buy licence plates for the car, and everything seemed set to go. The final destination was wherever the car could get them, with luck as far as Edmonton and perhaps even Vancouver.

Nicky's relationship with David was ambiguous. She had had sex with him, but didn't consider him to be her boyfriend. She felt he was sometimes too persuasive and forceful, especially in his sexual advances. Still, she looked on him as a friend, and had no hesitation accompanying him on the trip.

When David and Nicky went over to Ron Wilson's house to survey the car, they were in for a surprise. All the tires were flat, and the battery was dead. Undaunted, the three removed the tires and the battery, grabbed a toboggan and made their way to the nearest service station. Luckily, the tires had not sustained any major damage and were usable after they were thawed out and filled with air. They weren't so lucky when it came to the battery. The service station attendant informed them it was completely unchargeable, so they left it there and walked back.

"Ron and myself decided to steal a battery," David said afterwards, in trying to reconstruct the events leading up to the trip. "We went about one and a half blocks south in his back lane and went into a garage where we found a car. In the process of the theft we broke into the casing of the battery with our screwdriver and during the run back through the snowy back lane acid splashed on us."

With acid burns on his white shirt and grey pants, David changed into an outlandish pair of yellow-striped green pants. Once they had the stolen battery installed, they found the car still wouldn't start. So they had the car towed to the garage where it warmed up and was put into driveable condition.

When the three finally hit the road, it was roughly 12:30 a.m. on the 31st. All three jammed into the front seat for the voyage. They were anxious to leave and didn't even consider getting a good night's rest beforehand. David was the only one of the three who bothered to take along a suitcase, and by that time only Nicky had any money. Some vague and unrealistic idea of petty thefts was all they had in mind to finance the trip.

The first order of business for the three travellers was to go through Saskatoon and pick up one of David's buddies by the name of Shorty. David had first met Shorty at a park in Regina. Shorty had dropped out of school after Grade 7. He worked at odd jobs on farms and construction sites, but his main interest was having a good time with other young people. David recalls that Shorty used to tag along and want to be part of the scene.

Shorty had been immediately attracted to David. After all, David had seemed to have everything he envied – a smooth-talking manner, good looks, and plenty of girls chasing after him. After they had got together in Regina in March 1968, Shorty had followed David to his home in Langenburg, where they spent several days. The two then had returned to Shorty's crowded home in Saskatoon. They'd gone to the regular Friday night dance at nearby St. Mary's Church. The next day they'd walked downtown, with David sauntering barefoot and carefree through the puddle-filled streets, and Shorty gazing admiringly at the brazenness of his friend as David stopped in a diner to plead poverty and ask for a sandwich.

David hadn't spoken to his friend for some time. The plan was simply to drive to Shorty's house in Saskatoon and see if he wanted to come along for the ride.

Nicky dozed off during the ride north, but David and Ron tried to stay awake the whole time. They continued to discuss how they might scrounge some money to finance the trip. Finally they decided to stop in a small town along the way and break into a grain elevator. It wasn't clear what they thought they would find there, but the plan had one advantage. In the middle of the night, there would be no one around, and the two boys had no intention of trying anything that would involve a confrontation with anyone. They had earlier discussed possible purse-snatchings and break-and-enters in Regina, but they didn't have the nerve to carry them out. Finally, under cover of darkness, David plucked up his courage and approached the grain elevator. The only thing of value inside was a flashlight, which he brought back with him to the car.

On the way through another small town – Craik, Saskatchewan – the car got stuck. David took the wheel and tried rocking it back and forth. Much to Wilson's consternation, he threw the automatic transmission into reverse too quickly at one point, stripping the transmission of its reverse gear. After about an hour of digging and shoving, they finally got the car back on the road.

By everyone's best estimate, the three travellers arrived in Saskatoon sometime between 5:30 and 6:30 in the morning. Ron and Nicky had never set foot in the city before that, so David became the navigator. But it soon became clear to all of them that David had no idea where he was going, either. The only thing he knew was that he was looking for a teenager named Shorty, who lived close to a church in a district that David thought was called Peace Hill.

What happened in the next two hours has been the subject of controversy for the last twenty years. It has been scrutinized and studied by countless lawyers, judges, private investigators, and journalists. The truth is known only to three people – Milgaard, Wilson, and John – and two of those people, Wilson and John, have changed their stories on a number of occasions. Only David Milgaard has consistently stuck to one story, to one version of the events of that day. Based on the facts on which all three have agreed, it is possible to piece together an outline of what transpired on the morning of January 31 in Saskatoon.

David Milgaard had only a sketchy idea of how to find his way around Saskatoon. The extreme cold and fog that morning did not help matters. After driving around the city for a while, David guided Ron to an area he thought might be close to Shorty's house. As they were driving down a boulevarded street, they passed a woman on the sidewalk. Ron pulled up, and David, who was sitting by the front passenger door, asked the woman for directions to the Peace Hill or Pleasant Hill district. The woman couldn't help them out, and they carried on.

In the course of their search for the house, the trio passed by the Trav-a-leer Motel on 22nd Street. David was sent in to ask for directions and a city map. The manager, Robert Rasmussen, obliged by giving him a map. Later, Rasmussen would say that he didn't notice anything unusual about the visitor. He seemed an ordinary, polite young man. The only odd thing Rasmussen remembered was that the man ran into the motel in his stocking feet. As for the time, Rasmussen said, "It was just shortly after seven o'clock that I opened the door, and it hadn't been open too long when this car drove up."

With the help of the map and some directions from Rasmussen, the three turned around and drove about a dozen blocks east, not far from where they had asked the woman for directions. Still confused, they turned down an alley behind Avenue T between 21st and 22nd streets. There they saw a man struggling to get his car freed from the snow and ice in the alley behind his back yard. David and Ron had a brief discussion about whether to stop and give the man a hand. David was all for it, but Ron was afraid that it might harm their own vehicle. Finally, they agreed to push the man's car with their own in an effort to get it going. The result, as Ron feared, was that both vehicles stalled and became hopelessly mired in the alley. The time, by all accounts, was about 7:30 a.m.

The man, Walter Danchuk, invited everyone to wait in his home while he called a tow truck. It was clear there was no way he would get to work at Engineering and Plumbing Supplies in City Park by his normal 8:00 a.m. starting time. He chatted with Milgaard, who told him about their search for Shorty's place, mentioning that they had just come from Regina and were heading to Edmonton. Danchuk later said he noticed Milgaard had a fairly large tear in the seat of his pants. Aside from that, Danchuk didn't notice anything particularly unusual about his three visitors. At one point, David asked Danchuk's wife for a glass of water. She later remembered him as an ordinary and polite young man. In all, the trio stayed in the Danchuk home for close to an hour.

Eventually a tow truck arrived and extricated Danchuk's car. David and Ron had the idea that if they pretended not to have any money, Danchuk would offer to pay to have their car boosted as well. But the offer was never made, nor did Danchuk think he should risk using his own vehicle to get Ron's car going. Instead, he drove them back to the gas station where the tow truck was called once more, this time helping to free the second car.

After all this stumbling around in the fog and dark, the three finally located the church where David had attended the dance with Shorty. It was St. Mary's Church on 20th Street and Avenue O. From there, David was able to figure out that his friend lived a block away, at 334 Avenue O, across from St. Mary's School – and just one and a half blocks away from where Gail Miller's body lay. By now it was daylight, around 9:00 a.m. – about the same time that police were swarming the scene of the murder.

Shorty turned out to be seventeen-year-old Albert Henry Cadrain. He was the third oldest of the Cadrain's seven boys and two girls. For David, Shorty was "a guy that everybody liked in a way because he seemed overly friendly. Maybe a little simple in some ways, but a nice guy."

Ron parked the car on the wrong side of the street across from Cadrain's house, and David jumped out to see if his friend was home. Albert answered the door, pulled on a shirt and invited David in. They were then joined by Ron and Nichol. One of the first orders of business for David Milgaard when he got in the house was to change his clothes. He did so in full view of his friends, stuffing his ripped green and yellow pants into his suitcase. Ron also changed his acid-ravaged pants, borrowing a pair of burgundy slacks from David.

Shorty had no hesitation in agreeing to go on the trip. He was immediately called on to invest some money in fixing Ron's car, which needed transmission work. David, meanwhile, re-parked the car on the proper side of the street. Shorty's only request was that his three companions spend some time that afternoon helping him find a couple of friends to ask if they wanted to come along, too. When those friends couldn't be located, Ron, David, Nicky, and Shorty headed toward the highway and Alberta. Once again, no one bothered to inquire if anyone needed any rest. It was 4:30 p.m.

4

One Floor Down

Seventeen-year-old Linda Fisher flicked on the radio in her basement apartment on Avenue O. One floor above her, in the Cadrain household, David Milgaard and his companions were making the final preparations for their journey west. But Linda paid no attention to the stirrings in her landlord's house. She was riveted by the news of a murder that had occurred less than two blocks from her home.

A woman between eighteen and twenty-one years of age had been found in an alley behind the 200 block of Avenue N south, the announcer said. Although the autopsy was not yet complete, it was revealed that the woman had knife wounds to the throat and abdomen.

For Linda, the news report instilled no sense of fear. She was much too preoccupied with an argument she had been waging with her husband, Larry, for most of the morning. Larry had been out all night and had failed to come home even after the bars had closed. It was not an unusual event for the nineteen-year-old construction labourer. He often went out carousing with friends, leaving his wife and baby at home alone. What Linda found unusual was his apparent failure to report to work that morning. It was rare for Larry to miss a day of work, even after a night of heavy partying. Nonetheless, when Linda awoke around ten that morning, she found her husband sitting in the living room and wearing an outfit he normally saved for the weekends.

What followed was a loud and bitter argument, with Linda lashing out at her husband for his lack of responsibility. Obscenities were freely hurled, and anything became fodder for the bickering. The radio report of the nearby murder was no exception.

"My paring knife is missing," Linda screamed. "You're probably the one who was out stabbing that girl."

It was a spontaneous, albeit cruel, remark, completely in tune with the tenor of abuse that day. Linda's brown, wooden-handled paring knife indeed was missing; but she didn't believe for a moment that her husband could have had anything to do with such a heinous crime. That's why she was stunned at his response.

"My angry accusation stopped him cold," she recalls. "He looked at me like a guilty person who'd just been caught. The colour drained from his face and he looked shocked and scared. I will never forget his expression."

Larry Earl Fisher is a small, powerfully built man with green eyes and a confident smile. Linda first saw him at a sidewalk café in North Battleford, Saskatchewan, and was infatuated. For the fifteen-year-old farm girl, who considered herself plain-looking, it seemed too good to be true. Here was a handsome young man, two years her senior, paying lots of attention to her, offering to buy her Cokes and asking for dates. Her self-confidence soared when she realized he wanted her to be his steady girlfriend.

It was the summer of 1967, and for Linda it was the most romantic of times. Some days they would go horseback riding; other days Larry would drive her to the park where they sat and talked. Often Larry would come to the family farm, seven miles from the small town of Cando, and help her father with the haying. Linda and Larry wrote each other love letters, and talked about what it would be like to get married.

Their relationship took a more complicated turn when Linda discovered she was pregnant. The teenage romance had come to an end, and reality was starting to set in. Linda was terrified at the thought of becoming a parent at such an early age, but her own feelings were the least of her worries. Linda's mother was furious when she found out, and for her father it confirmed his worst fears. He had never liked Larry Fisher.

While the family tried to sort through the turmoil, everyone put up a brave front. A variety of different options were considered and discarded; the only solution that seemed possible was quickly arranged. Linda and Larry would have to get married. Linda had just turned sixteen.

It was a big wedding at the Third Avenue United Church in North Battleford, nine days before Christmas in 1967. Linda's parents were there, as were Larry's mother and stepfather. The family members and invited guests were in a festive mood, and a supper and dance followed the ceremony. Still, Linda was a reluctant bride. The wedding couple had to walk through a small archway in the church as part of the proceedings. For just an instant, Linda looked up at the archway and considered turning around. She didn't. Linda and Larry became husband and wife.

There was no honeymoon. Instead, the teenage couple immediately moved to Saskatoon, where Larry got a job with Masonry Contractors Ltd., hauling bricks and construction materials to bricklayers. Any lingering hopes Linda may have harboured for a romantic married life were dashed when she looked around the dingy apartment they moved into on Avenue F. It was a tiny, one-bedroom place with a bathroom in the hall that had to be shared with other tenants. Linda learned to cook on a hotplate.

It didn't take long for problems to surface in the marriage. Linda, whose pregnancy was showing even at the wedding, was getting bigger every day, and Larry was spending less and less time at home. He developed a fast friendship with Cliff Pambrum, Linda's uncle, and the two would often go out drinking, leaving their wives behind. Pambrum and Fisher both worked at Masonry Contractors, and when the two weren't drinking they would be out hunting duck or deer. If Pambrum was busy, Larry would find another friend to party with, or he would just go out by himself. It seemed to Linda she no longer had any place in his social life.

Linda didn't accept her fate silently. She criticized her husband for always leaving her behind, and the two had constant arguments. As the months went by, Linda clung to the hope that things would change once the baby was born. She was wrong.

Tammy DeAnne was born on April 25, 1968 – four months after the wedding. Larry was disappointed; he had wanted a boy. Despite having a newborn at home, Larry kept to his old routine – putting in his working hours during the day and leaving the house to party at night. Linda grew even more resentful at this behaviour. She suspected him of running around with other women, and even caught him once in a rendezvous with a girlfriend. Their arguments and fights grew uglier. Linda remembers one particularly painful incident.

"We were at my aunt and uncle's and he'd been out drinking," Linda said. "He came back, and I was just furious. I thought he was running around. We were outside, and he was hitting me, and I was hitting him back. After the fight was over I came in and sat on my aunt's couch. He came in. He had work boots on. I was sitting with my head down and he kicked me in the head. He cut my eye, and I hollered."

The violence of the encounter frightened Linda, but she didn't let it destroy their marriage. While Larry was unpredictable in his behaviour, Linda never actually feared for her life. Sometimes she would take the offensive and threaten him. On one occasion, she grabbed a butcher knife and promised to run him through if he came near her. He took hold of her hand and shook the knife free, but he didn't hurt her that time. He was too shocked at the prospect that she might carry out the threat.

There were days, though, when Linda felt the neglect and abuse were too much. January 31, 1969, was one such day. They had moved into the basement apartment of the Cadrain house the previous fall, giving the baby more room to crawl around. While money was never in great abundance, it was not a pressing problem either; Larry was a workaholic who kept the paycheques coming in steadily. But the sheer loneliness and frustration had driven Linda to consider moving out. When her husband had not come home the previous evening, she'd made a point of packing her bags before she went to sleep. She was seriously thinking of moving in with her relatives for a while. At the very least, she wanted to scare Larry into thinking she might leave him.

All of that was forgotten, however, in the swirl of insults that day. And when Linda saw the reaction that her accusation had triggered – an accusation that her own husband had been responsible for a murder – she glimpsed a side of her husband she had never seen before. "In retrospect, I know that the accusation was prompted by my intense anger and not really a belief that he had murdered someone," Linda said. "But his reaction was strange. . . . I recall thinking at the time that this strange behaviour was caused by his disbelief that I would say or even think something so horrible as that."

Linda Fisher did not realize it at the time, but there was another reason for her husband's mortified reaction to her accusation. While they lived together in the basement of the Cadrain home, Larry Fisher carried out at least three sexual attacks against women in Saskatoon. In all of the attacks, Fisher used a knife to threaten the women. In all of the attacks, he grabbed the women as they walked alone and attempted to drag them to a nearby alley or yard. And in each case, the women were assaulted just a short distance from their homes.

In every key respect, the *modus operandi* was similar to the assault launched on Gail Miller, with one important exception. Miller was slashed and stabbed to death, while Fisher's victims had "only" been sexually assaulted. Yet during the early months of 1969, there was another similarity among all the offences that was most frustrating of all for the families of the victims. The perpetrator, in each case, seemed to have gotten away undetected, and the crime remained unsolved.

Only in subsequent investigations by detectives, private

investigators and journalists, did the facts of Larry Fisher's prior offences become known – facts which show him to be a serial rapist in a city that saw fourteen reported rapes in 1968.

On October 21, 1968, about 7:30 p.m., Alice Baker (the names of Larry Fisher's victims have been changed to protect their identities) was walking home along Avenue H South, several blocks from Fisher's home. Baker, in her early twenties, had just visited a neighbourhood store and was a block and a half from her home when Larry Fisher grabbed her from behind. All she could recall later about the initial attack was that "someone came out of nowhere." Fisher put his hand over her mouth and threatened to kill her if she tried to scream. "You do as I say or else," she remembers him saying. "I thought I was dead." He was armed with a knife. Baker tried to push his hand away from her mouth.

Fisher dragged her into an alley and ordered her to take off her clothes. Terrified, she complied. As he was raping her, he was frightened by something and quickly fled. Baker put her clothes back on and ran to the nearest house, where there was no one home. She ran to the next house where there was a light on, but no one answered the door. Finally she raced back home, and from there was taken to St. Paul's Hospital, where she was treated. She had been slightly cut and although she was otherwise physically unharmed, the experience scarred her psychologically. "I didn't think I was going to get up alive," she said.

Baker didn't know her attacker, but Fisher may well have known her. Both of them took the same bus route on 20th Street West to work every morning.

On November 13, 1968, three weeks after attacking Alice Baker, Fisher was again on the prowl in the same neighbourhood. Shortly before 8:00 p.m., Cathy Shannon was walking from her home to meet her boyfriend. It was a few days before her seventeenth birthday. Somewhere between Avenues E and H, Fisher walked past her on the sidewalk, saying nothing. Then he grabbed her from behind and put his hand over her mouth. Shannon felt a knife at her throat, and Fisher told her, "If you want to live, do as I say." Fisher dragged the high school student into a nearby yard and ordered her to undress. Shannon recalls he told her not to scream and to "lie still and don't move." While she never saw the knife, she felt it at her throat throughout the rape. "I just lay there and obeyed. All I told him was, 'Don't kill me,'" she said.

After finishing the assault, Fisher quickly fled, taking most of Shannon's clothes with him. She ran to her home, about a block and a half away.

On November 29, 1968, Cindy Owen was walking home from an evening of studying at the University of Saskatchewan library. It was a cold night and dark outside. The nineteen-year-old was in her second year of college. Owen saw Fisher standing on the sidewalk as she made her way through the east Saskatoon neighbourhood. As she walked past him, Fisher stopped her and asked if she knew the name of the apartment building on the corner. She said she didn't, and continued walking. As she crossed the street, she realized he was following her. At first Owen thought he was heading towards the telephone booth on the corner. Then she saw he had gone past it and now was right behind her. Before she could turn around, Fisher grabbed her from behind and put his hand over her mouth.

Owen dropped the books she was carrying and began screaming for help. Fisher issued a warning. "Don't say anything," he told her. "I have a knife." He began dragging her towards the alley, but Owen struggled the whole time. Her hand was cut through her glove by Fisher's knife as they grappled. In the alley, he held her down and said he wanted her to come to a car he had parked nearby. As they continued to struggle, Fisher saw the headlights of a car coming down the alley towards them. It was a group of students who had heard the commotion and were coming to investigate. Fisher immediately fled, before he had an opportunity to rape her.

This case was unusual in that Fisher indicated he had a car in the area. Although he didn't own a car, he had ready access to one. Cliff Pambrum often lent him his '58 Chevrolet.

* * *

Rape was by no means a run-of-the-mill crime in Saskatoon. Investigators were assigned to each of the assaults, and were expected to solve the cases. Police interviewed all three of Fisher's victims, took them to lineups of suspects and checked all possible leads. But they were unable to come up with any clues.

Finally, they resorted to a measure that police are often loathe to use for fear of alarming the public. They issued a press release in the form of a warning. On December 14, 1968, the Saskatoon *Star-Phoenix* reported, "Police have issued a warning to women not to talk to strangers or walk in dark areas of the city if they can avoid it.

"They issued this warning after two instances of alleged rape and one assault were brought to their attention. Police said the alleged rapes took place in the Riversdale area and the assault took place in the university district.

"They said the alleged assailant first talks to women and then takes them into alleys."

Anyone familiar with the facts of the assaults would realize that the warning was pointless at best. Only one of the women had any prior conversation with the assailant, and all three were walking along illuminated city sidewalks and not in "dark areas of the city." More than anything else, the news release was an indication of the frustration police felt at being unable to catch the culprit – frustration that grew exponentially when a fourth victim was discovered in the person of Gail Miller.

Nearly two years would have to pass before Larry Fisher's involvement in the crimes became known, as his confessions only started flowing after he was caught in the act of attacking yet another young woman. For as long as he could, he kept the dark side of his personality a secret from everyone, including his wife. It was only with hindsight that Linda Fisher was able to put new interpretations on the events of January 31, 1969. Only years later did she realize that his failure to go to work that day, and his shocked and guilty response to her spontaneous accusation, were strong indications that he might be responsible for Gail Miller's murder.

Nor were those the only clues. A day or two after Miller's murder, Linda remembers a child coming to the door of their home with Larry's wallet. The wallet had been found beside a tree just down the street, between the murder site and the Cadrain house. And there was another unusual fact that also surfaced sometime later. Linda's uncle years later told her of the time he was burning garbage in a barrel in his backyard. Larry came over unexpectedly and threw a pair of nearly new work boots into the barrel. It seemed like a strange thing for him to do at the time, her uncle thought, but Larry offered no explanation.

With Gail Miller's murder, police were looking at many of the same elements they had witnessed in the three previous assaults. As in the other cases, the victim had apparently been dragged to an alley by a knife-wielding assailant and sexually assaulted. And Miller's body was found just a few blocks from the sites of two of the other assaults. In at least one of the other assaults, the victim was a frequent rider of the 20th Street bus line, as were Gail Miller and Larry Fisher.

The possibility that the Miller murder might be the handiwork of the same serial rapist – a rapist who had escalated his violence by using the weapon he brandished in his other crimes – did not escape the Saskatoon police. Some of the senior officers in the morality squad and other divisions speculated on just such a possibility. Yet they decided not to draw the link publicly. None of the local press coverage of Miller's murder so much as mentioned the previous assaults. Only one dispatch raised the possibility that the same person might be involved – a small story that ran, not in the Saskatoon newspaper, but in the Regina *Leader-Post* on February 4, 1969. The newspaper reported that "Police are investigating the possibility that the person who slashed a 20-year-old nurses' aide to death Friday may be the same person who attacked three women here last fall."

It was one day after that story appeared in print that the Saskatoon police came face to face with Larry Fisher. Officers were canvassing the neighbourhood for clues to the murder, interviewing anyone who might have been on the streets at that time. At 6:49 a.m. they found Larry Fisher waiting at the bus stop on 20th Street – the same bus stop that Gail Miller was headed to on the day she was killed. In a brief verbal exchange, they asked Fisher his name and address and asked what he had been doing the previous Friday morning. He told them he had caught the bus to work that day about 6:30 a.m. No, he said politely, he saw nothing unusual that morning.

More than twenty years would go by before police asked Larry Fisher any more questions about Gail Miller's murder.

5

A Break in the Case

In 1969, Saskatoon's police department was under the firm control of Chief James G. Kettles, a self-proclaimed "man of the soil," who exercised iron discipline and did not tolerate failure. Kettles was an imposing figure with rugged features and a thin, military-style moustache in the shape of an inverted V. An immaculate dresser, he always wore two huge diamond rings that earned him the nickname Diamond Jim. If ever an archetypal conservative Canadian policeman existed, it was Kettles. He was proud of his Scottish heritage, his respect for the laws of God, and his dedication to law, order, decency, and "justice swift and sure."

After pounding a beat in Ottawa for nineteen years, the forty-two-year-old Kettles was appointed Saskatoon's chief of police in 1954. He inherited a police force that numbered just forty-seven officers. Saskatoon, after all, was still a small city. It had 45,000 people at the time, and there wasn't a great deal for police to do. Traffic cops had just eighty-seven stop signs and three sets of traffic lights to worry about.

By 1969, Saskatoon's population had more than doubled, and Kettles had managed to increase his force five-fold. He knew everyone in the department by name, but he was careful never to mix business with pleasure. If he saw an officer at an outside social event, he wouldn't so much as nod in recognition. The next day at work, however, he would call the officer over and ask if he had enjoyed himself the night before.

Kettles was a hardliner, and he tried to instil those values in his men. Some of his views would make modern-day sociologists cringe. "Among many people there exists the idea that slums, poverty, and deprivation breed juvenile delinquency, drug use, and crime," Kettles once said mockingly. "I believe that one of the simple reasons for crime and violence as we know it today can be attributed to human nature, uncurbed human nature, human nature allowed to run rampant with fewer controls, more personal freedoms, and with increasing permissiveness."

His view of humanity spilled over into his analysis of crime in Saskatoon. Asked to comment on an increase of sexual assaults at the end of the sixties, Kettles blamed the miniskirt. "The way some girls dress these days, they are simply asking for trouble," he said. When it came to subjects such as capital punishment, which was a raging debate at the time, Kettles was uncompromising. "An eye for an eye and a tooth for a tooth, and if a person takes a life he must pay for it with his own. There is nothing unfair about that, not a thing."

By the late sixties, Kettles was feeling besieged. He was battling City Hall for more manpower and equipment, a new headquarters, and higher salaries. He was also struggling against a social trend that was bringing Saskatoon into the age of protest marches and student sit-ins.

Kettles looked at the upsurge in the youth and student movement as a dangerous threat to civil authority. For him, all the talk of rights and freedom were a cover to mask lawlessness. In the annual report of the Saskatoon police department for 1969, Kettles noted: "The greatest explosion now taking place in this country is not in the economy, but in crime arising from the inadequate lack of support for and disrespect of police officers. We witness acts of civil disobedience perpetrated by people who make use of the law for the purpose of breaking the law on the baseless pretence of protecting freedom. . . . Police forces cannot effectively combat white collar crime and organized criminals on the one hand with a younger generation challenging authority on the other, while operating in a society complacent and apathetic towards the police and the very laws which exist to protect the same society."

When it came to hippies, Kettles lost all patience. His attitude was clearly expressed in a report to the city's board of police commissioners at the time: "We find in this drug-saturated age of guided missiles and misguided people a segment of society identified as 'hippies,' who claim to represent love and peace but, on the contrary, those of us engaged in the profession of law enforcement know only too well that there is, in fact, little real love or so-called peace in 'Hippieville.'"

What Kettles was most concerned about were allegations of police brutality that surfaced in 1969, the very same year his men were trying to solve the mystery of Gail Miller's murder. R. A. Walker, a former CCF attorney general in Saskatchewan, charged that Saskatoon police were assaulting innocent people and perjuring themselves on the stand.

The charges caused an uproar. Kettles was quick to deny them, but the Saskatchewan government felt it had to take action. The attorney general appointed Justice J. H. Maher to head a Royal Commission into the allegations. Saskatoon lawyer Hugh Raney was one of the first to step forward with cases of brutality, and a number of young people also testified they had been assaulted and beaten by police. The commission investigated six specific cases of brutality and heard general submissions on the problem. In the end, Justice Maher criticized police for just one of those incidents.

Although his department's reputation had been tarnished by the commission, Kettles felt vindicated. Once again he jumped to the defence of his men and blamed society's ills on the public itself. "In my opinion we must become a lot more concerned about public brutality and irresponsible conduct on the part of its citizens and a whole lot less concerned and excited, in most cases, about baseless charges and those without foundation of alleged and inferred police brutality," he said.

With his department feeling pressure from all sides, Kettles turned his attention back to the vicious homicide that had shocked Saskatoon. He instructed his men to leave no stone unturned, to check out any leads that seemed promising. One of those leads eventually led them to David Milgaard.

It didn't take long for Saskatoon police to discover that a group of teenagers had left the Cadrain house for points west on the same day as Gail Miller's murder. It was one of hundreds of pieces of information that surfaced in the days following the slaying. It was a tenuous lead at best. There was nothing to suggest those teenagers had anything to do with the murder, but it was worth checking out.

Investigators had little trouble locating Albert Cadrain. He and his friends had spent a few days driving almost aimlessly around Alberta. They all returned to Regina around February 5. Soon after that Cadrain was arrested on a charge of vagrancy and sentenced to a week in jail. When Saskatoon police learned he was in Regina, they asked the local police department to question him about his activities on January 31. He was brought into an interview room, where a number of officers asked him to strip naked. They thoroughly inspected his clothes and conducted a full body search. Then they began to grill him about any involvement he might have with the murder.

This was the first time Cadrain had heard anything about a murder, and he was scared. Police left little doubt in his mind that he was a suspect in the case. They wanted to know why he had been in such a hurry to leave town on January 31. Cadrain told police about the trip and who his companions were. But he discounted any suggestion that he or any of them had anything to do with the murder. The officers, finding no physical evidence or any hint that Cadrain was lying, reported back to their colleagues in Saskatoon that there was nothing to pursue as a result of their interview. But they didn't share that conclusion with Cadrain. The strategy was to keep him on edge, and let him think he was still a suspect. At the end of their interview, Cadrain said one of the officers warned him he might end up dead in an alley if he continued walking the streets.

With no further leads to be checked, it seemed the Gail Miller murder was destined to become another unsolved case on the files of the Saskatoon police department. Detective Eddie Karst remembers the frustration of that first month after the slaying, the impotence police felt at having a murderer seemingly slip through their fingers. Then, at a time when many officers were on the verge of giving up hope, a break came in the case. It was March 2.

"All the suspects had been eliminated one by one," Karst recalled. "Then a fellow comes forward and talks to the desk officer at the station. He was turned over to me since I was one of the officers working on the case at the time. We checked his story out quite thoroughly, made sure he wasn't pulling our leg. We made sure he could have known all this, not just read about it. I ended up taking a statement from him."

The man told Karst he had seen David Milgaard in Saskatoon about 9:00 a.m. on the morning of the murder. He said Milgaard had blood on his clothes and seemed to be in a hurry to get out of town. Later in the day, the man said, he saw Milgaard dispose of a woman's cosmetics' case.

The man was Albert "Shorty" Cadrain. For his information, he ultimately collected the $2,000 reward.

Cadrain had returned to his Saskatoon home on March 1. It appears he heard about the reward for the first time then. He denies that money was his motivation for suddenly changing his story. Instead, he says he felt compelled to tell police what he knew. He spoke to his family about his intention of going to police, and they supported his decision.

The more he thought about the trip to Alberta, the more he felt there was something unusual about David's behaviour, Cadrain told police. The most puzzling comment came when, according to Cadrain, David took him aside and told him that he, David, was a member of the Mafia. Cadrain said that David had wanted him to get a gun and wipe out Wilson and John, because "they knew too much."

Police now had two conflicting stories from Cadrain – his statement two weeks earlier that no one on the trip had any involvement in the murder, and his new revelations about blood and guns. Police believed the latter.

"Cadrain put all the pieces together," Karst said. "He told us about blood on Milgaard. And he told us about the comment Milgaard made on the trip, about getting rid of the other two. He didn't understand it at the time, but he put it together later, that they knew too much."

Karst excitedly told his supervisor, Charlie Short, about the new lead. Even though it was a Sunday, the news was important enough to warrant a call to Chief Kettles. Staff Sergeant Ray Mackie was also briefed, and the officers spent all weekend going over Cadrain's second story. The only way to check out his allegations was to interview the other players, and they wasted little time in their effort.

On March 3, an RCMP inspector was dispatched to have a chat with Ron Wilson. Like Cadrain, he was not hard to find. Wilson had arrived back in Regina early in February and spent a few more days with Milgaard before they split up. The extended trip had taken its toll on his car, and a few days later he blew the engine. Out of money and without wheels, he planned and executed some petty crimes. His plans, however, did not encompass getting caught. Wilson was sentenced to the provincial jail in Regina on February 25 for a charge of theft over fifty dollars.

Wilson was surprised when he learned an Inspector Riddell of the RCMP wanted to speak to him. He was even more surprised when he found out that Riddell was interested in knowing about the car trip he and his friends had taken a month earlier. Nonetheless, Wilson cooperated fully and remembers that the hour-long discussion was a friendly one. It became clear early on that Riddell suspected David Milgaard had murdered a woman in Saskatoon, a murder Wilson said he heard about for the first time that day.

Following the interview, Wilson gave the officer a signed statement. In that statement, he tells of leaving Regina about 1:00 a.m. on January 31 and arriving in Saskatoon between

5:00 and 6:00 a.m. In searching for Shorty Cadrain's house, he says, the car came upon another vehicle which was stuck in an alley. Wilson then tells of their efforts to free the Danchuk car. He recounts how they finally arrived at Cadrain's place. Wilson says he and Milgaard both changed clothes at that point, and Milgaard then went outside to re-park the car on the right side of the street. They waited several hours while the car's transmission was being repaired, and then spent some further time looking for Albert's girlfriend. They finally left town, according to Wilson's recollection, sometime between 2:00 and 4:00 p.m.

The key part of the statement concerned Riddell's questions about whether Milgaard had blood on his clothes and had been separated from the others for long enough to have committed the murder. Riddell also wanted to know if Milgaard had ever been in possession of a knife.

On all of those points, Wilson was emphatic. "At no time during the time we were in Saskatoon was Dave Milgaard out of my sight for more than one or two minutes, the one time being when he drove the car around the block. This would be well after daylight. I never knew of Dave to have a knife. I am convinced that Dave Milgaard never left our company during the morning we were in Saskatoon. The coat he was wearing, a brown one, is now at my place as it also has acid burns and the pair of pants he changed is now in my car in the back seat. . . . All during this trip there was never any mention about the murder of a girl in Saskatoon. In fact, I didn't even know about this murder until the police told me today."

Nichol John told police virtually the same story. After returning from the trip, she stayed in Regina with Albert Cadrain until Cadrain was arrested for vagrancy. She, too, was surprised when police showed up at her door wanting to know all about the trip. And when she signed her statement, it contained no incriminating evidence against David Milgaard.

While Riddell was chasing down leads in Regina, Saskatoon officers were attempting to locate David Milgaard. They learned that he had left Regina around February 10 for Winnipeg. The sales licence David had been expecting finally came

through, and he was off to Winnipeg to sell magazine subscriptions for Maclean-Hunter. While his travelling companions were being picked up for vagrancy and jailed for theft,
David was beginning to earn a steady living at the age of
sixteen.

Early Monday morning on March 3, David's boss, Roger
Renaud, told him that police wanted to ask him some questions. David was taken aback. His brush with the law as an
adolescent had been a youthful indiscretion, he felt. He didn't
consider himself an angel – his recent theft of the car battery,
the flashlight at the grain elevator, and his dealings in drugs
testified to that. But now that he was removed from his circle
of friends in Regina and embarking on regular employment,
he thought he had begun a new chapter in his life. Now the
police were coming after him for something, and though he
didn't know what it was about, his main concern was how it
might affect his new job.

David was asked to come to the RCMP detention home for
boys. In an interview room, he was then introduced to Karst,
Staff Sergeant Edmondson of the RCMP and Constable
Kopang of the Winnipeg detachment. What followed was a
six-hour interview, with police asking him to account for
every minute of his time on January 31. David was not under
arrest, nor did police directly inform him that he was a suspect
in Gail Miller's murder. But the tenor and directness of the
questions made the point as clearly as any overt accusation.

There was no suggestion that David needed a lawyer at this
point. Whatever his legal rights might have been, he saw no
reason why he shouldn't cooperate with the police. He
patiently answered all the police questions, giving them
largely the same account that Ron Wilson and Nichol John
had given them. There were slight variations here and there,
but nothing police could seize on to establish that any of them
was lying. David even drew diagrams for the police in an effort
to explain his movements in Saskatoon on that day. Karst also
conducted a complete physical examination of the suspect.
He found no scars or scratches or remnants of injuries that
would indicate he had been in any type of struggle.

Following the interview, Karst asked if David had any objection to a search of his motel room. He didn't. David hadn't been back to his room since he learned police wanted to question him, so he had no time to prepare for the search. Karst spent the next hour rummaging through all of his clothing and personal effects. He was looking for ripped or bloodied clothes or any evidence that might link him to the crime. The search turned up nothing. No blood, no knife, no drugs – nothing to show that the story David, Nichol, and Ron were telling was not true. His interview and search complete, Karst returned to Saskatoon.

At the trial, Karst readily admitted that David Milgaard was polite and cooperative during his interrogation. He seemed willing to let police know as much as possible about his trip to Saskatoon. Privately, however, Karst had his suspicions. He had heard Cadrain's description of Milgaard and the suggestion that Milgaard wanted to wipe out his friends because they knew too much. And he was just naturally suspicious of any drug-using kids who wandered around aimlessly without any respect for the rule of law.

"Milgaard wasn't an ordinary guy," Karst recalls. "He was different. He was the scary type. A bit of a weirdo. People who dealt with him didn't trust him. I never turned around at one time for too long. Not that he ever threatened me or anything – nor did I ever hear him threaten anybody."

With their initial interviews complete, police were hardly further ahead. At the end of February, their investigation into Gail Miller's murder had reached a dead end. All possible suspects had been eliminated, and the hundreds of leads that were prompted by the reward and public appeals were exhausted. The only hope for a break in the case came when Albert Cadrain walked into the police station with his story. It remains surprising that no one on the investigating team treated Cadrain's second story with a dose of scepticism. Did the police not wonder whether the incentive of a reward played a part?

Now that police had checked out Cadrain's story, all they had were three largely similar versions of what happened from

Milgaard, Wilson, and John. Nothing in their initial statements suggested that Milgaard was guilty. It could be that all three were lying in order to protect Milgaard. But still, a murder in such circumstances didn't make much sense. There appeared to be no motive for Milgaard to commit such a horrible crime, nor was there any physical evidence linking him to it. Milgaard had no history of any violence, nor was there any reason to believe he had a proclivity for sexual attacks. If Cadrain's story was to be believed, why would Milgaard have lingered in the same area as the murder – no more than two blocks away from where Gail Miller's body was found – for about nine hours before leaving town?

All police knew for certain, on the basis of the various statements, was that David Milgaard was in Saskatoon at the time the murder was committed. They also knew that he was a drug-using hippie wandering through a town that didn't take kindly to long hair and mind-altering substances. Most of all, they recognized that David Milgaard was their only hope left for a conviction in a case that was starting to slip from their grasp.

Saskatoon police realized they would have to break Ron Wilson and Nichol John if they hoped to build a case against Milgaard. Cadrain's information was important, but it only provided a tenuous circumstantial link to the crime. Milgaard, after all, had arrived at Cadrain's house after Gail Miller had been murdered. Wilson and John, on the other hand, were with Milgaard the whole time they were in Saskatoon. Their testimony would be crucial in any court proceedings against Milgaard.

Police began putting pressure on Ron Wilson. While he was still in Regina, they visited him repeatedly. Karst and Short each grilled Wilson at least three times in Regina, and other members of the Saskatoon and Regina police departments also interrogated him. Armed with Cadrain's statement, they accused Wilson of lying to them and trying to cover up the truth. Police also made it clear to Wilson that he himself was a prime suspect in the murder. After all, he arrived in Saskatoon the morning of the murder and left town the same day. What alibi did he have? Why should police believe his story?

"I distinctly remember telling the detectives during this initial questioning that I knew nothing about the murder and hadn't even heard about it. They told me that they thought I was lying," Wilson says. "I was seventeen years old and very frightened because I felt that the police were trying to pin the murder on me."

Police made no secret of their suspicions, and the other inmates in Regina soon realized why police were visiting Wilson so often. This only added to the pressure on Wilson, but he stuck to his story.

Back in Saskatoon, the weather was turning warmer. By the beginning of April, the snow had begun to melt and residents were starting to forget about the deep-freeze of a few months earlier.

On April 4, eight-year-old Giles Beauchamp was coming home down Avenue O, kicking snow as he went. He had gone to the Cadrain house to call on one of his friends. His friend wasn't there, so Giles started to make his way back home. Three doors up from Cadrain's house, on the same side of the street, he kicked at the snow and saw something underneath. On the edge of the sidewalk and the snowbank was a wallet. He took the wallet to another friend's house, and his friend's mother called police. The wallet had no money in it, but it had identification papers. It belonged to Gail Miller.

The police officer asked Giles to show him the exact spot where he had found the wallet. Giles took him to the front of 326 Avenue O and pointed out the location. Giles noticed there were two papers which had fallen out of the wallet when he picked it up. They were hospital insurance cards belonging to Gail Miller.

The discovery of the wallet was greeted with excitement at the police station. All the other pieces of evidence had been found more than a block away, in the immediate vicinity of the murdered body. But here was the victim's wallet, a good distance away, strongly indicating that the assailant had been on that street and almost immediately in front of Cadrain's house. To Detective Karst and his colleagues, it was reassuring evidence that they were on the right trail in trying to build a case against David Milgaard. Of course, the wallet's location could just as easily have pointed the finger to someone else who lived in the Cadrain house.

The next day, Karst embarked on a door-to-door search for items on Avenue O. He canvassed the entire neighbourhood, asking people if they had seen anything unusual over the last two months. At 330 Avenue O, right next door to Cadrain's house, Karst met Helen Gerse. His inquiry prompted an immediate reply. Yes, she said, at the beginning of February she had found a blood-stained blue toque in front of her house. She thought nothing of it at the time. She had picked it up and dropped it in her backyard. With her permission, Karst retrieved the toque and turned it over to the department's identification section.

The retrieval of the toque was further encouraging news for the investigators. Although there was no evidence Milgaard had worn a blue toque that day – in fact, the evidence suggested he was wearing a green and yellow hat he had borrowed from Wilson's sister – the police were happy. They knew that the wallet and toque would allow a Crown attorney to paint a convincing picture in court of a trail of evidence leading to the Cadrain house – the house that David Milgaard was visiting on the day of the murder.

In the meantime, police were still working on Ron Wilson. He was scheduled to be released from jail May 9. Just before his release, Karst visited him again and tried to break him. Again Wilson denied any knowledge of the murder and refused to implicate Milgaard in any way.

Wilson felt besieged by the police. Over the next two weeks he would be interrogated again by police from Regina and Saskatoon, and by the RCMP. At times it seemed they were trying to force him to implicate Milgaard. At other times he felt they were interested in pinning the murder on him. He thought the interrogations would end as soon as he left jail,

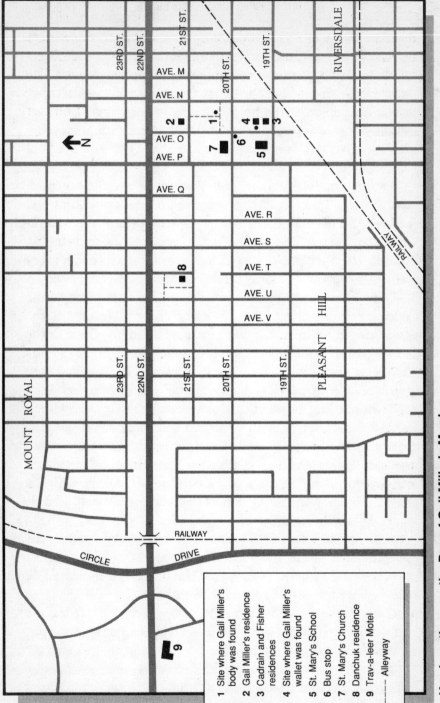

Key Locations on the Day of Gail Miller's Murder

1 Site where Gail Miller's body was found
2 Gail Miller's residence
3 Cadrain and Fisher residences
4 Site where Gail Miller's wallet was found
5 St. Mary's School
6 Bus stop
7 St. Mary's Church
8 Danchuk residence
9 Trav-a-leer Motel
——— Alleyway

but they continued without let-up. Soon after his release Wilson began drinking heavily. He would recall later that this was the beginning of a period of extensive drug use as well. He remembers taking LSD at least twice a week, sometimes injecting it directly into his blood stream with a syringe. Over the next few months, until a subsequent arrest for possession of drugs, he also used marijuana, hashish, mescaline, and heroin.

At one point he told the police what they wanted to hear, that it was possible Milgaard may have committed the offence. Yet his statement was unconvincing and was accompanied by no tangible proof. Finally, police suggested that he come with them back to Saskatoon. It might jog his memory if he saw some of the same streets again. Wilson complied.

Eddie Karst drove Wilson from Regina to Saskatoon in the third week of May. Along the way, Wilson pointed out the grain elevator where they had stolen a flashlight. Once in the city, Wilson was taken to the area where Gail Miller's body had been found. He was familiarized with all the landmarks in the area, and repeatedly asked what he could remember.

In the evening, he was taken to a room at the Cavalier Hotel, where Saskatoon police subjected him to further lengthy interview sessions. He remembers some lasting six hours at a stretch. Police used a variety of tactics to wear him down psychologically. They brought a polygraph machine into the room, hooked Wilson up, and fired questions at him. Did he kill Gail Miller? Did David Milgaard kill Gail Miller? Wilson remembers at least two sessions where he was grilled on the polygraph machine, both lasting as long as six hours. Police said they didn't believe him, that the polygraph indicated he was lying, that he had better come clean.

Police showed Wilson Gail Miller's coat, her white nurse's uniform, her blood-stained undergarments. Did he recognize any of the clothes? They trotted out an arsenal of different weapons, including a paring knife with a maroon handle. They told Wilson that a broken knife blade had been found under Miller's body. They showed him Gail Miller's purse, and told him it had been found in a trash can nearby. Later, they actually took him to the scene and pointed out where all the items, including the purse, had been found.

In the middle of an interview session at the hotel, Wilson received a jolt. Police brought Nichol John into the room and began questioning them both at the same time. He learned that she had been subjected to the same grilling as he had over the last few weeks.

Wilson had a vague suspicion of what was going on. Police were giving him every opportunity to implicate Milgaard in the murder, and they were also supplying him with details that he might use in doing so.

Finally, Wilson cracked. After a couple of days in Saskatoon, he proceeded to renounce his previous version of events, and began weaving a new story – a story that was to seal David Milgaard's fate.

"My mind was exhausted and I was mentally scrambled," Wilson said twenty years later, recalling the events of that day. "I remember it now being like brainwashing. Finally I began to implicate Milgaard in the murder, telling police the things they wanted to hear."

At the time, Wilson was a frightened young man, terrified at the prospect of spending more time behind bars, and anxious to shake the police off his back.

Wilson's first revelation was that he had seen David with a knife during the car ride between Regina and Saskatoon. He went further. It was a paring knife, with a reddish-brown handle.

Then Wilson recounted a story which, if true, showed how Milgaard had had a window of opportunity for killing Gail Miller. Wilson said the trio was driving aimlessly around Saskatoon before daylight when they saw a woman in a dark coat walking down the street. Wilson, who was driving at the time, pulled alongside the woman. Milgaard, on the right passenger side, rolled down the window and asked the woman for directions. She couldn't help them out, he said. Milgaard rolled the window back up and, according to Wilson, called her a "stupid bitch."

After that exchange, Wilson drove another three-quarters of

a block and attempted a U-turn. His car got stuck in the snow. Wilson then contended that he and Milgaard, after trying unsuccessfully to push the car out, went off in different directions in search of help, while Nichol remained in the car. Some time later, after failing to find any help, Wilson returned to the car to find Nichol "pretty well in a hysterical state," screaming. Five or six minutes later, Milgaard returned to the car. According to Wilson, Milgaard was cold, breathing heavily, and made the comment "I fixed her," or words to that effect.

Wilson said that all of this occurred around 6:30 a.m. At the trial, he was specific about the car's location as well. It was on Avenue N at 20th Street, just beside the entrance to the T-shaped alley where Gail Miller's body was found. Wilson went on to say that two men in their mid-forties pulled up in a cream-coloured Chrysler and helped get their car unstuck. He didn't know their names and couldn't provide a description of these men, nor did police ever locate them.

After emphatically insisting for weeks that Milgaard did not have any blood on his clothes, Wilson now changed his story on that score as well. He said he, too, saw blood on David's pants at Albert Cadrain's house.

On the trip to Alberta, Wilson now said, another incident of a suspicious nature had taken place. Nichol was looking through the glove compartment and found a woman's cosmetic case. She asked whose it was. Wilson said it hadn't been in the car when they left Regina. Without uttering a word, David leaned over, snatched the cosmetics' case from Nichol, and flung it out of the window. None of the other three people in the car questioned this action, nor was anything further said about it.

Perhaps the most damning evidence of all implicating Milgaard in the murder was Wilson's recollection of a conversation they had later during their travels through Alberta. They pulled into Calgary late in the evening on the 31st, and Wilson and Milgaard went into the bus depot to find the phone number of a friend who lived in the city. According to Wilson, David then admitted to him that he had "hit a girl" or "got a girl" in Saskatoon and went on to say that he had put her purse in a trash can and that he thought the girl would be okay. Wilson said no one else heard the conversation, and that he didn't bother pursuing it with David because he didn't believe it was true.

Police used largely the same strategy with Nichol John. They began repeatedly questioning her about the circumstances surrounding the trip. Everything Cadrain had told them was thrown back at her, and she was asked to confirm it. She would later say that from mid-February until October of that year, she was on an almost continuous LSD trip, taking the drug orally or injecting it every three days.

On March 18, a week after Nichol had told police she knew nothing about the murder, the investigators tried a different strategy. Charlie Short and Eddie Karst bundled Cadrain into a car and drove him to Regina. Short explained what happened next in his written report.

"Nichol John was located in a hippie house in Regina," he said. "She was, after considerable persuasion, brought to Regina gaol and interviewed by Karst and myself, and was placed in a room with Cadrain and allowed to discuss this matter, and it was learned from her after this discussion, through interrogation, that she was of the opinion that Cadrain was telling the truth and that everything he said was exactly what had happened on this trip."

It was a twist on the old police trick of dividing up suspects and interviewing them separately. In this case, the police were faced with the problem of two diametrically opposed stories from a pair of teenagers who had been on the same trip. Putting them together, they hoped, would convince them to come up with the same story – a story that they hoped would advance their investigation. The strategy worked.

Nichol was showing her first signs of wavering. She was frightened and confused and didn't want to be put in the position of calling Cadrain a liar. A month a half earlier they had been four friends travelling together and having a good time. Now, one of them was suspected of murder, and the others were being asked to substantiate those suspicions. She realized police wanted to hear her corroborate Cadrain's story. So she did. But she was still reluctant to go a further step and give a written statement to that effect. She never admitted seeing blood on David's clothes that day.

Police also probed Nichol about the nature of her relationship with Milgaard. Was she his girlfriend? That question scared her. Perhaps they were suggesting she might be his accomplice. She told police that David wasn't really a boyfriend, and that, in fact, she was afraid of him. She said he had pressed her to have sex on several occasions when she hadn't wanted it.

Nichol's statement made a lasting impression on the officers assigned to the murder investigation. In their minds, it provided the first tangible evidence that Milgaard might indeed be capable of a heinous crime. Still, it was a long way from being aggressive with a girlfriend to committing rape and murder. But for the officers, it was all they needed to begin forming a picture of a dangerous character. Once it was formulated, that picture became imprinted on the minds of all the police officers who came into contact with the case. Even Saskatoon officers who had nothing to do with the murder investigation learned over coffee or through chit-chat that David Milgaard was a weirdo, a sex-crazed hippie with shifty eyes.

An official Saskatoon police department investigation report written on March 22, 1969, by Charlie Short provides a good example of the bias that permeated the entire department. "It is my opinion that Milgaard is a dangerous person and it is known that he had a record as a juvenile for several serious offences," Short wrote. Milgaard, of course, did not have a record of several serious offences. His only conviction had been for his joy-riding episode when he was fourteen. As for being dangerous, there was simply no evidence. Milgaard had no history of any violent behaviour, and had been cooperative and polite when interviewed by Karst three weeks earlier.

The police realized that Nichol might hold the key to a more powerful case against Milgaard. They did not leave her alone, but kept interviewing her regularly, going over the same questions again and again. Finally, as they had done with Wilson, they brought Nichol to Saskatoon to "jog" her memory. She was driven around the city streets repeatedly and shown all the relevant locations. Then, on May 23, she was taken to the Cavalier Hotel, where she was shown the same assortment of Gail Miller's clothes and the same collection of knives as Wilson had seen. Although Nichol was never under arrest, she was confused about what police wanted of her and whether she had to go along with everything they were doing.

When police were finished questioning her for the day, they took her to the cell block of the Saskatoon police station. Terrified about being locked up for no apparent reason, she began to protest loudly. No one else was in the cell block at the time. She banged on the walls and started to scream. Police eventually moved her to the room normally occupied by a matron adjacent to the women's cells, where she spent the night. The matron gave her aspirins and tried to calm her down, but Nichol was in a state of near hysteria. She got no sleep that night.

The next day, after again being driven around by police, Nichol was returned to the matron's room in the jail. This time she was completely alone, and police didn't tell her what would be happening next. She waited. Eventually, police arrived and told her they wanted to take a formal statement from her. Following the statement, it was suggested, they would then drive her home.

Even the investigators who had spent months trying to break the Gail Miller case were flabbergasted at the statement Nichol gave. They were hoping and expecting her to confirm Albert Cadrain's story about seeing blood on Milgaard's pants, perhaps confirming Wilson's statement by saying that she saw the knife as well. What they got went much further than that.

The statement Nichol John gave to Sergeant Ray Mackie was ten pages long – ten pages of facts and recollections that were a complete contradiction of everything she had been telling police up to that point. After a day and night of confusion and fear in Saskatoon, here is what the sixteen-year-old girl told police about the morning of January 31, 1969:

After we got to Saskatoon we drove around for about 10 or 15 minutes. Then we talked to this girl. This was in the area where Sergeant Mackie drove me around. Ron was driving the car at this time. He drove to the curb where Dave spoke to this girl. Dave was on the outside passenger side of the front seat. Dave opened the door to talk to this girl as she approached along the sidewalk. Dave asked this girl for directions to either downtown or Pleasant Hill.

He offered to give her a ride to wherever she was going. She refused the ride. Dave closed the door and said, "the stupid bitch."

We started to drive away and only went about half a block where we got stuck and we ended up stuck at the entrance to the alley behind the funeral home. Ron and Dave got out and they tried to push the car. They couldn't get it out.

I recall Dave going back in the direction we had spoke to the girl. Ron went the other way past the funeral home. The next thing I recall seeing Dave in the alley on the right side of the car. He had ahold of the same girl he spoke to a minute before. I saw him grab her purse. I saw her grab for her purse again.

Dave reached into one of his pockets and pulled out the knife. I don't know which pocket he got the knife from. The knife was in his right hand. I don't know if Dave had ahold of this girl or not at this time. All I recall is seeing him stabbing her with the knife. The next I recall is him taking her around the corner of the alley. I think I ran after that. I think I ran in the direction Ron had gone.

I recall running down the street. I don't recall seeing anyone. The next thing I know I was sitting in the car again. I don't know how I got back to the car.

I seem to recall seeing Dave putting a purse into a garbage can. I don't remember which time it was or where I was when I saw this. I recall there were two garbage cans; the one on the left had the lid tipped; I don't recall which one he put it in.

The next I remember sitting in the car. I don't remember Ron being in the car or coming back. I remember Dave coming back and getting into the front seat of the car. I remember moving over towards the driver's side because I didn't want to be near him. I don't remember talking to Ron before Dave got back. I do not recall Dave saying anything.

There was more. Nichol maintained she saw David with a maroon-handled paring knife after they left Regina. And she also said that David had thrown a cosmetics' case out the window on the way to Alberta, after she had found the case in the car's glove compartment.

Police could not have obtained a more damning indictment of David Milgaard if they had written it themselves. It was all there – an eyewitness description of the stabbing, an explanation of the motive, a pinpointing of the location, even an account of how the purse got into the garbage can. What more could the prosecution need to press its case against Milgaard?

No one acknowledged it at the time, but there were some problems with Nichol John's statement.

Nichol said she saw the knife in Milgaard's right hand immediately before he stabbed the girl. That wasn't surprising, since medical and police experts had already determined that Gail Miller's wounds were consistent with having been inflicted by a right-handed assailant. It all made perfect sense, except for one fact. David Milgaard is left-handed.

There was another aspect of Nichol John's statement that should have raised some doubt about its truth. It had to do with the arrangement of Gail Miller's clothing when her body was found, a puzzling detail that police had not made public at the time of the murder. The top of her dress had been rolled down to the waist, and there were no knife cuts in the dress. But there were five cuts clearly visible in her overcoat. In other words, it appeared that Miller first had her clothes torn from her, after which she managed to pull her overcoat back on. Only then was she stabbed. According to Nichol John's account, however, Milgaard stabbed the girl while she was still fully clothed – an impossibility given the lack of any cut in her dress. Still, the police thought they, finally, had an eyewitness to the murder.

Two days after Nichol John signed her statement, police issued a warrant for David Milgaard's arrest. They had met with him two or three times before then – gathering saliva and blood samples and asking further questions. Each time David had been cooperative and willing to help, almost friendly with his interrogators. They didn't expect any problem picking him up this time.

At this time, David was working in the Prince George area selling magazines – the same magazines that would later feature articles on his own story. He had taken a definite liking to the job. "We would just sell on the street sometimes, or door to door – gift of the gab, and hope that somebody buys what you're saying more than they want the magazines. And you do pretty good.

"[On May 30] we were just finishing off a certain area I was working in. It's a nice place, really picturesque. The boss comes up, says 'They're taking you somewhere. They want to see you again.' I go down there, I walk in and say, 'Excuse me, I'm here to see someone.' He says, 'Who are you?' I say, 'David Milgaard.' He says, 'No, you're not David Milgaard. Are you David Milgaard?' I said, 'Ya.' He said, 'Don't move. You're under arrest for non-capital murder.' And then bang, that was it. Just in the cage."

David didn't believe what was happening. After all the information he had given them, after the samples he had provided, they had come back and were arresting him. He thought it must be a mistake. He believed it could all be straightened out if he kept cooperating and providing all the information he could.

"I had maps out. I was just a green kid inside the lockdown situation. And I was just sitting there, and I had maps out. I'm arrested, and I'm showing them the way we came into the city and all the routes. They must have just loved me."

May 30, 1969, was the last day David Milgaard was free to come and go as he pleased. Early the next morning, an RCMP and city police escort left Saskatoon for Prince George, to pick up the sixteen-year-old youth they said had murdered Gail Miller.

6

On Trial

Events moved quickly for David Milgaard in the next few months. It was like a horrible dream playing itself out, a dream he was powerless to control. In Langenburg, the news of David's arrest hit his parents hard. They weren't ignorant of his involvement with drugs and petty crimes, but they couldn't fathom a charge of murder. Instinctively they knew there must be some mistake. They were certain their son was no murderer. Unable to bear the cost of his defence, they turned to Legal Aid. A prominent Saskatoon lawyer and Queen's Counsel, Calvin Tallis, was appointed David's lawyer. It was an intriguing choice of counsel – Tallis also represented the Saskatoon Police Association at the time.

Milgaard was formally charged with murder on June 2. In 1969, the charge of capital murder was reserved for killers of policemen and prison guards, and a guilty verdict carried the death penalty. Milgaard faced a charge of non-capital murder, and a maximum sentence of life imprisonment with no mandatory parole.

Being in jail gave him plenty of time to reflect on what had happened to him. "Just sitting and waiting was a very, very trying time for me," he recalls. "I felt very worried. I didn't understand what was happening. And it didn't make any sense. I kept telling everybody, and they kept saying to tell the truth, it will come out, and all the rest of it. But I had that sense that things weren't right, because why would they arrest me if there was no reason to? They must have had some reason to arrest me. I was scared."

David's mother, Joyce, was scared, too. With her son in custody and the family finances in a shambles, she decided to move to Saskatoon to be nearby. She rented an apartment and found a job as a waitress in a small Chinese restaurant. She would work until two or three in the morning, catch a couple of hours' sleep, then visit David.

"I remember bringing milkshakes to him. I remember him wanting comic books. He was seventeen by that time, but he was still such a boy. I remember sometimes we prayed together because he was a scared kid at that time, too. But I can remember believing in him."

By mid-August the Crown had marshalled a formidable case. The Attorney General's department picked T. D. R. (Bobs) Caldwell to head the prosecution. He was thorough, interviewing a large number of witnesses in an effort to buttress the Crown's case. Tallis, meanwhile, was at a distinct disadvantage. The only potential witnesses were Milgaard's companions on the day of the murder, and they were all scheduled to testify for the Crown.

By the time the preliminary hearing began on August 18, 1969, public curiosity was at a high, and the media were quick to exploit the situation. All the elements for a dramatic story were there: a high-profile murder, a seventeen-year-old accused, an eyewitness account, drug-using teenagers. There were, as yet, no legal restrictions on reporting the testimony at preliminary hearings. The result was a media field-day, with every aspect of the Crown's case reported in full. How this might prejudice a potential jury was of no concern at the time. All the Crown cared about was mounting a convincing and effective case so that it could proceed to trial.

Over the next three weeks, Caldwell called forty-two witnesses – everyone from the little girl who had discovered Gail Miller's body to police officers who had come into contact with obscure bits of evidence. But for all his efforts, Caldwell could probably have convinced the judge of the need to commit Milgaard to trial with just three people: Albert Cadrain, Nichol John, and Ron Wilson. Here, after all, were Milgaard's friends and companions on that day. All would incriminate him, and all seemingly had no reason to lie.

Milgaard's friends seemed nervous and restless as they came into court to offer their testimony. They avoided eye contact with him. He felt betrayed and outraged when he heard their stories. Suddenly he was being painted as a ruthless killer who stabbed a woman he didn't even know while trying to grab her purse.

"I just couldn't believe it when I started to hear the testimony," Milgaard says. "It scared me. I wanted to jump up and say something, I wanted to tell the truth from start to finish. I wanted to do that badly, but I couldn't. My lawyer suggested that I not do that. His reason at the time, he told me, was that everybody was telling different stories. And he said, 'If you get up there and you tell the truth, it will be a different story.' I argued with him. I said, 'Why is one more different story going to be worse?' He didn't really say anything to that. He just asked me to sign a piece of paper saying that I made a decision not to take the stand, and I signed the piece of paper."

Tallis had his reasons for not wanting his client to testify. The purpose of a preliminary hearing is to determine whether enough evidence exists to warrant a trial. The defence generally uses the preliminary to learn the full extent of the Crown's case and to prepare to rebut it at the trial. It's considered bad strategy for the defence to reveal too much of its case at this stage.

Caldwell, for his part, was eager to reveal as much as possible. He encouraged his witnesses not to hold back, but to say everything they wanted. As a consequence, some of the Crown's witnesses seemed almost too eager to present evidence that would incriminate Milgaard. Albert Cadrain's testimony was one example. He excitedly offered a version of events that was clearly an embellishment of his earlier stories. When asked what happened after Milgaard and his friends arrived at his home on the morning of the murder, Cadrain, who to that point had only said he saw blood on Milgaard's clothes, answered, "Well, they were kind of nervous and running around, I guess, and Hoppy said, 'I got blood on my clothes and I have to change.' Well, first, before that, he said, 'We got to get out of town, we're going to Edmonton,' and he was kind of hinting for some money."

Never before had Cadrain revealed that Milgaard admitted to having blood on his clothes. It was a twist Caldwell wasn't eager to pursue, as he realized neither Wilson nor Nichol would corroborate that point. Instead, he moved the nervous Cadrain along in his testimony.

Cadrain went on to tell a strange tale about Milgaard signalling an unknown transport driver by flashing his lights on and off while Wilson and John were asleep during their trip. When the transport driver stopped, David handed him one of his suitcases. At another point in their trip, David had told him he was a member of the Mafia.

These were preposterous statements that did more to call Cadrain's credibility into question than to implicate Milgaard in the murder. Cadrain never mentioned them in court again.

Tallis did his best to raise doubts and point out contradictions in the evidence, but the fact remained that Milgaard's companions were all pointing the finger at him. When it came to the closing arguments at the preliminary hearing, there wasn't much doubt about the outcome.

"I think, in the light of the evidence which has been heard, that the accused is probably guilty, and that it is sufficient to commit him for trial," Caldwell told the judge. Tallis argued in vain that the possibility, or even probability, of guilt, wasn't sufficient to commit for trial. He pointed to the chronology of Milgaard's movements before and after the murder, which he said made it virtually impossible for him to have committed the crime. But his arguments were in vain. Judge H. J. Cumming committed Milgaard to stand trial for non-capital murder at the next Court of Queen's Bench sitting in Saskatoon.

*   *   *

The trial began five months later at 10:00 a.m. on January 19, 1970. David Milgaard sat nervously in the prisoner's box, wearing the new dark green suit, gold shirt, and tie his mother had bought after scraping together some money. His hair was short and he was clean-shaven. In all respects, he gave the appearance of being a neat and respectable young man. It was a small attempt to counteract the sea of negative images that all the publicity had generated. There was no motion to move the trial to a different venue, to a place where newspaper readers and television viewers might not have been exposed to all the lurid details of the murder and descriptions of the hippie suspect. Instead, a jury of eleven men and one woman was sworn, and they settled into what Chief Justice A. H. Bence told them would be a lengthy trial. It didn't take long for the jury to have the opportunity of assessing David Milgaard's demeanour. It came at the very start of the trial, when the charge was read.

"Do you understand the charge as it has been read to you?" the court clerk asked.

"Yes sir," Milgaard replied softly.

"And how say you? Do you plead guilty or not guilty?"

"Not guilty, sir."

Those were the only words the jury heard David Milgaard utter during the entire trial.

There's little doubt that the jury members were already aware of at least some details of the case. But even if they weren't, Caldwell wasted no time in telling them. Under the adversary system used in Canadian trials, the Crown presents as strong a case as it can, then the defence attempts to discredit the testimony and prove that the accused is not guilty beyond a reasonable doubt. A jury then makes the ultimate determination, with the assistance of a judge, who guides them on the weight they should put on evidence and the application of relevant law. The jury is the final judge of the facts.

But another tradition also exists in the Canadian judicial system, a tradition that often works against the rights of the accused. This calls for the Crown counsel to outline its case in an opening address to the jury. Even though the evidence during the course of the trial may be disputed or discredited, the Crown is allowed to summarize it before the jury has heard anything else. Bobs Caldwell took full advantage of this tradition in his address to the jury, giving a lengthy exposition of what he expected each of his forty-two witnesses to say when called to the stand. At the end of his presentation, the jury had before it a damning and convincing argument that David Milgaard had murdered Gail Miller.

Caldwell spent the first day of the trial setting the scene. He quickly entered into evidence police photographs of the murder site and of Gail Miller's body. The latter photographs showed in gruesome detail her slashed and mutilated body. An identification officer with the Saskatoon police, Thor Kleiv, was asked to confirm the different articles of Gail Miller's clothing that had been recovered following the autopsy. As if to demonstrate the certainty of the attack, Caldwell asked Kleiv to hold up the coat Gail Miller wore on the day of the murder and point out the five holes. He did it twice, once for the judge's benefit and once for the jury.

The central part of the Crown's case began in earnest the next day, when Ron Wilson was called to the stand. In many ways, he was considered the star witness, the accused's friend, who was in a position to know all the incriminating evidence. Caldwell made no mention of Wilson's signed statement to police on March 3, 1969, in which he denied any knowledge of the murder. Instead, he led Wilson into the story of how he saw a knife on Milgaard, blood on his clothes, and the other incriminating details he had provided in his final statement to police.

Throughout Wilson's testimony, there were hints that his evidence was too pat. It seemed almost tailor-made to fit the Crown's case. This appeared to become evident both to Justice Bence and to Tallis during the questioning. For instance, Wilson was suspiciously vague when grilled by the judge about his claim that he saw a knife on David during their trip.

Caldwell: Now, on the way to Saskatoon did you see anything in the car which might be a potential weapon of any sort?

Wilson:	I saw a knife.
Caldwell:	And where did you see that?
Wilson:	On David somewhere between Regina and Saskatoon.
Justice Bence:	Just a minute please; you say on –
Wilson:	On the way between Regina and Saskatoon.
Justice Bence:	Yes but you saw a knife in the car and I thought you said on David.
Wilson:	Yes.
Justice Bence:	On David?
Wilson:	Yes.

At this point, the Crown wanted Wilson to describe the knife, but Justice Bence still wasn't satisfied.

Justice Bence:	Excuse me just a minute – would you follow up by – where was it on him?
Wilson:	On him personally, I guess you could put it.
Caldwell:	Where was that? Just explain what you mean by that.
Wilson:	On his – I don't know how you would put it like but it was on him – in his clothes or something to that effect.
Justice Bence:	But how would you see it if it was in his pocket, for example?
Wilson:	Well, I don't know if it was in his pocket or not but at the time I saw it.
Justice Bence:	Where was it, in his hand or – ?
Wilson:	This I can't remember.

The judge still wasn't convinced that Wilson was telling the truth. Later on in the testimony he returned to the subject of the knife.

Justice Bence:	And on what side of him did you see the knife – on his left or his right side?

Wilson: I believe it was his right side.

Justice Bence: Well, if his right side was against the door of the car how could you see any object he might have?

Wilson: Well, he wasn't necessarily sitting up straight, like he was kind of slouched.

Justice Bence: Well, in view of the lighting conditions and the fact that it was dark outside, how were you able to see the knife?

Wilson: Well once your eyes get adjusted to the light you can see in the car pretty well.

In contrast to all the confusion about how Wilson could have seen the knife and where he actually did see it, the witness was certain about what kind of knife it was. In his very next answer, Wilson said, "It had a reddish-brown handle and was a sort of paring-knife type."

In his cross-examination, Cal Tallis tried to drive home the point that there couldn't have been enough time for Milgaard to have committed the murder. To do this, he had to challenge Wilson's contention that he and Milgaard had been separated for a long time when they went looking for help to get their car unstuck. According to Wilson's testimony at the trial, their car became stuck around 6:30 a.m., shortly after Milgaard had spoken to the girl in the dark coat on the street. Wilson then said he walked four or five blocks before returning to the car. Altogether, he said he was separated from Milgaard for about fifteen minutes.

But Tallis had before him Wilson's testimony at the preliminary hearing, where he told the court that he only walked about two and a half blocks before returning to the car. At the time, he said he and Milgaard had only been separated about five minutes. Tallis put the contradictions to Wilson:

Tallis: And then I suggest to you, witness, that you were only away from David for about five minutes at that time.

Wilson:	No.
Tallis:	You deny that?
Wilson:	Yes I do.
Tallis:	Just as you now say it was five blocks instead of two and a half?
Wilson:	Yes.
Tallis:	Why do you choose to double it under oath on this occasion?
Wilson:	Because since the preliminary I have been thinking about it a lot.

"I felt really bad when I sat in that courtroom and listened to him say things that weren't true," David later recalled. "I felt the guy just sold me down the river and he knew it wasn't the truth. I don't know why he did that."

When it came to contradictory evidence, Nichol John presented even more of a problem for the Crown. After signing the statement that had led directly to David's arrest, in which she said that she had seen the murder take place, Nichol again changed her story. In effect, she repudiated her statement, saying that she could no longer remember what had happened that morning.

Caldwell's frustration was evident when he asked Nichol to reconstruct the events of the morning of January 31, 1969. She reiterated the story of stopping a woman and asking her for directions. But, contrary to her written statement, she said she now couldn't remember David calling the woman a "stupid bitch." When it came to the key eyewitness testimony of seeing David stab the girl, Nichol again said she could remember nothing.

At this point, Caldwell asked for the jury and witness to be excused while he made a special application under a newly enacted change to the Canada Evidence Act. He argued that Nichol had given a previous signed statement that was inconsistent with her trial testimony. As a result, he said he should be given the opportunity to cross-examine the witness and then make an application to the court for a declaration that the witness is hostile. The purpose would be to allow Caldwell to pose challenging questions to his own witness. The net effect of this manoeuvre, however, would be to have the entire incriminating statement of May 24 read into the record, even though Nichol no longer agreed with it.

Tallis insisted that the cross-examination to determine the consistency of Nichol's testimony should be held in the absence of the jury. He argued it would be prejudicial to his client's interests if it were done in open court. But Justice Bence ruled that the cross-examination could take place in the presence of the jury. After the cross-examination, he ruled that Nichol was indeed a hostile Crown witness, and allowed Caldwell to read her entire statement to the jury. His judgement became known as the Milgaard Ruling, and would be quoted in countless cases thereafter. But for David Milgaard, it was a decision that allowed the jury to hear highly incriminating evidence, even though the person who provided the evidence no longer believed in it.

The entire experience was terrifying for Nichol John. She sobbed uncontrollably as Caldwell read back the statement she had signed in May. At each key point Caldwell asked if she remembered providing those details, and if she still believed them.

Caldwell: Did you tell Sergeant Mackie this: "The next thing I recall seeing Dave in the alley on the right side of the car. He had ahold of the same girl he spoke to a minute before. I saw him grab her purse. I saw her grab for the purse again." Did you tell Sergeant Mackie those things?

John: I don't remember.

Justice Bence: Do you remember any part of it?

John: No.

Justice Bence: Are you saying you didn't tell Sergeant Mackie that?

John: I'm saying I don't remember if I did or if I didn't.

Justice Bence:	Well, if you did see the accused grab the purse it's something you would have remembered, isn't it? Isn't it? Witness?
John:	I don't know.
Justice Bence:	Take a drink of water and stop crying.
John:	If I could tell you what happened I'd tell you. I don't know. I can't remember. . . . I don't remember anything. My mind is a blank. Nobody understands. Nobody wants to believe me.

Caldwell skilfully turned a difficult situation for the Crown's case to his best advantage. Ordinarily, it would be disastrous for the prosecution to have one of his own witnesses completely change her mind on the stand. But he used the occasion to elicit all of Nichol's earlier statement. He made no mention of the intense police pressure which had led to her statement in the first place, nor was he obliged to. Instead, by challenging her credibility, he made it appear that she was now changing her story in an effort to protect the accused. Not satisfied with simply reading Nichol's statement to the jury, Caldwell hammered home every critical point with individual questions to the witness.

Caldwell:	You don't know whether you saw him grab her purse and her grab for her purse again?
John:	No I don't.
Caldwell:	You just can't say one way or another, eh?
John:	No.
Caldwell:	And you don't know whether you saw Dave reach into his pocket and pull out the knife?
John:	No I don't.
Caldwell:	Or whether it was in his right hand?
John:	No I don't.
Caldwell:	And you don't recall him stabbing her with the knife?
John:	No I don't.
Caldwell:	And you don't recall whether or not you saw him taking her around the corner of the alley?

John: No I don't.

Caldwell: And as I understand it you don't even recall whether you ran after that?

John: No I don't.

Caldwell: I put it to you, Miss John, that those are all things that if you or anyone else saw them, you would absolutely have no trouble at all in remembering them, is that not right?

John: I wouldn't know. . . . As far as I'm concerned I don't know what happened. I don't even know if I was on that trip or not. . . . If you just stop and think how much this bothered me – I'm beginning to wonder if *I* even did it or not.

Only after the jury had absorbed the full extent of Nichol's previous statement did the judge warn them to be careful about what they had heard. Nothing in the earlier statement was to be considered evidence, he said, unless Nichol John admitted to it on the stand. Of course, Nichol had admitted to very little of it on the stand. But the damage had been done.

Interest in the trial was starting to peak. Day after day the courtroom was packed, with people lining the sides and back of the room and many sitting on the floor. For the people of Saskatoon, it was a novelty – the kind of entertainment usually seen only on television or the movies.

"I think it's fair to say that the focus of the whole city was on the trial and there was this intense interest to everybody," Bobs Caldwell said later. "It was a very big trial because there was a great deal of fear in the town that whoever did this was still out running around."

Saskatoon's politicians were also aware of the trial's importance and the necessity to assure people that police had indeed caught the right man. Mayor Sidney Buckwold chose the occasion to make a public statement praising what he called the police department's outstanding record, particularly in the area of serious crime. "The department has shown good performance as far as clearing offences is concerned," he said, in a statement that was carried by the media while the trial was in progress.

Like Buckwold, Caldwell was no stranger when it came to playing to the crowd. The thirty-six-year-old prosecutor was also an amateur jazz trombonist, and he once observed that the joy of playing comes from being in a group "where you're surrounded by compatible people and where you can tell how well the concert is going by the way everybody is moving."

With Caldwell conducting the prosecution, the Milgaard trial moved at a steady rhythm. Caldwell's strategy was to build his case in a methodical manner. He had, by this time, set the scene, shocked the jury with the brutality of the murder by entering the photographs and blood-stained articles of clothing, and had ensured that the jury had heard all of the damning, albeit circumstantial, evidence from Milgaard's own travelling companions. Caldwell now quickly moved to solidify that impact by calling Albert "Shorty" Cadrain to the stand.

Caldwell led his witness through the events of January 31, 1969. Cadrain had been sleeping on the couch in the living room when he heard a knock at the door. It was 9:00 a.m., and Cadrain was surprised to see his old friend standing outside. He quickly invited him in, and David waved at Ron and Nichol to join them.

Cadrain was nervous on the witness stand. He spoke softly, almost as if he didn't want Milgaard to hear what he was saying. From the time of his first interrogation by police in February 1969 he had been terrified of getting involved. Now the moment of truth arrived – he had to tell the court what he had told police over and over again.

Cadrain testified that he saw blood on David Milgaard's shirt and pants. He also corroborated the story the jury had already heard about David throwing a cosmetics' case from the car later in their journey. There was one further piece of evidence which the Crown wanted Cadrain to bring out, evidence that Caldwell felt would further incriminate Milgaard. It involved a conversation between Cadrain and Milgaard during their trip to Alberta. According to Cadrain, Milgaard had asked him to get a gun and wipe out Ron and Nichol "because they knew too much." Cadrain also maintained that David had told him he was in the Mafia. It was a strange tale which might have influenced the jury in one of two ways. Some might have drawn the conclusion that Milgaard was guilty; others might have concluded that Cadrain was suffering delusions and was untrustworthy. In any event, Justice Bence refused to allow the jury to hear the evidence.

During cross-examination, Tallis quickly pinpointed the obvious contradiction between Cadrain's first statement to police and his subsequent revelation. Like Nichol John and Ron Wilson, Cadrain at first was of no assistance to police. Only afterwards did he implicate his friend. Tallis pressed home the discrepancies, and Cadrain offered no real reason for his change in story.

Tallis: A week or two after you got back to Regina you had no recollection whatsoever of seeing any blood on any of David's clothes, did you? Isn't that correct, witness?

Cadrain: Yes.

Tallis: That's the truth?

Cadrain: Yes.

Tallis: And as a matter of fact you had every opportunity to recollect that for the police in Regina, didn't you?

Cadrain: I never thought nothing of it.

Tallis: No; you were trying to tell them the truth to the best of your ability at that time, weren't you?

Cadrain: Yes.

Tallis: And at that time you had no recollection of seeing any blood on David?

Cadrain: No.

The jury was left to decide on its own which version of Cadrain's story to believe – the one he had told police in February, or the one he related in March when he returned to Saskatoon. One fact that might have assisted the jury in its determination – a fact they were never told – was that Albert Cadrain was in line for the $2,000 reward for his incriminating information.

There was another fact about Albert Cadrain that might also have swayed the jury – a fact that didn't come to light until two decades afterwards. It involved the visions he was seeing at the time, particularly a vision with the Virgin Mary and a snake in the likeness of David. It was a vision which Cadrain interpreted as a sign that David Milgaard was guilty of murder. It was also one of the factors that led Cadrain to commit himself to a psychiatric institution, where he was subsequently diagnosed as a paranoid schizophrenic.

To this point in the trial, Caldwell had been relying almost exclusively on circumstantial evidence. He could hardly do otherwise, as all attempts to find some concrete physical evidence linking David Milgaard to the murder had been unsuccessful. In a case of sexual assault and murder, this is somewhat unusual. Generally there are clues – hair, blood, semen, fingerprints, or footprints – that are traceable to the attacker. In spite of the best police efforts, however, the search for clues led to dead ends. Foot and tire marks were nonexistent, and fingerprints could not be identified anywhere. Inexplicably, the reddish-tinged semen found in Gail Miller's body had been discarded without ever being tested for blood type.

Undeterred, Caldwell set out on a lengthy course to present the jury with physical evidence that he hoped would point a finger at Milgaard. Critical to the Crown's case were the two yellowish lumps of frozen snow uncovered by Lieutenant Joe Penkala at the scene of the crime four days after Gail Miller's body was found in the alley. The samples had been sent to the serology section of the RCMP's crime detection laboratory in Regina for analysis.

Staff Sergeant Bruce Ivan Paynter of the RCMP spent several hours telling the jury about the variety of tests and analyses that had been conducted on those lumps of snow. Just how much of the highly technical testimony the jury was able to

absorb is unknown. What is clear is that the Crown was putting considerable emphasis on this testimony, a signal to the
jury that it must be supportive of the case against Milgaard.

When he originally received the samples, Paynter was
instructed to test for the presence of semen. One of the yellowish lumps of snow was found to contain no human material. But the other lump, when melted down and analyzed,
was identified as having human semen in it.

On further analysis of the semen, Paynter found the sample
included blood group antigens from a person with type A
blood. The jury was told that the majority of people – about 80
per cent – secrete blood group substances, or antigens, into
their other bodily fluids. In other words, the presence of A
antigens in semen would point strongly to the donor having a
blood group of A. Paynter's discovery was greeted with excitement at the time by investigators. It seemed to narrow the field
to a suspect with Group A blood. They had already ruled out
the possibility that the blood came from the victim, as Gail
Miller was type O.

When David Milgaard became the prime suspect in the
case, police had quickly moved to collect samples of his body
fluids. He had complied without hesitation. But when the
results came back, the investigators had a problem. Sure
enough, he turned out to have type A blood. But analysis of his
saliva revealed no antigens. Milgaard was one of the 20 per
cent of people who do not secrete antigens into their body
fluids.

In other circumstances, the test results might have been
enough to eliminate Milgaard as a suspect. If the lump, found
so late after the discovery of the body, was to be given any
credence at all, it would have to point to a Group A secretor.
But police were reluctant to let things slip away so easily. They
were also reluctant to disregard the lump of snow, as it consti-
tuted the only possible physical evidence that could hold any
weight at a trial.

Paynter was therefore asked to do further tests on the sample, this time trying to determine whether there was any
actual blood present. The technique he used was later to come

under question. Paynter used the same test that hospitals employ for seeing if there is blood in urine, a method some experts question as invalid when it comes to testing for blood in semen. Complicating matters is the possibility of a false result if the sample has somehow come into contact with a variety of substances, including green vegetables or leather. In any event, Paynter completed the test and came to the conclusion that a minute amount of blood was indeed present.

For the police investigators and the Crown, this was all they needed to present to the jury. Caldwell argued that Milgaard must have secreted the blood together with his semen in his sexual attack on Miller. This would explain the presence of blood in the snow. It would also explain why type A antigens were found in the sample – not as a result of a person who secreted them into other bodily fluids, but directly from the attacker, who had Group A blood. The jury was told Milgaard's blood could have been secreted if he had a genital ailment or cut – a hypothesis that was never proved.

Caldwell made sure the point was hammered home a number of times to the jury – the blood at the scene was consistent with David Milgaard's blood. But that evidence all came down to Penkala's lump of snow, and to Paynter's inconclusive analysis of it. Even the trial judge had trouble seeing the value of Paynter's testimony.

Caldwell:	Now, when you on the second occasion tested the contents for the presence of blood as such, what result did you obtain?
Paynter:	I obtained a positive result for blood with this test.
Caldwell:	And is that the extent of what your finding showed you?
Paynter:	Yes sir; there was insufficient blood in this sample – or colouring in this sample that I was able to attempt any confirmation tests to absolutely prove that there was blood present.
Justice Bence:	It turned out to be useless then, didn't it?

Paynter: Chemically I could not say that it was defi-
                  nitely blood there.

Paynter's admission didn't stop Caldwell from trying to
press his point. He made a number of unsuccessful attempts
to ask Paynter to speculate on what the presence of blood in
the sample meant, each time being overruled by the judge who
objected to a hypothetical question about blood when no
blood had been conclusively identified. Finally, Caldwell tried
a different tack.

Caldwell: From the result you did get on that [test]
                  what could you narrow the item down to
                  being? From the result you got what could
                  you narrow down the cause of that result
                  to? . . .
Paynter: It would be blood or an extract from a
                  leather product or an extract from green
                  leafy vegetables such as lettuce, horserad-
                  ish, and vegetables of this nature.
Caldwell: If the result you got as I understand you was
                  caused by any of those causes, what can
                  you say about the effect of this second or
                  latter test, Staff [Sergeant], on the result
                  you got in your first test?
Paynter: If this test was caused as a result of blood in
                  the liquid, this would eliminate the neces-
                  sity of the antigens being produced by a
                  secretor that I found in the first test,
                  because the antigens could be there as a
                  result of blood being in the liquid.

As the trial moved into its seventh day, Caldwell was nearing
the end of his list of witnesses. It had not been a smooth ride for
the Crown's case, but the cumulative effect of the testimony was
having the desired effect. Witness after witness had pointed the
finger at Milgaard – sometimes directly, sometimes obliquely,
and always circumstantially. The role of the defence, mean-

while, was merely to react to each bit of testimony – without ever offering a plausible explanation for how this crime could have been committed by someone other than the accused.

For David Milgaard, the shock that he had felt at the preliminary hearing – when his friends took the stand to testify against him – had turned to numbness at the trial. It seemed to him as if a script was being read out, with all the players in a hurry to get off the stage so the audience could make its final determination. The frustration of not being able to testify kept building, but he was in no position to challenge the judgement of his experienced lawyer.

With the forensic evidence completed, Caldwell suddenly rose to notify the judge of a new development in the case.

"A matter has arisen, My Lord, that I think ought to be brought up in the absence of the jury," he began. To David, those words were a signal that the Crown intended to introduce some highly incriminating evidence, as long as the judge ruled it was admissible. Tallis knew what was coming, having been notified a few days earlier of the development. But for others in the courtroom, what followed was an eleventh-hour drama that helped to seal David Milgaard's fate.

As soon as the jury was excused from the courtroom, Caldwell dropped his bombshell. "On Sunday, January 18th [the day before Milgaard's trial began] the Saskatoon police learned for the first time of what in my submission amounts to an admission on the part of the accused to this offence. . . ."

Caldwell explained that two of Milgaard's acquaintances had come forward and told police of an incident in Regina the previous May. Alfred Melnyk and Craig Lapchuk, two friends of Ron Wilson, had gone to Milgaard's room at the Park Lane Motel for a party. Shortly after 11:00 p.m., a television news report regarding the Miller murder had come on. Melnyk and Lapchuk both later told police that Milgaard had responded to the report by re-enacting the killing, pretending to stab at a pillow repeatedly. At the time, it might have been seen as a macabre joke. But now, with Milgaard on trial for murder, the two were suggesting that it was an admission of guilt.

For the Crown, this was the icing on the cake – the final touch on what had started as a problematic case. The police had succeeded in turning three reluctant friends – all of whom initially denied knowledge of the crime – into prosecution witnesses. They had taken questionable physical evidence and made it appear damning for the accused. Now, literally at the last moment, the prosecution produced evidence that Milgaard himself had admitted to the murder. What more could the jury need?

All that remained was for Justice Bence to determine if the evidence should be presented to the jury. He had little hesitation doing so. "Well, gentlemen, I have decided that the evidence is admissible," he said at the end of brief submissions by both sides. "It's evidence which if accepted by the jury tends to inculpate the accused. I know that I have to determine matters of admissibility, and in this case to me it is clearly admissible; the weight to be placed in it is a matter for the jury."

Immediately after the judge's ruling, Caldwell called seventeen-year-old Craig Melnyk to the stand. A Grade 8 dropout who had worked at odd jobs for the last year, Melnyk testified he went to the Park Lane Motel on the outskirts of Regina sometime in May 1969. He and Lapchuk had heard that a party was happening there. When they arrived, they were greeted by David and two girls, Ute Frank and Deborah Hall. Caldwell quickly led Melnyk to the heart of his testimony. Melnyk said the television was on throughout the evening, and at one point a newscast mentioned that police were still looking for Gail Miller's murderer. He described David's reaction to the news item.

Melnyk:	He started hitting the pillow like he was stabbing something.
Justice Bence:	Just a minute please. Go ahead.
Melnyk:	He was hitting the pillow like he was stabbing something and he said, "I killed her" or something fourteen times.
Justice Bence:	"I killed her"?

Melnyk:	I'm not sure if it was "I killed her" but fourteen times was in there. It was either "I killed her" or "I stabbed her fourteen times."
Justice Bence:	You're sure it was either "killed" or "stabbed"?
Melnyk:	Yes.
Justice Bence:	Yes?
Melnyk:	And then he said, "I fixed her."
Justice Bence:	Yes?
Melnyk:	And then he sort of rolled on his side and started laughing.

Each word came like a hammer blow to Joyce Milgaard as she listened to the testimony. She gazed over to the jury, trying to gauge their reaction as she had done many times during the trial. They were listening intently, maintaining the same expressionless stare that is common among jurors. But for Joyce, the faces of the jurors told the whole story. She saw them looking at Melnyk, then looking back at David and convicting him right then and there. She looked in their eyes for some compassion, for some sense of doubt, for a hint that the story they were hearing was too glib. But there was nothing to indicate even an ounce of scepticism on their part. For the first time, Joyce Milgaard seriously began to confront the possibility that her son would be found guilty of murder.

George Lapchuk, eighteen, provided virtually the same testimony. He, too, remembered clearly what Milgaard did when the news report came on the air.

| Lapchuk: | Well, first of all he got a sort of funny look and then he jumped off the bed and straddled the pillow . . . and then he said, "Where is my paring knife?" . . . and then he went through the motions of stabbing the pillow, raising his arms and stabbing the pillow. . . . And then he said, "Yes I stabbed her, I killed her, I stabbed her fourteen times and then she died." . . . And |

> these aren't the exact words. The only part I can remember for sure is that, "and then she died." I can't remember whether it was "stabbed her" or "killed her" but "and then she died" stands out in my mind.

Caldwell: Now, what happened when the accused did these things in the room?

Lapchuk: Well, I was shocked, like I hadn't expected a display like that, you know; and I just started looking at him and I believe everybody else in the room was looking at him also; and then he looked up and saw that everybody – that I was staring at him with my jaw hanging down. . . .

Caldwell: What did he do?

Lapchuk: He just looked up and looked at me and then got up and shrugged his shoulders and smiled and sort of gave a little laugh and sat down.

Tallis had been forewarned about this testimony, but he didn't have much to work with. There was a slight inconsistency in the stories: Melnyk said Milgaard re-enacted the murder while still on the bed, while Lapchuk said he jumped off the bed for that purpose. But that discrepancy wasn't enough to persuade the jury they were lying. In fact, the variation in stories may have encouraged the jury to believe that the two were providing their best recollections, rather than fabricating evidence.

The only hope was to discredit the testimony by challenging the credibility of the witnesses themselves. In cross-examination, a picture emerged of the two friends that was not entirely favourable to the Crown's case. Both admitted to being frequent users of drugs – everything ranging from hashish and marijuana to LSD.

Both witnesses were out on bail at the time of their testimony, Melnyk for armed robbery and Lapchuk for forgery and uttering – passing bad cheques. Lapchuk had a string of convictions already recorded against him, including half a dozen charges of forgery, theft, and possession of a sawed-off .22-

calibre firearm. Both faced the prospect of imprisonment soon after testifying at the trial. What's more, they both testified that police had approached them in the past about acting as paid informers to catch drug dealers. Melnyk claimed he had been offered $500 a head for convictions he would help to obtain, and Lapchuk also said he was promised financial rewards for freelance undercover narcotics work. While both said they never went through with their jobs as informers, the jury was left to wonder what their motivation would be for providing their testimony at literally the last moment.

There was another unusual twist which was never fully explored at the trial. Lapchuk, together with Ron Wilson and others, had managed to get hold of David Milgaard's wallet and identification papers sometime in 1968. They had used the identification cards to write phoney cheques, for which they were never caught. Lapchuk said that experience showed him how easy it was to defraud people with bad cheques, encouraging him to do it again, which eventually landed him in trouble with the law.

The testimony by Lapchuk and Melnyk could be interpreted in a number of ways. It could have been a complete fabrication, cooked up by two young men who were eager to trade incriminating evidence for a favour from the prosecution in their own cases. On the other hand, it could have been true – an indication of Milgaard's perversity and the flippant attitude he took to such a heinous crime. Most likely of all, their stories had a grain of truth to them. An incident such as the one they describe almost certainly took place, but the key thing is whether Milgaard was at all serious or just playing out a bad joke.

Two other people who could have shed some light on the matter – the girls who were present in the motel room that night – were never called to the stand. One of them, Ute Frank, was in Saskatoon during the trial and available for either the Crown or defence to call. But neither did, for their own reasons. Caldwell saw no point in having her testify, as she didn't corroborate Lapchuk and Melnyk's story. As for Tallis, he realized that the lack of consistency in testimony might be offset by Frank's description of the events of that night, which he thought might prejudice the jury even more against his client.

Frank's statement to police illustrates the concerns of both lawyers: "I have known Hoppy (David Milgaard) since about the middle of 1968. I have gone out with him once or twice. About a day or two before May 10, 1969 I got tied up with Hoppy and on the night of May 10 stayed at a room with him at the Park Lane Motel. I think it was room 16, 17 or 18. Later on Gary Silljer, Bob Harris left but Craig Melnyk and George Lapchuk came to the room. Debbie Hall was also there. During the evening we watched TV there and I had sex relations with Hoppy and had several (about 4 capsules) of T.H.C. I was quite stoned and sometimes wasn't aware of what was going on around me. I was also hallucinating quite a bit. I recall asking Hoppy if he killed that nurse they were talking about, and he just looked at me and smiled oddly. I had become involved with David on this occasion because he offered me free drugs which he did in fact give to me."

The only other person in that motel room was Deborah Hall. She had a very different story to tell about the events of that evening, a story that directly contradicted Lapchuk and Melnyk's evidence. But she was never called to testify by either Caldwell or Tallis. Nearly two decades would have to pass before her version of events would become known.

On February 8, 1970, less than two weeks after testifying in the Milgaard trial, Craig Melnyk was sentenced to six months in jail for his armed robbery charge. According to a report by the Regina *Leader-Post* at the time, "the sentence is believed to have been the lightest ever handed out in Regina for armed robbery."

7

The Verdict

Justice Bence glanced at his watch as the final Crown witness was wrapping up her testimony. It was approaching noon on January 29, 1970, ten days after the trial began. Caldwell had marshalled every conceivable bit of evidence to prove his case, calling forty-five witnesses to the stand. Then, almost as an afterthought, he announced, "That's the case for the Crown, My Lord."

The judge immediately turned to Tallis for his response. But David's lawyer wanted a last chance to review his notes and decide on his strategy. He asked for an adjournment until 2:00 p.m., which was granted. For Tallis, the crucial moment had arrived. The jury had heard the Crown's case over and over again for the last ten days, while Tallis was restricted merely to sporadic challenges of the credibility and accuracy of witnesses. Now was his opportunity to present Milgaard's case in direct fashion.

Tallis had two options. He could call David to the stand, and let the accused tell his own version of events. Or he could call no witnesses, and thereby achieve the distinct advantage of being the last to address the jury before it retired. He chose the latter. He felt Milgaard could not help his own cause by presenting yet another version of what happened on January 31,

1969. At best, the jury would listen to a credible young man denying all knowledge of a murder that his friends and travelling companions were pinning on him. At worst, he would crumble under cross-examination and seal his own fate by looking guilty on the stand. It was a judgement that David and his family would later question, but at the time they went along with it.

Over the next three hours, the jury heard Caldwell and Tallis summarize the facts of the case and put their own interpretation on the testimony. Caldwell was blunt. Milgaard's attack on Gail Miller began as a purse-snatching attempt, he said. When she resisted, Milgaard pulled a knife and ultimately stabbed her to death. Then, Caldwell suggested, he raped her. Caldwell's hypothesis was designed to fit the facts of the case. He had to explain why there were no physical signs of forcible intercourse, so he postulated that rape took place after death. To explain why stab holes were found in her coat and not her dress, he ventured that Milgaard had ripped the top of her dress down, after which she tried to make a run for it while pulling her coat back on. Milgaard then pursued her and stabbed her in the back, he said.

Although Caldwell had been unable to prove conclusively that the so-called semen samples found at the scene were Milgaard's, he was unwilling to abandon the point. He reviewed all the testimony relating to the physical evidence, stressing that it did not eliminate Milgaard as a suspect in the case. The physical evidence also failed to eliminate thousands of other men in Saskatoon that day, but Caldwell did not mention that. By continuing to stress every possible link to the accused, he hoped to paint a picture of guilt. It was all part of Caldwell's thorough approach, designed to eliminate any possible doubt the jury might have.

And if any of the jurors was still uneasy that the case rested too heavily on circumstantial evidence, Caldwell had a reply. He readily admitted the point and went out of his way to make sure the jury didn't hold it against him.

"I always have the feeling that non-lawyers regard circumstantial evidence as being synonymous with unreliable or bad evidence, and in law this is not the case at all. His Lordship will be telling you that circumstantial evidence is perfectly good and proper evidence, so long as it is applied according to certain rules the law has laid down for its use, and those rules His Lordship will be explaining to you in detail. Suffice for me to ask you at this time not to leave this court room with the feeling that the Crown cannot prove its case, because it must rely to some extent on circumstantial evidence for that proof."

Tallis, meanwhile, tried poking holes in the credibility of the key witnesses. He pointed to the radical shifts and changes in their stories between February and May 1969. He noted the subtle changes in their testimony between the preliminary hearing and the trial. He contrasted their stories with the simple fact that David did not act unusually during the morning of January 31, 1969. He asked the jury to consider how a young man could rape and murder, then casually stroll into a motel and ask for a map, and then spend an hour chatting with the Danchuks, who noticed no sign of blood on his clothes or distress in his manner.

If Milgaard had raped a woman who had been stabbed so many times, why was he not completely covered with blood, he asked. Why did the Danchuks and the motel owner not notice any blood? Why did Nichol John not notice any blood? Why did the police not find a trace of blood in Wilson's car? Why did Ron Wilson's mother, who had washed David's clothes after they returned from the trip, not notice any blood on the pants he wore at the time?

Tallis's central argument rested on the critical time factor. The testimony, he said, showed that Gail Miller was still in her rooming house as late as 6:45 a.m. She normally caught the 7:00 a.m. bus to work. David, meanwhile, was seen at the Trav-a-leer Motel about 7:10 a.m. That left just a few minutes for David to cut his victim fifteen times in the neck, stab her twelve times, rape her, dispose of her boot, sweater, and purse, get his car unstuck, and travel more than a dozen blocks to the motel where he calmly walked in to ask for a map. "It defies common sense that all these things happened in this short space of time," Tallis said.

The jury was left with a difficult choice. They had the Crown's theory of an almost random purse-snatching that had escalated into murder and rape. Buttressing the Crown's case was testimony that Milgaard had had blood on his clothes. The trail of Gail Miller's possessions seemed to lead directly to Albert Cadrain's house, where David had spent the better part of January 31, 1969. His travelling companions all implicated him in one way or another. And the last-minute witnesses insisted he had re-enacted his crime less than four months after the murder. On the opposite side, they were faced with convicting a seventeen-year-old youth on the basis of purely circumstantial evidence – evidence that rested largely on the testimony of some drug-using, scared teenagers, who had all changed their stories during the course of the police investigation. And they were being asked to believe that Milgaard, a young man with no history of violent crimes, could brutally rape and murder a woman, then remain in the same neighbourhood for hours, showing no outward signs of agitation or distress.

Court adjourned at 5:10 p.m. on January 29, and the jurors were allowed to go home one final time before being asked to consider their verdict. All that remained was for the judge to deliver his charge to the jury – the all-important lecture on points of law, which inevitably includes an opinionated summation of the facts of the case. As court resumed at 10:25 a.m. on January 30, both lawyers waited anxiously for Justice Bence to begin. They knew that the way he reiterated the evidence, the interpretation he gave to key elements of the case – even his tone of voice – could have a critical impact on the jury.

The contrast couldn't have been more striking as a nervous-looking David Milgaard peered up from his prisoner's box to look at the man on the bench. Justice Alfred Henry Bence didn't need his regal judge's robes to exude authority. He had an aristocratic air about him. The son of a district court judge who had emigrated from Britain, Bence followed quickly in his father's footsteps. He graduated with distinction in law from the University of Saskatchewan, finding time along the way to become provincial tennis and badminton champion. He also excelled at swimming, water polo, and basketball. Bence dabbled in politics as well, serving as a city alderman, and later as Conservative MP for Saskatoon for five years. In 1961, Prime Minister Diefenbaker picked the fifty-two-year-old Bence to succeed Emmett Hall as Chief Justice of Saskatchewan Court of Queen's Bench.

Justice Bence had seen thousands of accused persons in his forty-year legal career, and he might have been forgiven if he had treated this trial as routine. But he was shrewd enough to realize that this was no run-of-the-mill event. Everyone in Saskatoon was waiting anxiously for the outcome, and he knew he could have an effect on how the jury came to its ultimate determination.

"You must banish from your minds anything that you may have heard concerning this case outside of this court room," Justice Bence said early in his charge. "It is obvious that this case has been of considerable interest to the citizens of this community. It is very obvious from the number of people that have attended here every day that it has created a great deal of interest. Things have been said over the radio, on television, reported in the newspapers and no doubt you from time to time prior at least to your being jurors in this case have heard persons expressing opinions about what might or might not have taken place. But please disregard all of that and reach your conclusions only on the evidence that was brought forth in this court room under oath. Everything else must be ignored."

In his review of the testimony, Justice Bence stressed that his role was merely to make decisions with respect to the law. The jury members themselves were in charge of determining the facts of the case. If he commented on the weight and relevance of certain evidence along the way, Justice Bence assured them this was strictly his own opinion, which they could accept or reject.

With that caveat, the judge proceeded to review all of the Crown's key testimony. At each juncture, he carefully pointed to the red flags the jury should heed when considering the evidence. For instance, in discussing Ron Wilson's testimony, Justice Bence noted that the witness had changed his story since testifying at the preliminary inquiry. In August, Wilson said he walked for two and a half blocks looking for help after he and Milgaard left their stuck car – about five minutes in total. Five months later at the trial, Wilson doubled the distance he had covered and tripled the time he and Milgaard were away from the car – allowing the Crown to argue comfortably that Milgaard had sufficient time to rape and murder his victim.

Justice Bence was shrewd enough to realize that in the eyes of the jury, the most damning piece of evidence against Milgaard was not really evidence at all. He had allowed the Crown to cross-examine Nichol John on her statement to police in which she had given an eyewitness account of Milgaard's attack on Gail Miller. Permission to cross-examine was really a legal technicality, designed to determine whether she was a hostile witness. But for the jury, the content of the statement was hard to ignore. In a case filled with vague and contradictory evidence, here was a girl who claimed to have seen the crime take place.

In an attempt to clear up any confusion about the statement, Justice Bence instructed the jury to ignore anything that Nichol John had not adopted as the truth on the stand. He even had the court reporter type out those portions of her statement that she had agreed were correct. After reviewing that part of her testimony, he warned the jury to be careful, not just with the testimony that should be ignored, but also with the evidence that was allowed to stand: "I repeat again that those things which she did not admit must be completely disregarded; and also with respect to those things that she did admit as being true that they are only the evidence of this girl and they may be true or they may not be true; it's entirely up to you to determine whether she was telling the truth when she admitted that she had said those things and that they were true."

David Milgaard couldn't help but be buoyed by much of what he heard in the judge's charge. Although he was always careful to use circumspect language, it seemed Justice Bence was showing contempt for many aspects of the Crown's case. Caldwell had gone to great lengths to show that Miller's wallet was found three doors away from the Cadrain house, while a bloody toque had been discovered just next door. He hoped that the proximity of the articles would convince the jury of some connection with Milgaard, even though there was no evidence of any link. But Justice Bence told the jury not to be fooled.

"The fact that the wallet was found near Cadrain's is not evidence really which you could link up with the accused," he said. "Whoever robbed her may have thrown it anywhere, and the fact that it was three doors away from Cadrain's doesn't, I suggest, implicate the accused to any degree at all. Anybody, any person may have dropped it in that particular locality." As for the toque: "The toque I suggest to you is of no consequence whatever. That toque might have been the toque of some small boy who got a nose bleed and dropped his hat and went running home . . . there is nothing in any way to connect it up with anybody in the car."

Justice Bence also told the jury not to jump to hasty conclusions regarding the cosmetic case, which all three of Milgaard's travelling companions testified was in the car's glove compartment after they left Saskatoon. Caldwell had invited the jury to draw the conclusion that Milgaard had stolen it from Gail Miller and hidden it in the car when he left Cadrain's house to re-park the vehicle. What Caldwell had failed to explain is why Milgaard would have methodically disposed of all other articles belonging to the victim, including her wallet, while hanging on to a seemingly valueless cosmetics' case.

Justice Bence said the jury would have to consider whether Milgaard took the cosmetics' purse from the accused. But he said there might be an entirely different explanation for its presence in the car. He reminded the jury that Gail Miller's purse had been found in a trash can, and it contained many cosmetic items. He warned them to be careful when assessing the significance of the purse that Milgaard supposedly flung from the car. "That purse may have had nothing whatsoever to do with the deceased," he said. "There were duplicates of those things that were contained in the . . . deceased's purse . . . so you might ask yourselves – well, isn't it quite likely that the purse in the car was from an entirely different source? What would be the necessity for so much duplication?"

Not only did Justice Bence chip away at the secondary aspects of the Crown's case, he also attacked one of its cornerstones – the suggestion that Miller had been raped when she was either unconscious or dead. With typical understatement, he told the jury that Caldwell's theory didn't appeal to him very much. But he went further, suggesting that if it had happened that way, it's unlikely Milgaard could have done it.

"One would have thought that if that was so, that whoever did the raping would be pretty well covered with blood; and if those were the circumstances and the accused had done it, surely the Danchuks, even though they weren't looking for blood, would have seen blood if there had been a profusion of it, because how could a person be in contact with a woman like that, bleeding as she must have been bleeding, and not become himself fairly well covered with blood?"

Justice Bence even took issue with Caldwell's suggestion that Milgaard went to the bathroom at the Danchuk house to clean up. There was no indication in the evidence that Milgaard had an opportunity to do so, he said.

If Caldwell felt his case was being eroded by the judge's comments, he must have been seething at the suggestion that his key witnesses were less than credible. But this is exactly what Justice Bence hinted at throughout his charge. The teenage witnesses were drug users, some were involved in criminal activity, and they lacked consistency in the stories they told to police. At one point, the judge went so far as to label Ron Wilson and Nichol John as discredited witnesses, though he was quick to point out that it was up to the jury to decide what weight to place on their evidence.

Justice Bence reserved his greatest venom for Melnyk and Lapchuk, the eleventh-hour witnesses who alleged that Milgaard incriminated himself by re-enacting the murder at a motel-room party. "You may ask yourselves what would be the motive in these persons of dubious character inculpating the accused, which they endeavoured to do. You have to consider whether the fact that they are both now charged with crimes might have something to do with it. They might have been trying to ingratiate themselves with the police, they might not. They might be telling the truth in this particular instance, they might not be telling the truth. That's entirely for you to determine."

Even if they were telling the truth, Justice Bence offered the jury an alternative explanation for Milgaard's statements. People have been known to boast and admit to things they didn't do, he said. So the jury must not only determine whether Milgaard made the statements, they must also decide whether those statements were true.

Joyce and Lorne Milgaard could barely contain their excitement. After months of anticipation and worrying, and after ten days of Crown evidence that seemed to paint a damning picture of their son, here was an authoritative voice raising serious questions. It gave them hope that the nightmare would soon be ended.

Even the guards who took David to the cell in the courthouse basement began to treat him differently. They let him speak to his parents in his cell with the door open.

The jury retired at 12:17 p.m. Word quickly spread in the community that the jury was out, and spectators began gathering at the court house. By evening, a large group of people was waiting for the jury to return. Included were a number of teenage girls who told reporters, "There is no other excitement in the city."

Years later, a juror would give reporters a glimpse of what happened in the jury room. At first, the panel was evenly split, he said. Gradually they began to lean in one direction, and eventually the lone remaining dissenter was persuaded to change his mind so that a unanimous verdict could be delivered.

Deliberations carried on until 1:00 a.m., when the jurors

decided to go to bed. They were kept under guard at a nearby hotel. They resumed sitting nine hours later, and before long they notified the guards that they had reached a decision.

David Milgaard smiled at the jury members as they filed back into the packed courtroom. At 12:15 p.m. on January 31, the jury foreman delivered the verdict: Guilty.

8

Life Imprisonment

A moment of stunned silence descended on the courtroom. The group of teenage girls who had watched the proceedings for the last few days suddenly began to cry. Joyce Milgaard, her face ashen, sat transfixed in her chair. Her husband, whose hand rested gently on her arm as the verdict was read, looked shaken.

"I don't remember actually hearing them say guilty or not guilty," David Milgaard recalls. "I just heard a bunch of noises behind me and kind of turned around. I looked at my dad. I never really saw my dad look anything but what he was – strong. At that point I looked, and he didn't look very strong. It scared me, too, and then I must have known that they had said guilty."

Justice Bence turned to the accused.

"Stand up please. The sentence in this case is mandatory. You are sentenced to imprisonment for life. Remove the prisoner please."

Joyce Milgaard could not believe what was happening. The judge's warning to the jury couldn't have been clearer, she thought. The witnesses were less than credible, and the evidence was circumstantial and skimpy. By the time the jury retired, everyone was hopeful that the ordeal would soon be over. What was going on? Joyce believed in David's innocence, and somehow had thought the entire experience might even be good for him. "I always told him that you have to be so careful about the type of people that you go around with. Because if you go around with people who have poor reputations, that's going to taint your reputation. I felt this would show him that if he had not been with those type of people, he wouldn't even be in jail. I really thought in a way it would prove a lesson to him."

As David was led from the courtroom, the enormity of the situation suddenly sank in. Joyce began to weep.

The four-hour drive home to Langenburg was one of the most difficult of her life. A million thoughts raced through her mind. How would they tell their other children what had happened? Chris and Susan, at sixteen and fifteen, might be able to understand, but could eight-year-old Maureen cope with a brother convicted of a brutal murder?

As it turned out, they didn't need to tell the children. Friends of the family were caring for them on a farm near Langenburg, and by the time Joyce and Lorne returned, the news had already arrived. If little Maureen needed to be told what the news meant, it came when she went to school. A group of children circled around her and kept her pinned down while shouting, "Your brother is a killer. Your brother is a killer." She struck out at them and they hit back. She ran home, her tear-stained face battered and bruised.

Many of the townsfolk were supportive, but the fact remained that the Milgaard family had been tainted by David's conviction. It was hardest on the children. After a few months, the pressure became so intense that the family decided to leave Langenburg and move to Winnipeg.

The trauma of the last year might have led the Milgaards to put the events behind them and heal the mental wounds that the conviction inflicted. But they were unwilling to do so. David had been forcibly removed from the family and shut behind bars at Prince Albert penitentiary, but he remained a part of them. The bond was perhaps strongest in the relationship that David developed with his youngest sister. Maureen never really knew her brother before he became ensnared in the events that led to his imprisonment, but she drew closer to him afterwards. They would write to each other faithfully, and David sent her cartoon pictures he drew.

Through it all, the Milgaard family's faith in David's innocence never wavered. That faith was first established when Joyce confronted David in 1969 on first hearing from the police that he was charged with murder. "When we first heard about it, I had to know if there were any drugs involved, or alcohol," she said. "I'm a realist, to the extent that if drugs and alcohol are involved, anything can happen. When we found out there were no drugs or alcohol, then we knew."

Joyce Milgaard harboured no illusions about her son. She knew he used drugs and engaged in petty crimes. She also knew he had a circle of friends who were capable of more serious offences. Yet she also knew how far David was capable of going. "David could never lie to me. He could never con me the way he could con other people. And when I asked him straight, I said, 'David tell me about this.' He said, 'Mum, I don't know anything about it.' David is not a vicious person. I mean it's just totally not in his personality. He was a tease; he was a torment. But never vicious."

After the initial shock of the guilty verdict passed, the Milgaards began planning for an appeal. There was no question of securing David's release pending the outcome, but the mere hope of a review by a higher court was enough to keep their spirits up. Money, as always, was a problem. They renewed their application to Legal Aid in June and secured Tallis once more to argue the case before the Saskatchewan Court of Appeal. To defend the jury's verdict, the Crown relied on Serge Kujawa, who would later earn fame by prosecuting Saskatchewan Conservative cabinet minister Colin Thatcher.

Many appeals are launched and won on the basis of the judge's charge to the jury. A prejudicial comment, an unbalanced review of the testimony, an error in directing the jury to the relevant law – all are grounds that appeal courts examine in determining whether to overturn convictions. But Tallis had no basis for taking issue with the charge. It was fair in almost every respect, and in many ways it urged the jury to be sceptical about key aspects of the Crown's evidence. Instead, Tallis took aim at the jury verdict itself. He advanced the simple argument that the verdict was unreasonable and could not be supported by the evidence. That put the onus on the Appeal Court to review the entire case and come to its own determination of whether sufficient evidence existed.

Tallis also formally objected to two decisions made by Justice Bence, which he said could have prejudiced the jury. The first was Bence's move to allow evidence regarding Ron Wilson's blood type. It had been a pre-emptive move on the Crown's part, to negate any possible defence contention that Wilson may have been responsible for the murder. The second was Bence's decision to allow cross-examination of Nichol John's original statement to be held in the presence of the jury. Tallis suggested that this should have been done with the jury absent.

For Joyce and Lorne Milgaard, the precise legal points of the appeal were never important. They hoped the court would review all the testimony and see that the jury's verdict was unjust. The appeal process was long and arduous. While David languished in jail, the judges deliberated. At the end of 1970, the Milgaards marked another Christmas and New Year's without their eldest son at home.

They didn't have much longer to wait. On January 5, the Appeal Court announced its decision. The jury had applied the proper principles of law to the evidence before it, and was justified in finding the accused guilty on that evidence, it said. The court could find no grounds to interfere with the jury's decision. The appeal was dismissed.

An attempt to appeal the case further to the Supreme Court failed. The Saskatchewan Appeal Court's sixteen-page written judgement became the final and authoritative word. David Milgaard was guilty and would spend the rest of his life in jail. His only hope for eventual freedom now rested with the parole board, but it would be years before it would even consider a hearing.

Two weeks after the Appeal Court decision was released,

Bobs Caldwell and Saskatoon city lawyer J. B. J. Nutting met to decide who should receive the reward for assisting in the arrest and conviction of David Milgaard. Three people had come forward to claim the money.

A decade later it was learned that Albert "Shorty" Cadrain received the $2,000 from Saskatoon's Board of Police Commissioners. The identity of the other two claimants has never been revealed.

9

Three More Victims

David Milgaard was behind bars, but the serial rapist who stalked women on the streets of Saskatoon was not. Just three weeks after Milgaard was sentenced to life imprisonment, the rapist struck again. If a mystery writer had been commissioned to develop the scenario for the next attack, he could not have come up with a more chilling message to police that the attack on Gail Miller was not an isolated event.

On the evening of February 21, 1970, Cheryl Nelson headed home from work. She was an eighteen-year-old high school student working part-time in the canteen at City Hospital – the same hospital where Gail Miller had worked. Like Miller, she took the 20th Street bus to work and back. She lived in the Pleasant Hill district of Saskatoon, just seven blocks farther west than Gail Miller had lived.

During the bus ride, Nelson noticed someone sitting directly across the aisle from her. He was a short, strongly-built man with dirty long hair and wearing heavy, orange-coloured work boots. She had a vague recollection of having seen the man somewhere before, perhaps on the same bus line, but couldn't place him.

As Nelson left the bus, the man followed close behind. She was walking down the sidewalk a few doors away from her home when he bumped into her, grabbed her from behind, and dragged her into a yard. Nelson started screaming, and the man hit her several times in the face. "I could easily break your neck," he told her. With Nelson struggling the whole time, he ripped off her angora sweater and green plaid skirt and raped her. He fled immediately afterwards.

Once again, an extensive police investigation failed to identify the culprit. Nelson was shown photos of suspects but could not make a positive identification. She remembers one of the detectives involved in the case commenting openly at the time that the rape was very similar to the attack on Gail Miller. That made it all the more baffling to her, since the man found guilty of that crime was behind bars. The rape has haunted her ever since. She still sees her attacker's heavy work boots in her dreams.

Several years later, when Larry Fisher's record of rapes and assaults were known, he wrote to his wife in an attempt to explain his behaviour. He described how he would almost black out when the attacks took place. In one case, he said, he was sitting near a woman on a bus when he suddenly got a headache. It was his explanation of what happened when he attacked Cheryl Nelson. He said he remembered following the woman off the bus, but his mind went blank from that point on. Only after he had raped her did he realize what he had actually done.

Whether Fisher's account was an accurate description of his mental state or an attempt to justify his behaviour is a question for psychiatrists to debate. But no matter what prompted his actions, he posed a severe danger to society – and seemed able to perpetrate his crimes with impunity.

Throughout his string of rapes and assaults, Fisher continued to live a uneventful life at home and at work. He showed no overt signs of distress or remorse. Indeed, his foreman at work, Jake Ketler, remembers Fisher as "a good worker and a good character." Ketler said Fisher was reliable on the job and doesn't ever remember him coming to work drunk. He did what he was told without complaining. But Ketler is also quick to point out that Fisher was a young man with a life of his own after work ended. "You have to know these people. They're party people. After work, what they did was their business. As far as I can remember, Larry was a good worker. But I didn't really know him after work. I learned years ago that when you're a supervisor you don't associate with the workers."

As the snow melted in Saskatoon during the spring of 1970, it was becoming clear that the construction industry was in a slump. Wheat farmers across the province were experiencing hard times, and the slowdown sent ripples through the farm-based economy. Building projects were scarce, and Masonry Contractors started to look out-of-province for jobs. That summer, the company successfully bid on a project in Winnipeg. Some of the regular workers in Saskatoon were offered the opportunity to move east and work on the project.

Larry Fisher jumped at the chance. So did Clifford Pambrum, his drinking buddy. Linda Fisher had no objections. It was a guarantee of work for her husband in an uncertain job market, and besides, he would be making even more money than he did in Saskatoon. The project was a temporary one, so Linda decided to remain in Saskatoon with Tammy and visit Larry occasionally.

Pambrum, Fisher, and four others from Saskatoon all lived in the same house in Winnipeg for a while. It was a chance for Pambrum to get to know his friend even better. "Larry used to like to be alone a lot," he said. "At night sometimes he'd just take off – wouldn't say where he was going. He was a real lady's man. He could get women like crazy if he wanted to. He seemed to have a way with them."

One of the nights Fisher took off by himself was August 2.

Shortly before midnight, nineteen-year-old Barbara Sullivan was heading home from downtown, where she was taking a nursing course. Sullivan caught the last bus to Fort Garry, her south Winnipeg neighbourhood. It took her only as far as the University of Manitoba campus. From there, she still had a lengthy trek to her home.

About a block from her house, a man approached her from the opposite direction and asked if she knew where to find a particular address in the area. She said she couldn't help him, and they both kept walking. Seconds later he grabbed her from behind and put his hand over her mouth. He warned her that he had a knife, which she could feel pressing against her neck. She screamed, but the street was deserted and her cries went unheard.

It was a remote location, far from downtown and any commercial activity. The man seemed to know exactly where to launch his attack – far enough from the activity at the university, and just before his victim reached her home.

The man was in a frenzy. He dragged Sullivan to a vacant lot that was heavily overgrown with brush and scrub trees. She continued to scream, and he repeatedly smashed her in the face in an effort to stifle her cries. He ripped off her clothes and brutally raped her, while continuing to hit her. He then made her lie on her stomach while he tied her legs and arms with her own clothes. He threatened to kill her if she continued screaming. He ordered her to lie still for the next ten minutes while he got away, warning her that he would return if she made any noise. Before he fled, the man rummaged through her wallet and made off with fifteen dollars.

Although her hands and feet were bound behind her back, Sullivan somehow managed to slide out of the yard and scream for help. Three young boys finally came to her aid.

The small Fort Garry police department was shocked at the brutality of the rape. Lorne Huff, now a private investigator, was a detective with the department at the time. In his twenty-six years as a police officer, he says he'd seen all kinds of offences, but this was a hard one to forget. "The utter savage brutality sticks out," he said. "Those things just didn't happen in Fort Garry in those days."

Police interviewed Sullivan and got a general description of the assailant – a description that matched Larry Fisher's. But other than the terrified victim herself, there were no eyewitnesses who could provide any information to the investigation. The Fort Garry department entered it on their books as an unsolved rape.

For Barbara Sullivan, it meant a radical change in her life.

Her battered face was unrecognizable. She left the city to escape further emotional trauma and humiliation.

Once again, there were no indications at Fisher's workplace that anything was amiss. He was working forty-hour weeks at the minimum, often putting in overtime, and saving his money. In September, the company was disposing of a number of pickup trucks and offered them to its employees. Fisher bought one, with the understanding that regular payments would be taken off his paycheque.

Fisher's wife visited him in mid-September and remembers nothing unusual about the trip. He had another few weeks' work in Winnipeg and then would be heading home. Masonry Contractors was actively bidding on more jobs, in Saskatoon and elsewhere, so the prospect of continuing work seemed bright. Linda remembers leaving Winnipeg on Friday afternoon, September 18.

Sometime after 1:00 a.m. on September 19, Mary Preston boarded a bus downtown for her south Winnipeg home. Preston, an eighteen-year-old first-year dentistry student, had been out dancing with her boyfriend at the City Centre pub. He lived in the north end of Winnipeg and didn't have a car, so they went their separate ways after the bars closed.

The bus let her off four blocks from her home. What happened next followed a familiar pattern. A man emerged from around the side of a house and walked toward her on the sidewalk, then passed her by. He quickly turned around and grabbed her from behind, putting his hand over her mouth and nose. She frantically tried to tell him not to hurt her, to take her purse and leave, but her muffled cries made no impression on him. He told her he had a knife, and started dragging her between two houses. Preston continued screaming, and in the ensuing scuffle the man dropped his paring knife in a flower bed.

Once he had dragged her far enough from the sidewalk, he began ripping away at her clothes. In his frenzy, he didn't notice that the lights had been turned on in a nearby house. The residents had heard Preston's cries and had called police, who arrived on the scene within minutes. For Preston, they didn't come soon enough to prevent the rape. But they caught her attacker. It was Larry Fisher. Police took both victim and assailant back to the station in the same car. Fisher's string of rapes and sexual assaults, for the time being, had come to an end.

The next morning, Detective Lorne Huff reported to work and scanned the early morning report written by the uniform branch. He saw there was a twenty-two-year-old labourer in custody, Grade 7 education, with no previous convictions. The facts of the rape struck him as amazingly similar to the August 2 attack on Barbara Sullivan, and before he ventured in to see Fisher he concluded that both crimes were likely committed by the same person. From the information police had already gathered from Fisher, Huff developed a strategy about how he would approach him in the interview room.

"It was a quiet interrogation. There was no yelling by anybody. He wasn't yelling or screaming for a lawyer. Fisher at the time was a family man, and I think some of that may have entered into it."

Huff asked Fisher how he would feel if someone tried to attack his wife. He asked him how he could do such things, given that Fisher himself was the father of a young girl. Fisher lowered his eyes and started talking. He confessed to both Fort Garry rapes.

"I think all he wanted was just somebody to be friendly towards him," Huff said. "And we treated him very well. It was just a straightforward, nice conversation, and he revealed all the details to us."

To Huff, Fisher was something of an enigma. He came across as a loner, a meek and introverted character who was soft-spoken and seemingly repentant – someone who was looking for a friend to confide in. At the same time, Huff never let himself forget that this mild-mannered individual had been savage in his attacks.

Fisher told Huff that his problem derived from his drinking. He would be out drinking and would start to feel aroused, so he'd go out looking for women. But Huff never believed the explanation was so simple. When he looked at this seemingly shy character with the powerful forearms, Huff saw a man with the potential to do terrible things.

"He always gave me the impression that he was a very dangerous man, and eventually something would occur. Who knows if it would happen tomorrow when he got out of jail, or ten years from now? Just from talking to him it was a feeling that I had and that my partner had, that this man could potentially be very explosive."

At Fisher's workplace, meanwhile, his employer was starting to be concerned. It was late Saturday morning and Fisher had not shown up for work. On the Monday he again did not show up. Jake Ketler started to wonder if it had anything to do with Fisher's purchase of the company truck. He was worried that Fisher had taken off with the vehicle, after not so much as one payment. By the middle of the week, Ketler was demanding that Cliff Pambrum and Fisher's other friends tell him what was going on. "They said he was drunk in a bar and beat up a detective," Ketler recalled. "I never found out until about a week, week and a half later what really happened."

Cliff Pambrum knew exactly what had happened to Larry but was intent on protecting him. He conveyed a similar phoney story to his niece back in Saskatoon.

"I was at my aunt's when I first heard about the charges," Linda Fisher said. "My uncle said Larry had been picked up because he had been driving without a licence, and slugged a cop."

It didn't take long, however, before the truth came out. Linda was genuinely shocked. She went through a period of denying that it was possible. "I never would have believed him capable of doing it. In fact, I didn't believe it until he was charged and convicted."

Fisher's life of crime became harder and harder for Linda to deny as more news filtered out of Winnipeg. Huff had not only elicited a confession to the two Winnipeg rapes with relative ease, he had also learned more. Fisher had admitted to similar crimes in Saskatoon.

Saskatoon police sent two detectives to Winnipeg to interview Fisher. They were armed with a list of the unsolved rapes and sexual assaults in the city over the last few years. Again, no heavy-handed interrogation techniques were required. One by one, Fisher confessed to attacking four women, providing sufficient detail to convince the detectives that he was telling the truth.

He admitted to raping Alice Baker on October 21, 1968. He admitted to raping Cathy Shannon on November 13, 1968. He admitted to assaulting Cindy Owen on November 29, 1968. He admitted to raping Cheryl Nelson on February 21, 1970.

During the interrogations, the detectives made no apparent attempt to question Fisher about Gail Miller's murder. It was no longer an unsolved crime. David Milgaard had been tried and convicted. As far as police were concerned, it was no longer open to question.

But there were compelling reasons for police to reopen the investigation on the basis of what they had just heard. Fisher had confessed to crimes that bore a striking similarity to the Miller assault. In almost every case he had stalked a woman on her way to or from a bus. In almost every case he had brandished a knife and had dragged his victim to an alley or secluded spot. He had a history of stealing money from his victims after attacking them. And three of his Saskatoon victims lived, and were attacked, within blocks of Gail Miller's home. In the Miller case, the trail of evidence that had led directly to the Cadrain house could now be seen in a new light. Milgaard had been a chance visitor to the Cadrain residence for a few hours. Fisher lived there.

Fisher's confessions were embarrassing for the Saskatoon police. It showed they had been incapable of defending the city against a serial rapist, and only became aware of his identity after his involvement in another jurisdiction. To have reopened a murder case for which a man had already been convicted would have been doubly traumatic for the department – and for the entire system of justice in the province.

Lorne Huff was not aware of the Miller murder at the time. But in retrospect, he says it was strange that Saskatoon police would not have immediately reopened the investigation once Fisher fell into their hands. "You can't overlook the fact that the man has committed this number of rapes, and he lived nearby where this rape and murder took place. It's obvious you have to look into it," he says. At the same time, Huff says he can understand the type of mentality that would resist the desire to reopen an apparently solved case. "I think what happened in the Miller rape was the police already had a suspect, and people said that he did it. So I guess they just closed their eyes to that end of it."

Even Fisher's wife was convinced that he could have been responsible for the murder, especially when she reflected back on the events of January 31, 1969. "After hearing about the Winnipeg rapes, I told everyone that I thought Larry might have done the Gail Miller one," she said. "It was possible. But everyone said they wouldn't convict a guy without proper evidence. The friends and family members I talked to about this were telling me that I didn't have any real evidence. I even talked to my doctor, and he said I'd be better off forgetting about the whole thing. He said if there had been a dishonest investigation and a cover-up of the truth, police would be protecting someone in a high position, and not someone like Larry."

Fisher spent the next few months awaiting trial in Headingley jail, just outside Winnipeg. His fellow inmates quickly found out the nature of the charges against him and made his life miserable at every turn. More than once he begged Huff to help him while in jail, to get him transferred into protective custody where he wouldn't have to put up with taunts and attacks from other prisoners. Throughout his ordeal, Fisher still had the support of his wife. She visited him in Winnipeg and told him she still loved him.

Lawrence Greenberg was hired to defend Fisher, but there wasn't much any lawyer could do. Fisher had confessed fully to both Winnipeg rapes, without giving any indication there had been mitigating factors. Although he had no previous convictions, Fisher had shown a brutality in his rapes that would count heavily against him with any judge.

In February 1971, during a preliminary court appearance, a judge recommended that Fisher be detained at a psychiatric hospital or other suitable institution where he could get medical care. But Manitoba was and remains a province with a severe shortage of appropriate psychiatric facilities. Fisher never received the kind of sustained medical attention the judge thought necessary. Instead, he was returned to Headingley jail, where he continued to wait for the court case backlog to clear.

Finally, in late May, Fisher was brought before Mr. Justice Roy Matas in Manitoba's Court of Queen's Bench. He pleaded guilty to two charges of rape, one of robbery, and one of possession of an offensive weapon – the paring knife he had used. Matas sentenced him to six and a half years on each of the rape charges, and concurrent terms for the other offences, for a total prison term of thirteen years.

Curiously, Fisher was not sent to Saskatoon to stand trial for his prior offences. After a direct indictment that was signed by acting attorney general Allan Blakeney, Fisher was transferred to Regina where he pleaded guilty to the four Saskatoon crimes. Appearing for the Crown was Serge Kujawa, the same prosecutor who had argued against Milgaard's appeal less than a year before. Despite his familiarity with the cases against both Fisher and Milgaard, Kujawa did not connect the two. As he told a reporter twenty years later, "It may be a case of myself and others simply not being able to put two and two together."

The judge, feeling that Fisher had received a harsh enough sentence in Winnipeg, didn't add to his burden. He imposed four-year sentences each for the rapes of Alice Baker, Cathy Shannon, and Cheryl Nelson, and a six-month sentence for the indecent assault on Cindy Owen. But he made them all concurrent to the time Fisher was already serving.

The case went virtually unnoticed in Saskatchewan, as there was no press coverage of Fisher's sentencing. There has never been a satisfactory explanation as to why Fisher was tried in Regina, rather than Saskatoon. It was almost as if authorities were unwilling to rekindle any of the fears that the original string of assaults had generated. Perhaps they were also unwilling to publicize the accidental capture of a man who had eluded them for so long – a man who would have been the most natural suspect in a murder case for which someone was already serving time behind bars.

Curiously, the arrest of Fisher in Winnipeg and his subsequent confessions may not have been immediately made known to some of the Saskatoon police officers. There is evidence that at least one officer continued his investigation into one of the rapes as late as February 1971, four months after Fisher had already confessed to the crime.

So reluctant were the Saskatoon police to publicize the case that they even failed to notify the four victims of Fisher's assaults. These four women didn't find out that Larry Fisher had been arrested and convicted of assaulting them until 1991 – twenty years after the fact. In an interview, one of the victims said the fear of not knowing that her attacker had been caught has made her life painful. "When someone looks at me, I wonder if he's the person who raped me," she said.

In the end, for his string of five rapes and one indecent assault, Larry Fisher received thirteen years in prison – making him eligible for parole in 1980. He was transferred to the institution where he would spend most of his term, Prince Albert penitentiary. The same institution that housed David Milgaard.

10

Catch-22

"He claims his innocence vehemently and does not appear to me to be the criminal type." So wrote a penitentiary psychiatrist about David Milgaard early in his prison stay. For more than twenty years, Milgaard continued to claim his innocence, not just to prison officials, but also to fellow inmates, friends, family members, and, most importantly, to himself. Despite pressure from many people that he admit to the murder as an initial step to rehabilitation, Milgaard has remained steadfast.

The first two years of his imprisonment were perhaps the most difficult for David. At age seventeen, he was thrown into a world of hardened criminals at the overcrowded Saskatchewan penitentiary in Prince Albert. He believed strongly that his appeal would be successful, and therefore for his first year behind bars didn't concern himself with adjusting to a lifelong prison sentence. The regimented procedures inside the institution only fuelled his anger, and he lashed out at any vestige of authority. The other inmates viewed him with a mixture of amusement and respect. Here was the convicted killer they had read about in the papers, a killer who had sexually assaulted his victim, a man who wouldn't stop insisting he was innocent, and who defied any efforts to restrain his independence.

David remembers one incident early in his term. "When I first came in the institution a great big black guy came up to me because I'd been typing away on the typewriter all hours of the night. And he asked me – he said, 'You know, the guys are pissed off at you making a noise and that you're going to have to stop. Right?' And I started to explain to him how I had to do this because I had to get out, because I was fighting for my life. And I guess he believed me. Because usually in a situation like that, where all the newspaper stories were out and everybody knew who I was, a guy wouldn't last very long. He'd be stabbed or something."

A staff psychologist who visited David in Prince Albert remembers that he had an unusual relationship with the other inmates. "When he was first incarcerated he didn't seem to be afraid of what would happen in prison," said Ken Howland, who later went on to the National Parole Board. "I recall I told him I was surprised that he wasn't subject to repercussions or physical abuse by other inmates. Given the inmate views and attitudes, and the inmate code at that time, which was very much to be harsh with sexual offenders and very unaccepting of them, it was surprising David had no problems. I still recall him saying, 'Well that's easy. The inmates know I'm not guilty, and I just wasn't able to prove that in court, but I will be able to when it gets to the appeal.' Normally if the inmates had any belief or feeling that he had been involved in a sexually related offence, he would have great difficulty and be subject to physical harm from other offenders – particularly a young, relatively small, defenceless inmate."

But a maximum security institution with five hundred inmates, most of whom are destined again to get in trouble with the law once they are released, is far from a rational place, and David eventually was subjected to a variety of approaches and attacks. He adamantly stood his ground, priding himself on the toughness he quickly developed. That toughness and defiance of authority was often designed to prove himself in the eyes of other inmates, to show that he could hold his own even among the most hardened men in the institution. In the first eighteen months of his stay, he was charged with thirty-one institutional offences – everything from swearing at guards to refusing to obey direct orders to hurling water on prison staff. Once he threatened a guard with a knife. Though he quickly became a disciplinary problem for prison officials, David never actually harmed anyone.

Two factors soon combined to increase the mental torment that Milgaard was experiencing – his family's move to Winnipeg, and the dismissal of his appeal. Suddenly, the hostile and aggressive posture he had adopted while waiting for his appeal gave way to depression. He began to see the prison psychiatrist, and was put on an ever-changing course of sedatives and stimulants – whatever chemicals could be found to control him to the satisfaction of his keepers.

A number of suicide attempts followed. On one occasion he jumped from a second-storey window. There were a few wrist-cutting incidents. In the fall of 1971, he swallowed some wires, necessitating emergency surgery to remove them from his stomach. Each attempt was accompanied by a demand: Transfer him to Stony Mountain Institution near Winnipeg, where he could be closer to his family. He even staged a hunger strike at one point, "I will not speak, nor eat," he declared, until his demands were met. His demands were ignored, and he continued his self-destructive behaviour.

Prison officials were at a loss to understand him fully. The first of many contradictory psychiatric assessments was made of David Milgaard. He has an asocial personality disorder, one doctor said, though no psychotic or neurotic symptoms could be pinpointed. How much of this was brought on by his prison stay and how much pre-dated it was anyone's guess.

What was clear was that Milgaard often was confused in his thinking and jumped to wrong conclusions. At one point, Milgaard confided to a doctor that he was behaving poorly in order to get transferred to an isolation unit of the prison. A senior convict had told him that this would improve his chances of eventually being moved to Stony Mountain penitentiary near Winnipeg. The doctor replied that this was bad advice. The best way to earn a transfer would be to improve his behaviour as much as possible. Milgaard was unconvinced. The doctor concluded that his patient was easily led by "evil forces."

"I didn't know what was happening around me," Milgaard says of his early prison years. "I was worried. I don't think it's any different for anybody that comes inside a penitentiary. Everything is kind of topsy-turvy; you don't really know. And as you look out and reach around and try to understand stuff, you're not really sure just what it is that you're trying to understand, because you're just trying to get along. You know you don't want to make any big waves or cause any problems. . . . No person would normally walk into a penitentiary convicted of the crime that I was convicted of, and actually even survive very long, because people that are criminals that commit those kind of crimes, rape, or anything like that, you know, nobody wants nothing to do with them inside penitentiaries."

In March 1972, Milgaard was notified he was being transferred. Instead of going to Stony Mountain, however, he was told he was headed for Dorchester penitentiary in New Brunswick. It came as a blow to his hopes of being near his family. He challenged prison authorities on the decision, and was told that he could expect to be transferred to Stony in a year. When he entered Dorchester on March 24, 1972, Milgaard began marking his calendar, fully intending to hold the officials to their word.

Dorchester is far from the ideal place for an inmate to learn how to cope with institutional life. While Milgaard was there, it was racked by violence and discrimination, much of it coming from the penitentiary staff. In his first few months in Dorchester, there were numerous incidents of stabbings and beatings. In one case, a prisoner was said to have been beaten by five guards. Charges of discrimination against black inmates and French-speaking inmates were rife. This was the atmosphere in which Milgaard attempted to chart a new course for his life.

Now just out of his teens, Milgaard began showing signs of maturity. He had a goal to look forward to, and he was intent on achieving it. The number of institutional offences dropped drastically, to less than half a dozen a year – all of them minor. He successfully completed a Grade 8-10 upgrading course and enrolled in the University of New Brunswick mature student program. He signed up for a university philosophy course, and managed a grade of B – remarkable for someone who had scored 27 out of 100 in Grade 9 social studies as a youth. Milgaard was intent on keeping his part of the bargain.

As the first anniversary of his admission to Dorchester drew nearer, however, Milgaard realized that prison officials were not keeping their part. There were no plans to transfer him. The correctional service still viewed him as a difficult case, a man convicted of a brutal murder who showed no signs of remorse and who had made life problematic for his keepers at the Sas-katchewan penitentiary. Earning a transfer from the maximum security Dorchester prison to the medium security Stony Mountain would take considerably longer than a year, though no one was telling Milgaard just how long that might be.

After a year of trying to turn things around, Milgaard felt betrayed. It was psychologically important to him to move closer to his family. He saw it as moving one step closer to eventual freedom. Now that door seemed closed. The most frustrating thing of all was not being told how or when he might earn the privilege.

About the same time, word started spreading around the ninety-three-year-old institution that a prison break was being planned. It wasn't the first time such plans had been hatched. Usually they came to nothing, as security in Dor-chester was rigorous. Previously, David had ignored offers to join in the conspiracy. It's not that he didn't relish the idea of being free; he just didn't want to jeopardize his chances of being transferred back to Stony Mountain.

But this time, he hinted that he would be willing to join in.

Larry Harvey and Michel Satel, two inmates serving lengthy armed-robbery sentences, briefed him on the plan. David knew Harvey from Prince Albert; they had been transferred to Dorchester at the same time. The plan called for the three inmates to scale the prison wall, with the assistance of two other prisoners who would remain inside. The break was set for March 24, exactly one year after Milgaard's arrival in Dorchester.

Dorchester guard L. H. Winters would later try to explain to an official board of inquiry what happened that day. "I came on duty at 2300 hours March the 24th and was posted to B-7 Cell Block. I went around with CX-4 Toole [another guard] to make the rounds. He checked the landings and counted the bodies in the cells. The count was 205 – a correct count. The next round was made by CX-2 Niles and myself and that was made around 0100 hours. I did the counting and the count was again correct. The count was taken again at 0200 hours and again the count was correct at 205. We counted again at 0300, 0400 and 0500 hours – the count was correct at all times."

The count, however, was not correct. The cells on B-7 had solid doors with six-by-nine-inch windows. Winters and the other guards checked each cell by peering through the window, occasionally shining their flashlights in. What they didn't realize was that Milgaard, Harvey, and Satel had constructed dummies to make it appear they were in their beds. Two of them were not even supposed to be in the B-7 range. They had switched cells with other inmates to facilitate their escape, as their original cells had bars, not doors, which would have made detection of the dummies easier.

All three had been among a group of inmates who were taken to the gymnasium at 6:30 p.m. Saturday for exercise and weight-lifting. Instead of returning to their cells at 10:30 p.m., the trio hid in the gym. With the dummies in place in their cell beds, they waited for an opportune moment to leave the gym and scale a wall out of the prison. One of them had a .32-calibre gun.

Although the dummies kept guards fooled for several hours, the escape did not go as smoothly as planned. Shortly after midnight, inside patrol officer Elphege LeBlanc began his routine search of the gym. He had a dog with him called Mike. Mike was unleashed and began roaming around the gym, sniffing for anything unusual. The dog made his way to the weights room and suddenly gave out a yelp, then came scurrying back to the guard. LeBlanc rushed into the room and then into a corridor where he saw a door close. He tried to open the door but felt pressure, as if somebody from inside was pushing against it.

"Who is there?" he yelled. Nobody responded.

He ordered the dog to stand guard as he went back into the weights room to radio for help. At that point the inmates burst through the door and overpowered LeBlanc, tying him up and holding him at gunpoint for the next few hours. The prison board of inquiry would later place some of the blame for the escape on the unfortunate dog: "It is considered the guard dog (Mike) did not fully fulfil his role in the face of danger. He was much too passive under the circumstances."

The inmates forced LeBlanc to maintain his regular two-way radio reports so as not to arouse suspicion. Then they used an electric extension cord to climb the prison wall and escape. At 5:30 a.m., LeBlanc freed himself and notified authorities of the incident. There was delay in calling RCMP while the embarrassed prison officials determined exactly which inmates were missing. Every cell was opened and inmates roused. Only then were the dummies discovered, face down in the beds with human hair hanging from their heads for added effect. Finally, police were notified and an exhaustive search began of the immediate area. Roadblocks were set up across the province, and police brought in tracking dogs and a helicopter. Police stations throughout the Maritimes were notified.

Free for the first time in nearly four years, Milgaard was at a loss what to do. He had never completely believed the escape would be successful. Now that it was, he had to figure out how to survive. As it turned out, neither he nor his fellow escapers were any match for the massive manhunt that was organized to track them down.

The trio made their way to the outskirts of Sackville, where they stole a truck. They managed to elude police that day, but realized they couldn't drive out of the area without being stopped at a roadblock. Early the next morning, they drove their truck up the long driveway of a farmhouse on Walker Road, just outside the Sackville town limits. There, they politely knocked on the door of Corey and Florence Estabrooks, an elderly retired couple.

"I answered the knock and one of the men asked if he could have some water for his truck radiator, which presumably was leaking," said Florence, aged seventy-six at the time. "We gave them a bucket of water and he returned to his truck, but the next thing we knew the same fellow stepped into the kitchen and ordered us to hold it."

Florence immediately realized she was facing the three escaped convicts. What followed was a comical episode that saw three nervous escapers facing a feisty couple who had no intention of being pushed around.

The first order of business was to search the house, and the inmates quickly determined there was no one else in the basement or main floor. By this time Corey Estabrooks, seventy-eight, was running out of patience. He said they were telling the truth about being alone in the house, and refused to allow them to search the second storey. The convicts complied.

Milgaard, Harvey, and Satel hadn't eaten since getting out of prison. They demanded breakfast. Florence showed them where the food was and suggested they make it themselves, which they did. While food was cooking, they took off their wet clothing and dried it over the woodburning stove in the kitchen.

In searching through the cupboards, one of the inmates discovered a bottle of brandy. As he started to open it, Corey became enraged. "That's my medicine, young man. You put it right back where you found it," he shouted. The inmate sheepishly put it back.

Milgaard and his friends somehow thought they could take over the farmhouse and live there until the roadblocks came down. It was an impractical idea born of desperation. The Estabrooks had children and numerous relatives in the area. It didn't take long for the phone to start ringing.

With a gun to her head, Florence Estabrooks gave curt answers to the callers. Her relatives realized something was amiss. Everyone in the area knew about the prison escape, and it seemed prudent that police be notified. Within two hours of receiving their uninvited guests, the Estabrooks' farmhouse was discreetly surrounded by police. But the authorities were not about to storm the house and endanger anyone's life. They kept a safe distance, watching the scene with binoculars and a helicopter.

When they realized their predicament, the trio made a dash for the woods, about a hundred yards from the farmhouse. Before they did, they took a pair of Corey Estabrooks' rubber boots and some food. They paid cash for them. Police let them go, knowing they would have them cornered in a matter of minutes. At about 11:00 a.m., the three were spotted on a sideroad near the TransCanada Highway not far from the Estabrooks' home. They were easily recaptured, offering no resistance. The escape had been accomplished without violence, and the arrest was also peaceful.

In a subsequent investigation, Milgaard was judged not to have been the instigator of the break. Yet he had gone along with it, and that was to count heavily against him in the future. Along with the other two inmates, he received a three-year sentence for the prison break and an additional six years, to run concurrently, for armed robbery committed while at large. When they filed into the Moncton courthouse for their appearance, Florence Estabrooks approached the men and asked how they were doing. There were no hard feelings.

The escape was the start of a long period of reassessments, reports, and appraisals for Milgaard. His family now seemed far removed. They were getting on with their lives. With all avenues of appeal exhausted, they all but accepted David's life sentence, hoping that parole would one day give him his freedom. Joyce moved through a series of sales and promotional jobs, and Lorne advanced to a senior position with a quarry near Winnipeg. Their financial crisis of the late sixties was finally behind them. With the children growing up and the parents in different, full-time jobs, the Milgaard family's relationships were changing. But David was no longer part of the family unit; his only relationship was by long distance, and it became tenuous. He never gave up the objective of being closer to them, but he realized that his escape would delay its realization.

In 1974 he was sent back to Prince Albert penitentiary in Saskatchewan. Again he was told that a period of good behaviour would put him in position for a transfer to Stony Mountain. Again he applied himself with that goal in mind. He made a serious effort to improve his institutional work skills. His record of minor offences inside the prison improved, and he enrolled in more continuing education university courses, achieving an A in sociology.

This time, prison officials took note of his effort, and in August 1976 he was finally transferred to Stony Mountain. It was a significant milestone, and the whole family celebrated. Two weeks later, there was another momentous occasion. David was granted a three-hour temporary absence, his first since being convicted more than six years earlier. It was a humanitarian gesture to allow him to visit his ailing grandmother in a senior citizen's home. But the memory of his escape three years earlier was still fresh. Prison staff insisted on posting two guards with him. Milgaard made no effort to flee, and he was rewarded two months later with another temporary absence, this time to visit a medical clinic in Winnipeg.

After an initial period of adjustment, Milgaard's proximity to his family seemed to give him a renewed sense of hope. But there were difficulties along the way. His parents were experiencing marital problems, and a separation was on the horizon. In May 1977, his grandmother, who had provided him with strong support through the years, died. The troubles at home didn't deter him from his long-range plans. It had taken six years for Milgaard to achieve his goal of entering Stony Mountain. He was now ready to take aim at his next objective – parole. The first opportunity would come in 1977.

Gail Miller in a community
college yearbook photograph.

Gail Miller's body lies in the alley where it was found on
January 31, 1969.

Joyce Milgaard with her children David and Susan, *circa* 1956.

David Milgaard, aged sixteen, shortly after his arrest for Gail Miller's murder. (Saskatoon *Star-Phoenix*)

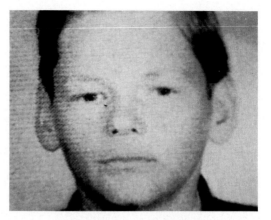

Ron Wilson, David's friend and travelling companion at the time of the murder, testified against him at the trial.

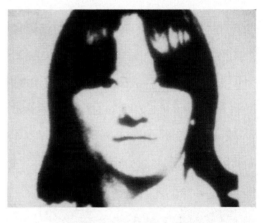

Nichol John, who was with Ron Wilson and David Milgaard on January 31, told police she'd seen David murder Gail Miller, but at the trial said she could remember nothing.

David's friend Albert "Shorty" Cadrain in 1969. He eventually received $2,000 for information leading to Milgaard's arrest.

Joseph Penkala, the Saskatoon police lieutenant who found what were taken to be lumps of frozen semen at the scene of the murder. The lumps, it now appears, may have been dog urine. (Saskatoon *Star-Phoenix*)

Eddie Karst, one of the principal investigators of Gail Miller's murder, as he is today.

James Kettles (left), the hard-line Saskatoon chief of police in 1969, had no use for hippies. (Saskatoon *Star-Phoenix*)

Calvin Tallis, David Milgaard's defence lawyer, advised his client not to testify at the trial. (Saskatoon *Star-Phoenix*)

T. D. R. (Bobs) Caldwell, David Milgaard's prosecutor, seen here enjoying his hobby – the trombone. (Saskatoon *Star-Phoenix*)

Mr. Justice Alfred Bence, who presided at the trial, cautioned the jury not to believe everything they had heard. (Saskatoon *Star-Phoenix*)

Craig Melnyk (left) and George Lapchuk (right) testified they saw David Milgaard re-enact the murder in a Regina motel room in 1969 after seeing a TV news item.

Linda and Larry Fisher on their wedding day in 1967.

Larry Fisher, *circa* 1969.

Stony Mountain prison, home to David Milgaard since 1976.

David Milgaard, one of Canada's longest-serving prisoners.

In the summer of that year, Milgaard applied for day parole so he could attend the University of Manitoba. It would be the first of nearly twenty applications to the parole board. It would also be his first lesson in the politics, the inequities, and the bloody-mindedness of officialdom in the correctional service.

Perhaps the most frustrating aspect of his incarceration for both Milgaard and his family has been the parole board's attitude that his protestation of innocence is holding back any chance of release. According to the logic of parole officials, it is both healthy and positive for an inmate to admit his crime and make a clean break with his past before rejoining the community. This makes sense when the inmate is guilty of the crime. But what about those cases where the inmate has been wrongly convicted? No provision is made for such a case, since they are officially deemed not to exist.

The attitude is summed up in the report prepared by Milgaard's parole service officer in 1977. "The subject has applied for a temporary absence program and therefore the institution and myself are in the process of preparing such a proposition to the Parole Board. Any temporary absence program is however felt to be far too premature considering the subject's attitude toward this offence, and failure to admit the offence. He is an unknown quantity and it is not felt that any commitment should be made to him with regard to any form of release."

Calling Milgaard an "unknown quantity" after seven years of incarceration, appraisals, psychiatric probes, and daily observations may be more of an unwitting criticism of the Canadian prison system than Milgaard's chance of reintegrating with the community.

Just as startling is the official attitude toward Milgaard's family. Here, too, the argument is advanced that their belief in his innocence is slowing down the process of his re-education. The following comes from a penitentiary service document summarizing Milgaard's parole application: "There is no question Milgaard's family are concerned and supportive. They firmly believe in his innocence and have indicated, in numerous correspondence, their willingness to do anything to effect a TA [temporary absence] program or release. Mrs. Milgaard, in particular, has illicited [sic] the support of a number of influential community members. This writer questions how constructive this familial support is. First, if subject is guilty, familial belief in his innocence provides a firm block to subject ever admitting to or working through intrapsychic aspects of offence. Second, although support is strong, it is at times overpowering, dominant, inhibits independence, stress producing high expectations and demands on David to obtain release – demands often unrealistic."

What the writer ignores is the possibility that Milgaard is innocent, and the severe psychological trauma that an unsupportive family could produce under those circumstances. He even admits to not really being concerned whether Milgaard is innocent or not. As long as he is in custody and in the care of penitentiary officials, he will only be released when those officials deem it appropriate: "It is this writer's opinion that whether guilty or innocent, Milgaard's behaviour is poor . . . and he is therefore a poor parole risk."

Milgaard was caught in a Catch-22. Not only were prison and parole officials using his protestations of innocence against him, they were also using his incarceration at such an early age as further reason to keep him locked up. The same 1977 parole assessment noted: "Confinement occurred at a very crucial stage in subject's developmental years. Incarceration has further debilitated skills Milgaard may have had. Many socializing experiences which are crucial to subject's satisfactory reintegration into community have not taken place."

While this may be an accurate assessment of Milgaard, it is also a powerful indictment of the failure of the prison system even to begin rehabilitation of someone it had in its care, at that point, for more than seven years.

Milgaard was formally denied day parole on October 5, 1977.

The failure to get parole was not a crushing blow. Milgaard knew he was serving a life sentence for an uncommonly vicious murder. He had hardly been a model prisoner, and his escape had tacked two more concurrent sentences onto his record. Parole officials might have feared a public backlash for releasing an inmate under those circumstances.

Milgaard was no longer an angry and impulsive teenager. He had already spent nearly a third of his life in prison, and was hardened to its realities. But his desire to get out never diminished. He recognized that his chance to get full parole in 1979 was very real. By then, he would have been in custody for ten years and could argue that it was an opportune time to be returned to the community.

Over the next two years, Milgaard made headway in all the categories parole officials consider important when determining eligibility. He became an apprentice mechanic in the prison's tailor shop and developed skills fixing sewing machines. In the process, he achieved the best work records of his entire prison stay. He avoided all institutional offences for more than a year and resisted the urge to use the hospital as a refuge during stressful times. He also made great strides in his education. He finished his eighth university course and earned a complete first-year credit towards a B.A. degree, with an impressive 3.2 grade point average. He also took an active part in the prison's student advisory committee.

Another milestone came in June 1978, when Milgaard applied for a regular temporary absence to visit with his grandmother at his mother's house. After much deliberation, the absence was granted. It was a special moment for Joyce Milgaard, who enjoyed the company of her son in her own home for the first time in almost a decade. And for David, it was a demonstration that he could be let out of prison and return peacefully, without trying to flee.

Everything seemed to be proceeding smoothly on the road to the next parole hearing. On the critical issue of whether he would finally admit to his crime, however, Milgaard remained adamant. It was not something that could be bargained away or used as a negotiating chip. It was a matter of simple pride and self-esteem. There was no way he would ever admit to something he didn't do, particularly something as horrible and gruesome as Gail Miller's murder. In a 1978 psychological assessment, it was noted that Milgaard had shown signs of maturity with respect to his academic work and institutional employment, the social life of the institution, and relationships with his family. When it came to the question of the murder, however, the doctor noted, "He made it quite clear to me that there should be no room for supposing that he would change his mind on the issue of his innocence or guilt."

His good record over the last few years notwithstanding, Milgaard still faced an uphill battle. Every time prison and parole officials opened his file, they saw an array of conflicting assessments. Some of those assessments judged him perfectly normal, except for the stresses that prison conditions themselves had imposed. Others had him bordering on the psychotic. Which should they believe?

One of the people who sympathized with Milgaard's plight and saw the injustice of his situation was Frances Deverell, the supervisor of education at Stony Mountain. She had worked with him since coming to the institution in May 1978. In her written evaluations, she spoke highly of his workmanship and the seriousness with which he took his university classes, and his role on the advisory committee on which they both served. But she also noted the frustration he felt at always trying to stay optimistic in a world without hope. She reserved most of her criticism for those officials who left Milgaard without a clear idea of what he needed to do to rehabilitate himself and earn his freedom.

As the date for Milgaard's 1979 parole hearing approached, Deverell felt compelled to write to the parole board with her views. "It is my impression that no one in this institution feels qualified to assess whether David is imbalanced and sick or not," she wrote. "Furthermore, it is my impression that no one in this institution is willing to take the risk of saying that he is healthy. I don't know what the solution is to this problem. However, I do believe that it is destructive to David to be continually left in the position that no matter what he does it can't be good enough. An assessment should be made and a decision should be made as to whether or not David will ever get out on parole. If he is to get out he needs to know what he has to do to be considered successful, and he will need a lot of personal support at every stage. Personally I believe that the rehabilitative work necessary to take David to the street should be begun."

On January 22, 1979, Milgaard was sent to the Regional Psychiatric Centre in Saskatoon for a month-long assessment. Dr. R. F. Rockstro was asked to do an intensive examination for the purpose of deciding the suitability of a release program. As in previous examinations, Rockstro came up with a complex diagnosis, capable of a variety of interpretations. He saw no indication of delusions, hallucinations, misinterpretations, or thought disorder. While noting some manipulative tendencies in Milgaard, he also observed the patient was well oriented to time and place, and showed no compulsive traits. He also took note of Milgaard's passionate insistence that he was innocent and his desire to take a truth drug so he could prove it. Rockstro said this would be a natural reaction if Milgaard were really innocent. But if he were guilty, it could either be bravado, or a request for a gentle way to come to terms with his criminal behaviour.

Though he could point to no violent behaviour on Milgaard's part, or any signs that he would be a danger in the community, Rockstro also was unwilling to take a chance on the inmate's release. His final diagnosis makes the case for continued confinement: "Mr. Milgaard is a man of average intelligence, who does not suffer from any of the major psychiatric illnesses. It may be said however that he has a defect of personality and that this defect is of the psychopathic type. He does not demonstrate the features of the psychopathic personality to extreme degree and at least during the last two or three years his gross behaviour has not been violent nor did we witness any incidents suggestive of his inability to control aggressive tendencies here. Nevertheless he does exhibit some of the features of the psychopathic personality to a moderate degree."

Rockstro concludes that Milgaard isn't yet ready for release. He suggests he be transferred to the social therapy unit at the Oak Ridge division of the Penetanguishene Mental Health

Care Centre in Ontario. After a regime there of perhaps two years, he writes, Milgaard might then be sent for a further life-skills program before any release is contemplated.

The psychiatrist concludes his report with a statement that is sure to send shivers down the spine of any person who is accused of a crime that he didn't commit. "There is a possibility – although not in my view a strong one – that Mr. Milgaard is innocent of the offence of which he was found guilty. *Even if this could be demonstrated to be the case, it would still be necessary for him to receive treatment as referred to above*" (emphasis added).

Surely if it could be demonstrated that Milgaard were innocent, the logical course to follow would be to set him free, provide some sort of compensation for his wrongful imprisonment, and arrange whatever psychiatric or psychological assistance he needed – assistance to cure a problem that incarceration itself has created. In view of what would happen in the coming months, after Milgaard agreed to go to Penetanguishene, Rockstro's statement takes on a particularly ironic colour.

Armed with Rockstro's report, Milgaard's parole officer prepared a negative recommendation for the parole board. "It is readily apparent," the officer wrote, "that the subject is in need of serious treatment which unfortunately Stony Mountain Institution is unable to provide at this time and date." No mention is made of why, then, Milgaard was transferred to Stony Mountain three years earlier in the absence of such a treatment program.

On June 19, 1979, the parole board confirmed what Milgaard and his family already knew was coming. It turned down his application. In its comments on the decision, the board states, "Milgaard is an intelligent, personable individual who has been doing quite well over the past few years. He continues to claim his innocence of the offence. He would appear to have had a mixed-up background prior to the offence and ten years in penitentiary has complicated his maturing processes."

A claim of innocence, a mixed-up background, a decade in prison – these are not crimes but, rather, powerful reasons to set a truly innocent person free. All are reasons cited for the continued incarceration of David Milgaard.

11

A Taste of Freedom

Milgaard did not last long in Penetanguishene.

Forlorn at losing his parole bid, he accepted the board's recommendations and agreed to a transfer to the Ontario mental health centre. There was just one problem. Because Penetanguishene is a provincial institution, doctors insisted that Milgaard be certified as mentally ill under the Ontario Mental Health Act. After he had already been moved to Ontario, Milgaard underwent the certification assessment. The psychiatrists could find no evidence of any psychiatric disorder and promptly ordered him back to Stony Mountain.

Milgaard now faced the preposterous situation of having been denied parole because he required treatment at a centre – while the centre wouldn't accept him because he wasn't sick!

Rather than admitting there was a problem, prison officials tried to make the best of an embarrassing situation by transferring Milgaard to the regional psychiatric centre in Abbotsford, B.C., under the direction of the same doctor who had suggested he go to Ontario – J. F. Rockstro. Milgaard and his family could take no more. They lodged official protests with his parole officer and the board.

David sent an emotional letter to his parole officer protesting his treatment. "My institutional behaviour of the last five years has been good, my academic endeavours superior, and instead of looking in this direction as a way of moving me towards the community, you have me feeling like a little white ball in a bureaucratic game of ping-pong," he wrote.

After lambasting the series of psychiatric assessments and shuffling he had been subjected to, Milgaard challenged officials to address the real issues involved in his parole.

"Why not ask me the three questions that all this qualified effort seems directed towards:

"1. Can I cope with the changes a person must make in the transition from institutional life to that of the free person?

"2. What has been the actual effect of eleven years of imprisonment?

"3. Am I seen as a violent person in relation to the offence? . . .

"Do I have to undergo actual mental anguish to convince everyone I am well? Should this go on, [I might] lose the motivation towards my freedom and find myself stagnating to the point of total collapse or acceptance of what I consider human warehousing."

He made a final plea for administrators to understand that any emotional problems he may be suffering were as a result of his imprisonment, and that they would slowly heal after he was removed from that environment.

"Do you think possibly that someone will realize that I am in fact a product of my environment, stunted in growth, care enough to admit it and still not be getting anywhere? The way I see growth as possible is with my support where it is strongest, and that of course is with my family and on campus. I want to see sunshine and fresh air, which would definitely enhance the development of good healthy relationships with new people and friends. The idea of those inside a mental institution, another total institutional setting, and some program that sees a person moving again with the confines of a bureaucratic framework away from where I am strong, will not work."

Joyce Milgaard, for her part, demanded that a proper community assessment be done in preparation for the next parole hearing. In such an assessment, parole officials determine what sort of support system the inmate will have if he is released. Family members are interviewed to determine how they will interact with the inmate. In the past, the sporadic community assessments of Milgaard's family had been negative. Prison and parole representatives wrote on a number of occasions that the family was a dominant and unconstructive force in his life. They questioned the stability of the family unit and alluded to family problems before the murder as a reason for Milgaard's "mixed-up background." Most of all, they took issue with the family's support for his claim of innocence, an attitude they felt merely perpetuated his inability to admit to the crime.

Milgaard's parole officer reacted to the criticism by asking that he be reassigned. In a written explanation of his dealings with the inmate, he gave a detailed account of Milgaard's movements in and out of the various psychiatric institutions. Nowhere does he explain why Milgaard was transferred back to Stony Mountain from Penetanguishene after such a brief period, and even in mid-1980 this information was still not available to members of the parole board. Trying to deflect any criticism from himself, the officer says, "I wish to state and have this on record, that I do not wish to be known or placed as the scapegoat and therefore am strenuously requesting from my latest supervisor that a new parole officer be immediately reassigned." As a final act, he proposed that an updated community assessment be conducted by the John Howard Society – an agency that deals with inmates and their reintegration to society – "to ensure that no bias is shown."

Less than three weeks later the community assessment had been completed, this time with a very different result. For the first time, the supportive posture of Milgaard's family was viewed favourably. David Kennedy, executive director of the John Howard Society, summarized his findings as follows: "We were favorably impressed with the strength and quality of the support that this family was prepared to offer the subject. His mother stated that she will be prepared to spend several months with her son to teach him and help him in his social integrating process following his release. His father will be glad to offer him moral support, material help and assistance in locating suitable employment. His siblings are ready to do anything required to help him in his re-establishment in the community. On the basis of the strength available in the community it is felt that perhaps serious consideration could be given for the arrangement of temporary absence programs for the subject at this time."

The Milgaard case was starting to become a political football inside the prison and parole system. Frances Deverell's admonitions began to ring true for many people – but still no one was willing to take a chance and say that he was ready to go free. There were other factors at work. Jim Kettles, the hardline police chief who had presided over the Saskatoon department at the time of the Gail Miller murder, became a temporary member of the parole board for a short period in 1980. And years later, it was revealed that Bobs Caldwell, Milgaard's prosecutor, made submissions to the parole board to warn against releasing Milgaard.

Milgaard has always considered his escape from Dorchester as a turning point. After he was recaptured, he had a long talk with a fellow inmate who convinced him that he must settle down. Innocent or not, the only way to get out would be to play by the rules of the system, he was told. Over the next few years, that's exactly what he attempted to do. But it was becoming increasingly obvious that playing by the system's rules was not working.

August 22, 1980, was to be another turning point in David Milgaard's life. It was his brother Chris's birthday, and he was given a temporary absence to mark the occasion. Two days before the escorted absence was to take effect, Milgaard sat down with a member of his case management team to discuss his future prospects for parole. He was told the prison had enough confidence in him to grant what it called "resocialization" absences, passes of a few hours' duration, with an escort, to enable him to get reacquainted with members of his family in their home environments. As for day parole, the situation was less promising. Milgaard was told he shouldn't expect to be released for another four years.

It was by no means an official determination of Milgaard's status. But the discussion drove home the helplessness of his situation. Despite years of improvements, he wasn't getting anywhere.

Milgaard's living unit officer at the time was Ben Dozenko. The living unit officers dressed in plainclothes and maintained their offices within easy access of the prison ranges. Eight or ten inmates would be assigned to each officer, whose job involved counselling and assisting the prisoners. They were also expected to assist in the security of the institution. In many cases, the officers developed close relationships with the inmates on their caseload.

Dozenko had always had a good rapport with Milgaard in the four years he served as his living unit officer. He had accompanied him on his escorted absences in the past, and everything had gone smoothly. So it came as no surprise when Dozenko was asked to escort Milgaard once more.

On the 22nd, Dozenko took a staff car from Stony Mountain and drove Milgaard to an apartment at the Quail Ridge complex in West Winnipeg, where his family had gathered for a barbecue. Dozenko had taken him there before. On a previous occasion, David had gone swimming in the pool. The complex also had an exercise and sports room that featured a pool table. While Lorne Milgaard barbecued T-bone steaks on the patio, David and his youngest sister asked Dozenko if they could play a game of pool. The three walked across the parking lot and into the games room.

"I waited around until they were down to two or three balls left on the table," Dozenko recalls. "I trusted him. I said I'd walk back to the apartment, and they should follow when they were done."

"Tell Dad we'll be there in a few minutes," David said to Dozenko. "The steaks should be ready by then."

It was the first time Dozenko had ever let Milgaard out of his sight during an absence. "I got back to the apartment and expected him to be there any minute. Five minutes went by. I thought maybe they had started another game. I figured I better go back there and check. When I got to the sports room, they were gone. I went all around the complex calling his name, looking everywhere. Nothing."

When Dozenko came back to the apartment, Joyce looked up and asked where David was. "I think David's escaped," Dozenko told them. He recalls their reactions clearly. "She was in shock. His father was very surprised, too. I don't think they had anything to do with it at all. It wasn't a planned thing for David, he just took the opportunity."

David fled in the family car. Dozenko drove downtown in a desperate attempt to spot the car. He checked at a McDonald's restaurant and a number of nearby hotels. Finally he called Winnipeg police. The police told him that an escaped federal inmate, even one who was convicted of murder, didn't fall under their jurisdiction, and that the RCMP should be notified. An exasperated Dozenko then called his superiors at Stony Mountain, who notified the RCMP. By this time, Milgaard was long gone, experiencing his second taste of freedom since being imprisoned.

Years later, David expressed regret about the escape. But his desperation drove him to seize the opportunity when it arose. "I did the wrong thing. But I felt I was losing a little bit of myself every day in this place, and that's why I did it."

Police across Canada were put on the alert, and the FBI was also notified. There were no indications Milgaard was ever armed, but all the bulletins warned that he should be considered dangerous. Initial media reports had Milgaard heading west, and the news caused considerable alarm in Saskatchewan.

In fact, he went east, deciding to lose himself in the anonymity of downtown Toronto. Suddenly, he was an adult in a foreign world, expected to act like a twenty-eight-year-old man but with only teenage hippie experiences on the outside to draw on. Adopting the name Dave McAdam, he rented a room in a downtown rooming house and got a job doing what he thought he could do best – selling encyclopedias for the Grolier book company. It was a telephone sales job, so he didn't have to risk going out on the streets and knocking on doors. He managed to hold onto the job for about five weeks, after which he was let go because of absenteeism. Milgaard was trying to keep afloat, but it was difficult without the support of a network of family and friends. Above all, he needed a companion to share his experiences with, someone he could confide in.

He soon found that companion in Rhonda Hicks, a sixteen-year-old Grade 11 student in Toronto. Milgaard spotted her coming out of a record store on Yonge Street one day. He stopped her and asked for directions to the Holiday Inn. Rhonda was taken with his boyish good looks and clean-cut demeanour. She gave him the directions, and they kept talking. He told her his name was Dave McAdam, and that he had just arrived in town from Calgary. She accepted his invitation for a coffee at the Eaton Centre.

Milgaard successfully steered the conversation away from himself. He asked Rhonda about her life. It was his first time on a date in eleven years, and he was trying to determine the right way to act. Were young people the same as they were in the sixties? It was a slow process of trying to find out, and Milgaard didn't want to rush it. Rhonda said she had to leave, but she gave Milgaard her phone number, not expecting him to call. But he did call, and they began seeing each other daily.

"I was in no financial good shakes then," Rhonda later said. "The two of us would wander up and down Yonge Street, panhandling for an hour or so every day. When we had enough money for a meal, we'd go into a local bar or restaurant."

Rhonda also spent a great deal of time at Milgaard's room, but she never moved in. She would go home to her mother's place every night and then join up with David the next day. Some days he would take a day job with a labour agency to earn some cash – enough so he could keep paying for his rented room. Mostly, though, they made their way by panhandling.

For Milgaard, it was a throwback to his life in Regina a dozen years earlier. Once again he was "just hippying it," surviving from one day to the next with no particular long-range goals. When he was sixteen, there was no need for such long-range goals. He was young and free, with plenty of time to think about his future. This time there was another reason for not looking too far into the future. He knew his freedom would be temporary, a brief respite from the hard life of prison that he was certain he would return to. All he could do was enjoy life on the outside while he had the chance.

Less than a week after they met, David took Rhonda aside and told her that he hadn't been completely honest with her, and proceeded to tell her the whole story.

"I didn't do it Rhonda, I swear to you. I was out driving with my friends and we ran into car trouble. The next thing I knew I was charged with murder. I still don't understand how they could have found me guilty. I know it's just a matter of time before it's all worked out. I know the truth will surface sooner or later."

Rhonda recalls the conversation clearly, and the sincerity that shone through as Milgaard told it.

"I'm innocent Rhonda, you have to believe me. If you want to walk away and never see me again, I'd understand, I'd respect that. But I'm just not capable of something like that, killing someone, I mean. I never did it."

Rhonda was taken aback by the enormity of the revelation. But she could find no reason to disbelieve him. After all, he hadn't had to tell her a thing. But he had, and had insisted on looking her right in the eye when he did. In the brief period she knew him both before and after his confession, they never had an argument, and she never observed even a hint of violence in him. She told him she believed him, and the issue was never raised again.

"In all our time together, and we did spend many hours together on a daily basis, he was never violent or abusive," Rhonda recalls. "In fact, just the opposite. I found him to be kind, gentle, and concerned about my welfare."

Milgaard never acted like an escaped inmate who was wanted by police forces across North America. He just seemed happy to be free, and didn't shy away from being on the streets and meeting new people.

"He was realistic about his situation," Rhonda says. "He knew he wasn't out for good. He knew he would be caught. He was not trying to escape and stay out for good."

Rhonda didn't tell anyone of the secret Milgaard had confided in her. But at least one of the other acquaintances Milgaard made in Toronto found out and passed the information along to police. Along with the tip was an outlandish suggestion that Milgaard was in possession of a sawed-off shotgun and was planning to commit an armed robbery.

After three or four weeks, Rhonda and David didn't see each other for a couple of days. They hadn't split up, and Rhonda was waiting for him to call when she heard a news item on the radio. David Milgaard, alias David McAdam, had been shot by police.

It happened on Saturday, November 8. According to police reports, a joint operation of the RCMP and Metro Toronto police had pinpointed Milgaard's whereabouts and were tracking him. They had information that he was intent on committing a crime. At 10:25 p.m., he was spotted walking down Queen Street West near Roncesvalles, in the west end of the city. Police claimed that he was armed and dangerous, and that he had told people he would blow the head off anybody who got in his way.

Corporal Jack Briscoe of the RCMP began chasing Milgaard, who turned north through an alley. Briscoe thought he saw Milgaard reaching for a gun. He took aim and shot the fleeing suspect, hitting him in the buttocks. Milgaard was captured and taken to St. Joseph's Hospital. Police found no weapon on him or in the room he was renting. Two weeks later Briscoe – even though he had shot an unarmed man in the back – was cleared of any wrongdoing in an investigation into the shooting.

Rhonda Hicks wrote to Milgaard a couple of times while he was in custody in Ontario, and he responded. They gradually lost contact, but she has followed his case with interest over the years. She remembers him fondly as a "very caring, very loving, gentle man." Now a single parent still living in Toronto, she is just as convinced today as she was in 1980 that David Milgaard is innocent.

12

The Gumshoe Mom

Sitting at David's hospital bedside in Toronto, Joyce Milgaard underwent a qualitative change in her thinking. In the beginning, she had placed her hope in appeals and parole. More recently, she had written to politicians, parole board members, and anyone else who would listen to plead her son's innocence. But now everything had changed. David had escaped, and police had gunned him down in the back to recapture him. His chances at getting out were severely diminished.

The time had finally come to prove that he was innocent. Joyce Milgaard set out on a course of action that would later spark an American television show to dub her "the gumshoe mom."

"Once David escaped, that's when I really took on the role as an investigator," she recalls. "Really, at that point the whole family did. We sat down and we thought, David has escaped. There's no way they're going to let him out. They're going to throw away the key once they get him back in there now. The only way we're going to get David out is to find out who really did it."

Taking on a new career was nothing new for Joyce. At age fifty, she had cycled through dozens of different jobs, from serving on restaurant tables to doing promotional work for the Royal Winnipeg Ballet. Like David, she was blessed with a persuasive, silver-tongued approach to selling. It would stand her in good stead over the years, as she tried to coax reluctant witnesses to step forward and reveal what they really knew about David's involvement in the murder.

"I had an RRSP for $10,000 and I talked to the rest of the family and I said, 'What do you think about offering this reward? I'll put the money out, what do you think we should do?' We had a family conference and they all said, 'Let's go for it Mom, let's go, let's do it.'"

Joyce printed up a leaflet offering a $10,000 reward for information leading to the true killer of Gail Miller – information that would exonerate her son. She even offered to resign her job as an administrator with a property management firm before announcing the reward, to spare her employer any repercussions the publicity might bring. But her boss kept her on and offered his support for her efforts. Just before Christmas 1980, she distributed the leaflet all over Saskatoon, sparking immediate media interest. Joyce gave interviews, passionately pleading her son's case and calling on anyone who had information about the murder to step forward.

"Of course I don't like the publicity," she said in one interview. "It's a chapter that I would like to push under the carpet. But that would mean pushing my son under the carpet, and I could never do that."

At this stage, Joyce had nothing concrete to offer the media as proof of David's innocence. But that was soon to change.

She ordered transcripts of the original preliminary hearing and trial, and she set about studying them line by line. She had sat through the entire trial proceedings, but passions were running high at the time; now she subjected the Crown's evidence to a logical analysis. The errors and inconsistencies seemed to jump off the page at her.

The Crown's case was preposterous, she concluded. It assumed he had gotten his car stuck, raped and murdered a complete stranger, somehow gotten his car working again, and had driven eighteen blocks to a motel where he showed no signs of agitation, all within a few minutes. Even if someone had planned such a crime, it would have been impossible to complete it in such a time frame, she thought.

To prove the point, the family staged a re-enactment of the crime at the scene, while Chris, David's younger brother, taped everything with a video camera. Actually going through the motions proved to the family that an injustice had been perpetrated on David.

"This was a very important day in all our lives," Joyce says. "Suddenly when we got out there and we tried to do what the Crown said that they had done, it was impossible. And I knew, I knew intellectually that David had not done it. I knew it with my brain instead of with my heart, suddenly. And at that moment the whole family knew it. We went through the transcripts and we were so sure. Well, once you're sure, that fired us up. We *knew* he was innocent and we just jumped right on."

The reward offer brought a stream of letters and phone calls, most of them leading to dead ends. Joyce recognized that the key to the case rested in the hands of the witnesses who had offered testimony against David. She would have to find them and get them to change their stories, to tell the truth about what really happened on January 31, 1969.

In tracking down the witnesses, Joyce received invaluable help from Peter Carlyle-Gordge, a freelance journalist and Manitoba correspondent for *Maclean's* magazine at the time. Carlyle-Gordge had just finished writing an extensive article on a twenty-one-year-old murder case which helped lead to the arrest and conviction of the real murderer. As soon as he became acquainted with David Milgaard's conviction, he saw the potential for another journalistic exposé. As he learned more about the facts, he became convinced that the case cried out for justice. He would later sum up his attitude with the comment: "In my view David Milgaard is as much the victim of a heinous crime as Gail Miller was. The only difference is that the state, not an individual, was the perpetrator of the crime against him."

Searching through old city directories, making phone calls

to neighbours and friends, they made slow progress in discovering where all the witnesses were. But locating a witness was one thing, and getting him to talk was another. For a witness who may not have told the truth at the trial, it was a terrible sight to see David Milgaard's mother show up on the doorstep.

In January 1981, Joyce and Carlyle-Gordge located Ron Wilson in Regina. He agreed to talk, but he was extremely careful about what he said. David Milgaard had been his best friend a decade earlier, and he had helped put Milgaard in prison for life. He seemed uncomfortable talking about the case. Still, snippets of information were revealed in the interview. Wilson gave a glimpse of the pressure that he was under at the time of the investigation.

"How did they get you involved in the incident? Was it through Shorty Cadrain?" Joyce asked him.

"Yep," replied Wilson.

"So Shorty must have told them something at that point, and then they came down and started to lean on you."

"Started to lean on all of us, yeah."

In his original statement to police, Wilson had insisted that he was never separated from Milgaard for longer than a few moments on the day of the incident. Under those circumstances, it would have been impossible for Milgaard to have had enough time to commit the murder. But by the time he got to trial, Wilson was saying he and Milgaard were apart for as long as twenty minutes.

A decade later, Wilson was unwilling to point the finger at Milgaard.

"Do you really think that David did it, yourself?" Joyce asked.

"Honestly speaking?"

"Uh-huh."

"No. I don't know," Wilson said.

Soon after speaking to Wilson, Joyce found the Danchuks, the young couple who had invited Milgaard, Wilson, and Nichol John into their home while a tow truck was called on the morning of the murder. The Danchuks told Joyce how surprised they had been at learning Milgaard had been charged with a murder that must have been committed only minutes before he was in their home. Mrs. Danchuk said she was certain she had seen no blood on Milgaard at the time and had observed nothing in his demeanour to suggest he had just been involved in a vicious rape and murder. They also remembered the very ordinary behaviour of Nichol John – a far cry from the hysteria the jury was told she was exhibiting as a result of having witnessed the attack.

Nichol herself was a little more difficult to find. She had married and changed her name, then separated from her husband. She initially refused to speak to Joyce and Carlyle-Gordge when they confronted her in Regina, but later agreed to a meeting. She insisted on having her lawyer, Larry Leslie, present.

While a tape recorder ran, Joyce tried to take Nichol back twelve years to the day of the murder. Her recollections were foggy. She didn't remember seeing a knife on the trip to Saskatoon. She didn't remember seeing anything in the lane after their car got stuck. She didn't remember giving a written statement to the police or being locked in a cell during the interrogation. What she did remember was fragmentary, like segments of a dream that had long since started to fade.

As she had at the trial, Nichol intimated that she had been afraid of Milgaard. Something had terrified her before or during the trip, but she was unable to say what it was. Joyce had her own theory about this. Perhaps Nichol had actually witnessed the real murderer in action and was suppressing the memory of it because it was so traumatic.

"Do you remember anything?" Joyce asked in frustration. "You're obviously frightened about it. There must be something that's really blocking it out in your mind. Do you think you're subconsciously blocking it out because you don't want to remember?"

"I know something happened," Nichol said. "I know that I saw something, but I don't know what I saw. You want the truth, that's the truth."

"That's really what I want, Nicky, the truth. I don't want lies."

"Mrs. Milgaard, there's too many things I don't remember, there's too many holes."

Joyce's strategy was to try to put Nichol at ease and get her to see the injustice of her son's plight. She adopted a sympathetic tone that sounded patronizing to Nichol. She kept calling her "Nicky" until Nichol emphatically told her she didn't like that nickname and would appreciate if Joyce stopped using it.

In vain, Joyce tried to get Nichol to say she had been pressured by police. Again, her recollections were sketchy, and Nichol said what she felt, if anything, was that she had been treated well.

"This statement that was read to the court," Joyce said, "that you signed on every page, if we looked at it logically, then you would say that that statement probably could have been true?"

"It depends on the circumstances that the statement was made," Nichol said. "I'm no dummy. I'm twenty-eight years old. If a person is emotionally upset, or mentally, or under stress or strain. . . . Let's face it, you could probably say anything."

"Do you think that was the case?"

"I don't know, because there's too much I can't remember. There's too much I don't want to remember."

What emerged most clearly from the interview was that Nichol still harboured some fear and resentment towards David, a feeling she had conveyed to police when they were originally investigating the murder.

"He raped me," she told Joyce, repeating the story she had related to police a dozen years earlier. "Well, maybe rape is too strong a word," she added. "He forced me. David forces his will on people. Excuse the pun, but David's a con artist. He makes – I have trouble explaining myself – "

"I think the word you're looking for is manipulate," Joyce offered.

"Okay, David manipulates," she said. "Whether you think something or not, he can make you think the other."

Nichol's assessment of her son was no great surprise to

Joyce, who knew that David could be manipulative and a bit of a con. But that was a far cry from being a murderer.

Despite her assertion about being forced, Nichol admitted that she may have had sex with David on several occasions after that, and she had no qualms about travelling with him. "I have a tendency of doing things I don't want to do." It was all part of Nichol's contradictory personality which Joyce was trying to understand.

As the interview ended, Nichol had one question of her own for Joyce. "Why did you wait so long?"

The question drew blood. Joyce had long harboured feelings of guilt for not acting sooner. "It's a hard question," she finally said. "I've asked myself a thousand times. . . . I don't feel as a mother I really did what I should have done at the time."

The interview left Joyce frustrated. She didn't think Nichol was lying about any aspect of her recollections. The problem was she remembered so little. Joyce felt the answer to the puzzle might be locked somewhere in Nichol's mind. Nichol agreed to Joyce's suggestion that they hire a qualified doctor to explore the possibility of removing the mental block.

Arrangements were made for Dr. Charles Messer to administer a truth serum to Nichol. A number of preliminary meetings were held, and Joyce agreed to absorb all the costs, including the expenses of Nichol's lawyer. At the last minute, however, Nichol changed her mind. She refused to take the serum. Instead, she left Regina and moved to Kelowna, B.C., resisting all further efforts by Joyce and others to get her to speak in detail about her experiences.

The failure with Nichol didn't deter Joyce and Carlyle-Gordge from their mission. They continued tracking down anyone who might offer some new insight into the case.

They found Roger Renaud, David's supervisor with Maclean-Hunter at the time of his arrest. Renaud told them that he had considered David a responsible and mature employee; he had trusted him sufficiently to ask him to baby-sit his two children when he and his wife went out at night. Renaud had no direct knowledge of what occurred in Saskatoon on the day of the murder, but insisted that from what he knew of David, there was no way he could be responsible for the murder. He offered to give David a job the day he walked out of jail.

They found George Lapchuk, who admitted he was on drugs the night he had seen Milgaard re-enact the stabbing in a Regina motel room. He also confirmed that he had received a light sentence for an armed robbery charge just days after the trial had concluded.

They also spoke to Deborah Hall, who had been in the same motel room at the time. She told them that Lapchuk and George Melnyk's story of what happened that night was a lie. David had joked about the news item that told of Gail Miller's murder, she said, but had not performed any re-enactment of the stabbing, as the jury was told. These last-minute witnesses who came forward a day before the trial began, in her view, were lying. Hall had never been called to testify at the trial.

Finally, after considerable effort, they found Albert Cadrain, the Crown's star witness, who had initially pointed an accusing finger at Milgaard. They learned that he, too, had come under considerable police pressure. In Cadrain they found a confused man, terrified that Milgaard might get out of jail and ruin his life or kill his wife and kids. "As far as I'm concerned he was possessed by the Devil," Cadrain said of Milgaard. He repeated his assertion from the preliminary hearing, that Milgaard was connected with the Mafia.

Dennis Cadrain, Albert's younger brother, threw some further light on the case for Carlyle-Gordge. He said the police questioning of Albert had contributed to his brother's mental instability. "He had to go to a psychiatric ward afterward, because they screwed him up. . . . You have to watch what he says, too. I wouldn't take everything that Albert says as gospel."

Joyce Milgaard's sleuthing had exposed a number of holes in the Crown's case. The timing of the murder didn't make sense. The credibility of the prosecution's star witness was in question. The pressure exerted on Milgaard's friends may have influenced their final statements. And a woman who was never called to testify at the trial directly disputed the testimony of the eleventh-hour witnesses who had sealed David's fate.

The probing struck a nerve within the Saskatoon police department. This was a closed file as far as its senior officers were concerned. Any attempt to exonerate Milgaard, after all, would reflect badly on the men who had laboured to convict him in the first place. As soon as the department became aware of what Joyce and Carlyle-Gordge were doing, they contacted various original trial witnesses, telling them not to talk to David's mother about the case.

Carlyle-Gordge publicized some of the findings of the detective work, but it drew limited media interest. Joyce was an ardent champion of her son's cause, but there is no shortage of mothers in the world who believe their sons have been wrongly jailed. The media's attitude was generally one of cynicism.

"I think that if I knew then what I know now, I probably would have got a good investigator to do what I was doing, instead of getting out there as a mom and my kids," Joyce says. "I think witnesses tend to be intimidated by someone that's personally involved. I think from that perspective, I wasn't doing our case any good in seeing these people."

What Joyce did realize at the time was that she wouldn't be able to navigate the legal problems on her own. She needed a lawyer, but she couldn't afford one. Fortuitously, an offer came along that she couldn't resist. Howard Shannon, who had worked with David at Maclean-Hunter, and who passionately believed in David's innocence, offered to pay the legal costs for Joyce to retain Regina lawyer Tony Merchant. Joyce didn't know Merchant, but she couldn't afford to be choosy. He was hired.

Merchant had a high profile in Saskatchewan and a solid record in criminal law. He also had political connections and couldn't easily be ignored if he argued strongly on an accused's behalf. Like his mother and grandfather before him, he had served as a Liberal member of the Saskatchewan legislature. He knew the lawyers involved in Milgaard's trial personally and was familiar with police practice at the time of the murder.

"While many of us have some questions about current police methods, and think they're inappropriate, they pale in significance in comparison to police methods in the sixties," he says.

After listening to Joyce's story and conducting his own investigation, Merchant recognized the police's behaviour with the prosecution witnesses. "There was considerable reason to believe that they took these witnesses and sweated the living heck out of them because the police were under tremendous pressure with their inability to solve this crime. There might well have been some motive to put pressure on some people."

All of Joyce's detective work, however, served to raise more questions than it answered. There were many inconsistencies in the case, but was there enough to prove that David Milgaard did not murder Gail Miller? Merchant didn't think so. After all, a jury had convicted Milgaard on the evidence, and their decision was upheld on appeal. It would take something far more concrete to reopen the case, something like an admission of perjury by a witness, or solid evidence that someone else was responsible for the murder. Fresh evidence was needed, as opposed to a re-examination of the old evidence, he concluded.

Merchant travelled to Millhaven penitentiary in Kingston to visit Milgaard and get a first-hand view of his new client. He saw a man whose personality had been distorted by his years in prison. At the same time, he saw nothing to convince him that his client's protestations of innocence were anything but genuine.

As Merchant delved into the case, he encountered more than a few stumbling blocks. Perhaps the most puzzling was the attitude of Cal Tallis, Milgaard's lawyer in 1969 and 1970. Tallis was a personal friend, a man Merchant considered to have the highest personal and ethical standards. But Tallis adamantly refused to discuss the Milgaard case with him, citing solicitor-client privilege. Merchant pointed out that he was now Milgaard's solicitor and would treat any information with the same confidence, but Tallis still refused. "I thought it unusual," Merchant said. "I thought there was nothing unethical about his discussing it. I just wrote it off as an insoluble riddle."

A cooperative Tallis might have revealed why he had never asked Milgaard to testify in his own defence. But Merchant deduced that Tallis didn't want his client admitting to drug and alcohol use and a hippie lifestyle before a straitlaced Saskatoon jury. Merchant couldn't bring himself to believe that Tallis had mismanaged the case, deliberately or otherwise. He surmised that Tallis made the right decision in not calling his client to testify.

"He would have said in his mind that this individual is going to have to testify to drugs, to alcohol, and things which were sort of anathema to the nice forty-five-year-old uptight citizens who would have been on the jury. These are not juries from 'L.A. Law' with seven blacks sitting there who know how the real world works. In a small community like Saskatoon or Regina as they are now, but particularly as they were then, the Attorney General's department does a pretty close investigation of the jury. There isn't a big turnover, and the Attorney General's department has the right to stand aside a whole lot of jurors in a murder case. So they basically get a jury that they pick, which is a pretty upright, unctuous group of individuals. I think it would have weighed heavily on Cal's mind when he thought about it: Will I expose this guy to cross-examination, when I think I've got a pretty good case as it is?"

In the end, Merchant realized that the best chance in reopening the case lay not in second-guessing Tallis, but in pinning down the original witnesses and getting them to tell the truth. He saw the strong possibility of an argument that the police put undue pressure on them. "They put the witnesses through a far worse interrogation than we would now permit someone to put an accused through," he said.

But for the argument to carry any weight, the witnesses had to come forward and make the complaint. It wasn't happening, and Merchant began running out of leads to pursue. About the same time, the money to fund his expenses also ran out. The case was at an impasse.

While Joyce was embarking on her crusade, David Milgaard continued to serve time behind bars. Consigned to Millhaven penitentiary following his escape, he again had to fight for an eventual transfer back to Stony Mountain. His years of good behaviour and steady progress inside the institution had been wiped out by the violation of his temporary absence.

In a way, Milgaard had proved in practice that he was not a danger to the community. During his seventy-seven days of freedom, he had found a job and had done nothing violent. No one he met would have suspected that he was a convicted murderer. At worst, he seemed a little immature – not an unusual thing for someone tasting freedom for the first time in ten years.

The parole board, however, was not impressed. In denying him parole once more in 1981, it commented: "While he may have been offence-free during his period at large and employed, this does not counter-balance the impulsive decision to escape."

Despite a recommendation from a parole board member two years earlier that Milgaard be given an independent psychiatric evaluation, prison officials weren't eager to let him out of their grasp. Instead, Milgaard continued to be assessed and probed by institutional psychiatrists from B.C. to Ontario. The following 1981 comment from a psychiatrist in Kingston, not only sad and ironic, is typical: "I doubt any prison is the best place for him, but alternatives are hard to find."

13

Almost a Murder

Prison, it seems, was the not the best place for Larry Fisher, either.

Despite the urgings of a Winnipeg judge, Fisher was not put in a psychiatric centre. Instead, he was thrown into Prince Albert penitentiary, a maximum security institution, where other inmates did not take kindly to any sort of sex offenders, much less serial rapists.

Fisher's wife remembers several times seeing him cut and bruised when she visited him in prison. He never spoke about his tribulations inside, but she realized what he must have been going through. With all the tension he faced inside the prison, his only sense of calm and normality came during her visits. But those visits gradually tapered off.

"He wrote me letters saying that if I lose you, I just might commit suicide like this guy and that guy. I didn't want him to commit suicide. I still cared about him, but I didn't love him. I told him I still loved him, but I really didn't. I didn't want to see him get hurt.

"At first I visited him a little more often, and then it got to be about once a year. He thought I had a boyfriend, which I did, but I told him I didn't."

After Linda Fisher had a child with her boyfriend, Fisher

saw no reason to continue the marriage. They were divorced in 1976.

In 1977, some of the inmates at Prince Albert were canvassed to see if they wished to apply for a treatment program at the new regional psychiatric centre, which was opening in Saskatoon. Some jumped at the opportunity to escape the regimentation of the penitentiary. Others genuinely felt the treatment might help them with their problems. Fisher apparently fell into the second category.

The selection process was a rigorous one, and Fisher's hearing wasn't scheduled until April 1978 – some ten months after he had applied. A fellow inmate, who shared a dormitory with Fisher in the prison's protective custody unit, recalled what happened after Fisher returned from his hearing.

"Larry came back to the dorm, and he was visibly upset. And at that time we asked Larry, 'What's the problem.' He said, 'They denied me my transfer. They said it was because I've only got a short period of time left on my incarceration, and they felt I needed a long-term treatment program, so therefore it would do me no good to transfer now.'"

The inmate remembers the rage Fisher exhibited at being denied the transfer.

"I'll show them bastards," Fisher shouted. "I'll get out and I'll do it again. I sat here for seven years with no treatment, none at all. And I'm just the same way I was when I came in. I'll just get out and do it again, and they'll have to take me then."

On January 6, 1980, after serving two-thirds of his thirteen-year sentence, Fisher was released on mandatory supervision.

Fisher went back to his hometown of North Battleford, where his mother lived. He made no attempt to contact Linda, although he kept in touch with his daughter. After nearly a decade in penitentiary, he spent the first few weeks at his mother's home, trying to adjust to a life of freedom. But he knew from the start that the old urges, which had driven him to attack women, were still present.

On March 31, around 9:00 p.m., fifty-six-year-old Ellen Samuelson (not her real name) was on her way home from a club meeting in North Battleford. The sidewalks were still icy, so she walked down the centre of the road. When she saw two young men headed towards her on the street, she thought it would be prudent to move to the sidewalk. A few moments later, as she walked past an abandoned house, Fisher jumped from behind a hedge and grabbed her around the neck.

"He dragged me through the gateway and into the yard and he told me not to yell, that he had a knife at my throat, and I could feel something at my throat with my hand. I grabbed it, grabbed ahold of the blade, and he pulled it through my hand and sliced through my leather glove and my finger."

Fisher dragged her to the back yard and raped her. Then he pulled her into the vacant house where he raped her again. As he had after some of his other rapes, Fisher then rummaged through her purse and stole the money. This is how Samuelson described what happened next:

"He ordered me to roll over, then tied my hands behind my back with my nylon stockings and bound my feet with my scarf. When he was finished, he dragged me to my feet and hauled me into another room. I was also gagged at this time. Without any explanation, he placed the sharp object to my neck and slit my throat. Then with the same instrument he stabbed me several times in the chest. I sank to my knees and he then attempted to suffocate me by putting his hand over my mouth and nose. I lost consciousness. I remember heavy breathing and thinking to myself, 'My God, he's still here.' Somehow I was able to untie my foot and got to the back door and across the yard to the neighbour's yard. I remember knocking on the back door with my elbow, then being told by someone inside to come around to the front. Then someone came around from the front and helped me into the house. I remember sitting on the couch while the lady called for an ambulance. I also remember that I was nude, and that the same neighbour lady put a blanket over me. I remember the siren, being put onto a stretcher, and the bright lights of the operating room. I don't remember being operated on. I was hospitalized for more than a week, and I was told by my doctor that I came very close to dying that night."

During the assault, before she was stabbed, Samuelson had had a brief conversation – one that terrified her more than anything else about the incident. "I asked him why he did such terrible things, how he would like his mother treated that way. He said, 'Never mind my mother. I've done this – I've spent ten years for doing this same thing, only I slit her throat.'"

As soon as she related the conversation that evening to police, they had their suspect. Larry Fisher was the only person in town who had just served ten years for attacking women. They went immediately to his mother's house, where they found Fisher in the basement washing blood from his boots. They also found some of the victim's clothes, which Fisher had hidden under the floorboards.

In a 1991 interview, Ellen Samuelson said, "At the time of the Gail Miller murder, I was living with my first husband on a farm. I recall the David Milgaard conviction, but thought little of it until seeing on TV within the last year that Larry Fisher had been accused of committing the Miller murder instead of Milgaard. When I learned this, something clicked and I had a gut feeling that Fisher was the one, and that Gail Miller was the murder victim he was referring to when he tried to kill me."

Samuelson today is terrified at the prospect that Fisher might soon be released once more. "I feel that it is outrageous and despicable that the government would release Fisher without conducting a thorough and honest investigation into mounting evidence that he murdered Gail Miller, as well as trying to murder me," she says.

It was a horrific crime that shocked North Battleford. But Fisher was not as quick to admit guilt as he had been in Winnipeg ten years earlier. There were no witnesses to the attack, and he offered no formal confession to police. Ellen Samuelson was forced to relive the rape in testimony at a preliminary hearing, with Fisher's lawyer challenging her to recollect and repeat every detail. Fisher, meanwhile, sat in the courtroom with a newly-grown moustache, making it difficult for his victim to make a positive identification.

The argumentative tactics of Fisher's lawyer led to some testy exchanges during the hearing. He did not dispute that a rape and stabbing had taken place, only that there was sufficient proof to link his client to the crime.

But Fisher's hopes faded altogether when Crown attorney David Arnot called RCMP Constable Charles Thompson to the stand. Thompson testified that he had accompanied Fisher to Saskatoon for a psychiatric assessment the day after his arrest. During the trip, he had pulled out his notebook and recorded a conversation with Fisher right in front of him – a conversation that he proceeded to relate word for word in court.

"You must have been pretty relieved when you found out she was okay," Thompson said to Fisher.

"You want to believe it," the accused replied.

"It's always made me wonder when a guy gets himself into a position like this, all of a sudden he's into it, and then once he's into it, he doesn't know how to get out of it."

"I know," Fisher responded. "That's what I did nine years for."

"Is that what happened to you last night?"

"Yeah."

"How long did you think about it before you did it last night?"

"I just did it, that's all."

"Was she walking down the street?"

"That's why I want to see a lawyer."

"Did you know the lady last night?"

"No."

"That house, how far away from your mother's house was it?"

"About four or five blocks."

"Do you remember what the woman was hurt with?"

"I don't know."

"Where did you hide your clothes?"

"I don't remember."

"Is it that you remember hiding them, but that you don't remember where they were hidden?"

"That's possible."

"What do you think would have happened if that woman had have died?"

"I probably would be doing a twenty bagger."

"What's that mean?"

"I'd do twenty."

There was little question that Thompson was hoping Fisher would make an incriminating statement, and it seemed he might succeed. Later on, he tried to get Fisher to be more specific. "What's bothering me," he told Fisher, "is that the psychiatrists let you go in the first place. I wonder if what happened the other night was as much their fault for letting you out or yours for being there."

Fisher, who thought he had found a sympathetic ear, took the bait.

"I told them I wanted to go to a halfway house, but they wouldn't let me. I think it's 75 per cent their fault and 25 per cent mine."

"I can go along with that. Another thing that bothers me is that I don't know whether or not this woman kind of went along with you or not. What I'm trying to say is that I have to make a decision as to what charges are going to be laid and in order to do this I have to know exactly what happened, but I would like you to confirm it with me. I'll relate to you what I think happened and if you disagree with me, I want you to stop me and tell me where I was incorrect. What I think happened is that without any forethought, and what I mean is you didn't plan it, you found yourself in the hedge and grabbed Mrs. S. Is that right?"

"Right."

"Then I think you kind of blacked out for a while and you don't remember anything until finally something clicks and you realize that you are raping this woman. You realize that you're in serious trouble and you don't know what to do about it. Am I right or wrong?"

"You should have been a psychiatrist."

"Am I right or wrong?"

"You're right."

After hearing this conversation related at the preliminary hearing, Fisher's lawyer realized there was no point in going ahead with the trial. Months went by, and after some plea bargaining, a deal was struck with the prosecutor. In return for a guilty plea, the Crown would recommend a ten-year prison term and the defence would concur. As far as Fisher was concerned, it was far better than the maximum life sentence the judge was entitled to mete out.

The judge, J. H. Maher, agreed with the arrangement, sentencing Fisher to ten years' imprisonment on charges of rape and attempted murder. Arnot told the press that he was satisfied with the outcome of the case, calling the sentence "one of the severest ever imposed in Saskatchewan for such charges."

For Fisher, it meant he had to complete his original sentence and only then start serving his new one. Barring parole, he could look forward to staying in prison until 1994.

Unlike his previous offences in Saskatoon, Fisher's new conviction and sentence were not ignored by the media. By this time, however, Gail Miller's murder was a hazy memory for most people. Few people would draw any connection between the facts of the North Battleford case and Miller's murder.

One of the people who did draw the connection was Fisher's former wife, Linda. Reading about the attack in North Battleford rekindled her suspicions that Fisher had been involved in the Miller case. With those suspicions constantly at the back of her mind, Linda opened her mailbox late in 1980 and pulled out a flyer – the flyer that Joyce Milgaard hoped would convince someone to come forward and help get her son out of prison.

"A total $10,000 reward is offered to any person or persons able to provide information that will exonerate David Milgaard, convicted on circumstantial evidence, of the murder of Gail Miller in Saskatoon, Saskatchewan on January 31, 1969," the flyer read.

"David has spent over eleven years in prison, where he presently remains. His family, who pledge this money, believe David is innocent and that justice must prevail! If you know anything, it may help. Please write or send your name and phone number to: Box 309, Stonewall, Manitoba."

Linda brought the flyer back into her apartment and showed it to her boyfriend, Bryan Wright. They started discussing the reward excitedly.

For Linda, the discussion stirred a strange mixture of emotions. Fisher's recent court case had still not concluded, and she was genuinely afraid of what might happen when he got out of prison. They were divorced, but Linda still felt a connection to her former husband. He was the father of their daughter, and Tammy still held him in high regard. At the same time, Linda felt strongly that the wrong man had been convicted of the Miller murder. Now, the lure of a cash reward was added to the equation. Bryan encouraged her to go to the police immediately with her story. Yet Linda was still hesitant. She said she wanted to tell her story, but preferred to wait a day and think about it. "No," her boyfriend said. "If we don't do it now, you'll never go."

Bryan was insistent. Finally, that same evening, they both went to the Saskatoon police station. Linda announced that she had new information on a 1969 murder.

"I gave the police a one-page statement, listing the reasons I could think of why I felt that David Milgaard was innocent and that Larry Fisher had committed the crime," she said. "They didn't look at me as if I was lying," she says. "They took it seriously, I thought."

But there is no evidence that police took the statement seriously at all. The Saskatoon police department was well aware that Joyce Milgaard had been distributing flyers offering a reward and was trying to track down people who had testified at the trial. All the senior officers involved in the Miller case were still on the force, now in positions of authority. They did not take kindly to any suggestion that they had jailed the wrong man for the last eleven years.

Linda's statement did not lead to a reopening of the Miller murder. Police didn't even bother questioning Fisher about the allegations. As far as they were concerned, the case was firmly closed. Linda never heard from the police again.

14

Asper's Little Project

After an initial period of excitement and progress, Joyce Milgaard's career as a private investigator now seemed to be
stalled. Most of the key witnesses had been found and interviewed. The pages of the transcript were dog-eared from reading and re-reading. The family members, friends, and
volunteers who had tramped around Saskatchewan doing the
legwork were tired. And David was still in prison.

In Joyce's mind, the evidence was powerful. But nobody
seemed to be listening. Attempts to persuade the national
media to pick up the story were unsuccessful. Even her lawyer
seemed to think there was not enough new information to
force the issue.

As months began to slip by with no further progress, Joyce
became alarmed. Some of the witnesses were moving elsewhere. If something wasn't done soon, they might never be
found again. Despite her disillusionment with lawyers and
the legal system in general, she thought it was time to try that
avenue again. This time she looked for a lawyer closer to
home.

Hersh Wolch has the reputation of being one of the best
criminal lawyers in Winnipeg – a lawyer who isn't afraid to
stand up for the rights of his clients, no matter who they are.

He has extensive experience with the criminal justice system, having served as a Crown prosecutor for six years and Justice Department lawyer for two before entering private practice. When a high-profile accused goes shopping for a lawyer, Wolch is usually on the short list. Armed with the transcripts from her son's trial and appeal, Joyce marched into Wolch's office in early 1986 and introduced herself.

Wolch was intrigued. He already knew the name Milgaard from legal texts. The case itself was not an important precedent, but the set of procedures that had been used in questioning Nichol John about her police statement at David Milgaard's trial had become enshrined in Canadian legal practice. It was known as "Milgaarding" a witness. Beyond that, Wolch knew nothing about the facts of the case, but was curious to find out why the inmate's mother had come to see him.

"Tell me how much you would charge to read these transcripts," she recalls saying. "And tell me, am I banging my head against a cement wall? Is there anything in here to prove that my son is innocent? Is there a chance?"

Wolch studied Joyce's face and saw the fierce look of determination in her eyes. He knew the odds of overturning a conviction by a jury – a conviction that had been upheld on appeal and that the Supreme Court had refused to review – were practically nil. Yet he was not averse to taking on a challenging case. He glanced at the transcripts – more than a thousand pages – and said he would read through the material and provide an opinion for $2,000.

Joyce wrote out the cheque. It was a financial burden for her at the time. Devoting nearly all her time to her son's case was rapidly depleting her savings. And the government would not assist her in trying to clear her son's name. An application to Saskatchewan Legal Aid was turned down; they suggested she try Manitoba, where David was currently residing. But an application to Manitoba Legal Aid was also rejected; they insisted he apply in Saskatchewan, where the offence originally occurred.

If Wolch had actually sat down and read through the transcripts, he would probably have written a legal opinion stressing the problems and weaknesses of the Crown's case. In all likelihood, he would have pinpointed the areas that could be pursued in appealing the case to the minister of justice. He may even have highlighted the contradictions that could best be exploited in doing further research. But Wolch didn't read the transcripts – not at first, anyway. Instead, he turned them over to David Asper, a twenty-seven-year-old junior lawyer, who had just joined the firm.

When Joyce found out, she was neither shocked nor upset. Over time, she realized that the move was the best thing that could have happened. "David Asper became our knight in shining armour," she says. "He was really gung-ho. You could see that this guy was not going to be deterred. He's a fighter."

Joyce had found the perfect tonic to revitalize her campaign. In Asper, she had a partner. When she got mad, he got mad. They would phone each other excitedly over every bit of fresh news. She pestered him constantly, at the office and at home, but he tolerated it. Fresh out of law school, Asper did not have much experience with clients. But even he recognized that this was no normal client. After a while, he didn't bother turning on the billing clock when she called or came to visit him. It was obvious he was spending far more time on the case than could ever be recovered. His colleagues in the law office looked on in amusement, dubbing the Milgaard case "Asper's little project."

Asper is the son of millionaire businessman Izzy Asper – a private broadcasting czar who controls Global Television and once dabbled in politics by serving a short stint as leader of the Manitoba Liberal party. Izzy is a lawyer, too, and encouraged his son to follow in his footsteps. But the Asper name carried little weight with the admissions committees at Canada's law schools. David couldn't get in, so he travelled south and earned his degree at the California Western School of Law in San Diego. He returned to find Hersh Wolch willing to give him a chance in his home town.

The Milgaard case was Asper's first assignment of any significance and he was determined to do a good job. Perhaps he was too inexperienced to be cynical about a mother who insisted that her convicted son had done no wrong. He devoured the transcripts and emerged with a genuine sense of outrage. An injustice had been done, he thought.

"I was one of those people who graduated from law school believing that by practising law one had a great opportunity to do good in the world and to right the wrongs," he said. "So I had that pretty fresh in my mind. And then all of a sudden somebody presents themselves as being wrongly convicted, and it's entirely consistent with my mindset at the time. So I didn't think, here's another guilty guy who insists he's innocent. I lunged at it and thought, holy smokes, this is what it's all about."

Asper drove up the highway to Stony Mountain and visited Milgaard. He was impressed by his client's attitude. Milgaard didn't beg or plead for help; he insisted on it. Asper then travelled to Saskatoon. In order to test the validity of the Crown's case, he felt it was important to follow the route taken by David, Nichol John, and Ron Wilson on the day of the murder. He drove from where Wilson's car supposedly first became stuck to the murder scene, and then to the motel where Milgaard had asked for directions. From there, he drove to the spot where Wilson's car stalled behind the Danchuk residence. He measured all the distances and figured out how long it would take to drive between them at a reasonable rate of speed, not even accounting for delays due to stoplights or weather conditions. After doing all the calculations, he was convinced. It was physically impossible – a fact he considered mathematically demonstrable – for David Milgaard to have committed the crime and then travelled to all those places in the brief time frame the Crown had alleged.

The more Asper drove around the neighbourhood and surveyed the scene, the more senseless the Crown's case appeared to him. Later he would summarize his findings this way: "At 7:00 a.m. the neighbourhood was likely very still. To suggest that Milgaard grabbed Gail Miller at any point, cut her fifteen times about the neck, stabbed her twelve times, raped her, arranged her clothing as it was found, disposed of the boot, sweater, and purse, without himself being covered with blood, without having made any noise that anyone heard, and without leaving signs of a struggle having started at one point and carried on up the alley, is absurd."

Asper reported his findings to Wolch, and they discussed how to proceed. Wolch realized that something more was needed than a new interpretation of the known evidence. The Crown's theory about the timing of the murder might be strange – it might be downright wrong – but it had been accepted by the jury. All of the facts surrounding the timing were known to the jury, and they still found Milgaard guilty. It would be pointless to re-argue the facts of the case, since the Canadian judicial system doesn't allow for such a procedure once a verdict has been rendered and all appeals exhausted.

What the system does allow for is a direct appeal to the federal minister of justice for a review of the case. At the time, Section 617 of the Criminal Code gave the justice minister the power to reopen cases and order new trials if the evidence warranted. But the only hope of convincing the minister even to consider such a course of action was to come up with fresh evidence – pertinent facts the jury wasn't told during the trial.

The only fresh evidence of any significance had come when Joyce had interviewed Deborah Hall. Their meeting was directly attributable to the flurry of publicity that Joyce had generated in late 1980 and early 1981. Hall was working as a men's hairstylist at Rudy's Hairstyling in Regina when a customer noticed her nametag. Was she the same Deborah Hall who was involved in the David Milgaard case, he asked. The customer was Chris O'Brien, a radio reporter who had become well-versed in the Milgaard case. Hall was taken aback. Of course she knew Milgaard, but she had no idea he had been convicted of any crime.

O'Brien showed her the transcript of evidence given by George Lapchuk and Craig Melnyk, the last-minute witnesses who claimed Milgaard re-enacted the stabbing at a Regina motel-room party in 1969. Again Hall was shocked. She was at the same party, and took issue with Lapchuk and Melnyk's statements. Nothing of the sort they described ever happened, she said. Hall contacted Joyce Milgaard and told her the story.

That was in 1981. Asper now realized the importance of taking a sworn statement from Hall and including it as part of an application to the justice minister. He went to Regina in November 1986, hoping that her story was still the same.

Hall explained that she remembered the events of that night very clearly, because it was the first time she had ever experimented with drugs. That in itself was a double-edged sword for Asper, but her precise recollection of who was there and what was said convinced him that she was a credible witness. Hall described the scene that night in the Park Lane Motel, where she, Milgaard, Ute Frank, Lapchuk, and Melnyk were partying. Milgaard and Ute, his girlfriend, were lying on the bed. It was the latter part of May 1969, four months after Gail Miller's murder.

Hall's sworn affidavit left no room for doubt about what she had seen: "I remember seeing news pictures of the Gail Miller murder on the television set but could not hear what was being said. As I previously indicated, everyone in the room was chattering back and forth. At one point, Craig Melnyk said to David Milgaard, 'You did it, didn't you?' As Craig Melnyk was saying this, David Milgaard was punching the pillow, trying to fluff it up. I remember him saying, in response to Craig Melnyk, 'Oh yeah, right,' in a sarcastic or joking manner. David Milgaard then put the pillow back against his chest. I believe his response to the comment made by Craig Melnyk was in a joking manner. At no time did David Milgaard use the pillow to re-enact the murder. My interpretation of David Milgaard's response was that it was a completely innocent and perhaps crudely comical comment. I know that if I had thought he was serious I would have left immediately. No one in the room thought anything of that particular conversation. Craig Melnyk and George Lapchuk both lied when they stated in their evidence at trial that David Milgaard re-enacted the murder by going through a series of stabbing motions against the pillow."

Asper was pleased. The statement was a convincing refutation of Melnyk and Lapchuk's testimony – testimony which itself was suspect because of the perception that they had come forward at the last moment to win favours in the treatment of their own criminal charges.

The unanswered question was: Why was Deborah Hall never called to testify at Milgaard's trial? The Crown had been aware of her identity, but hadn't interviewed her or attempted to produce her at the trial. One explanation is innocent enough. Her surname was misspelled as "Hull" in the initial police reports. As she left Regina in June 1969, police may simply not have been able to locate her in time for the court proceedings. Then again, with two incriminating statements in hand, police may have believed they need go no further in investigating what really happened at the Park Lane motel room.

While in Saskatoon, Asper had a chance to sift through the original exhibits at the Milgaard trial. For some reason they had not been destroyed, even though all legal appeals had long since been exhausted. There, in an old shopping cart in Saskatoon's courthouse, were Gail Miller's coat, her undergarments, the knife blade, and all the other articles that were tendered as evidence.

It occurred to Asper and Wolch that new evidence might also be unearthed by a careful re-examination of the exhibits, as well as of the original laboratory analyses that were carried out by police and RCMP. The physical evidence that was presented at the trial was confusing at best. If it could be shown that the forensic evidence had not been interpreted properly, or if it had been explained incorrectly to the jury, a case could be made that a serious miscarriage of justice had occurred.

Another possibility occurred to the lawyers. New techniques of DNA-typing might be used to go over the exhibits in an effort to exonerate Milgaard. These techniques involved isolating minute traces of DNA on clothing and tracing them to individuals involved in the crime. If any DNA still existed on Gail Miller's clothing, it could provide a clue to the true assailant. It was a slim chance, but there was nothing to lose.

To assist them, they turned to an internationally recognized expert in forensic pathology, Dr. James Ferris. Head of forensic pathology at the University of British Columbia, Ferris had performed more than six thousand autopsies in his career – including six hundred and fifty cases involving homicide. He was a leading researcher into the use of DNA in forensic biology. He had also recently earned widespread attention by testifying at the Royal Commission of Inquiry into the Chamberlain conviction in Sydney, Australia – the famous "dingo murder" case, where a woman who was convicted of murdering her baby insisted that it had been carried off by wild dogs. She was exonerated.

Ferris agreed to review the evidence at no charge. A motion was made in Saskatchewan Court of Queen's Bench to release some of the key exhibits. Once he obtained them, Ferris set out to retrieve DNA from samples of Gail Miller's clothing, particularly her panties and girdle.

Much to Wolch's and Asper's disappointment, Ferris reported that he couldn't obtain sufficient DNA to carry out a genetic typing analysis. Even a new technique that allowed for the artificial manufacture of DNA from tiny traces recovered at the scene would not have succeeded, he said. In any event, he said there was no evidence the DNA would have remained unaltered during its long period of storage.

Undaunted, Wolch and Asper asked Ferris to continue with his review of the physical evidence as it was presented to the trial. This involved a considerable investment of time on Ferris's part. But when he finally completed his analysis, the lawyers were not let down.

"On the basis of the evidence that I have examined," wrote Ferris in his report of September 1988, "I have no reasonable doubt that serological evidence presented at the trial failed to link David Milgaard with the offence and that, in fact, could be reasonably considered to exclude him from being the perpetrator of the murder."

How did Ferris come to this conclusion eighteen years after the fact?

At the trial, the Crown had spent a great deal of time discussing the implications of the semen found near the scene of the murder. This was the sample derived from the two frozen yellowish lumps of snow recovered by Lieutenant Penkala on February 4, a full four days after Gail Miller's body had been found.

Laboratory testing of the semen at the time showed that it contained type A antigens. This suggested that it came from a person with type A blood who secretes his antigens into other bodily fluids, such as semen and saliva. While Milgaard was identified as having type A blood, he was also one of the 20 per cent of people classified as non-secreters. In other words, he could not have transferred the antigens into the semen.

The Crown had come up with an alternate theory. Type A antigens would also be present in the semen if some of Milgaard's blood had actually mixed with it, perhaps as a result of a genital infection or injury. This was the suggestion the Crown left with the jury, without offering any proof that Milgaard had such an infection or injury.

The first problem Ferris identified was the integrity of the sample itself. He noted that a platoon of police officers had trampled through the area for days, shovelling and melting snow and greatly disturbing the area. "In view of the extensive disturbance of the scene and the obvious potential for contamination of the scene, I find it quite remarkable that two small pools of semen were identified four days after the initial examination. On the basis of the forensic testing that was done I have no doubt that semen was recovered and described. However, it would be most unusual for this semen not to have been contaminated by all of the tampering which had gone on with the evidence around the scene. I am surprised that with this clear inability to prove either the continuity or the integrity of these seminal samples, they were considered admissible evidence."

If the sample did contain some elements of blood, Ferris said the most likely possibility was that the blood was the victim's. "The fact that when this frozen semen was melted down in a tube and appeared to be slightly bloodstained is not a surprise. I would find it hard to believe that any object that had been recovered four days after the murder from the area immediately adjacent to where the body had lain would not have been stained by blood derived from the area adjacent to the body."

Even if the sample was uncontaminated, Ferris had further concerns. To begin with, he said there is no positive proof that blood was ever found in the semen. He then pointed out that there was no evidence whatsoever that Milgaard had an injury or infection, thereby contaminating his semen with blood. In any event, he would be sceptical of such a thing ever happening. "I have also spoken to a number of personal contacts in other forensic science laboratories and on the basis of their experience and my own experience, we are not familiar with a single case where seminal fluid or stains have been found to be contaminated by blood from the alleged assailant. It would be my opinion therefore that even if the contamination of the seminal sample can be proven to be blood, there is no evidence that this blood came from David Milgaard and therefore there is no evidence that this type A semen can be linked with David Milgaard."

The lack of sophisticated modern testing techniques in 1969 also affected the Crown's case. Ferris noted that, at that time, laboratories in Regina were unable to differentiate between type A and type AB blood in a case where only A antigens were detected in the semen. That meant there was still a possibility the semen sample came from a person who had type AB blood, again excluding Milgaard.

Ferris summed up his conclusions succinctly. Either the semen sample had been contaminated and was therefore useless as evidence, or it was valid and should have been reasonably used to exonerate him.

Joyce Milgaard was elated. An independent expert, with far more experience in pathology than anyone connected to the original investigation, had discounted the only physical evidence that purported to link David Milgaard to the crime. It did not constitute new evidence in the strictest sense, but was a new interpretation of the existing evidence. Had someone with Ferris's expertise testified at the trial, the jury would surely have been hard-pressed to put any credence in the Crown's assertion that the so-called semen sample linked Milgaard to the murder.

Much to the delight of Joyce and her lawyers, however, Ferris went even further in his report. As an expert who had been involved in hundreds of homicides, he couldn't help commenting on some of the other aspects of the Crown's case. Ferris noted that the victim had died as a result of bleeding from the lung tissue into the chest cavities. In such cases, unconsciousness occurs at a relatively slow speed. He conjectured that Miller could have survived for at least fifteen minutes following the injuries; they were almost certainly not immediately fatal or even immobilizing.

"[T]he circumstances of the rape/murder were complex, probably prolonged, and in my opinion, incapable of having occurred within the time frame suggested by the evidence at the trial," Ferris wrote. As a footnote, he added: "I have real concerns as to the practicalities of a rape/murder as apparently described taking place at -40 degrees C in the environment described."

Ferris went on to suggest a theory that others have also considered likely. The offence, he said, might have taken place elsewhere, and the body later dumped in the alley. He was quick to point out, though, the lack of clear evidence to support this conclusion.

There was another possibility. Perhaps Gail Miller had been taken into a building or a car, forced to undress and raped. Then, after putting her coat back on, she might have tried to flee, precipitating the rapist's fatal attack. That would certainly explain the knife cuts in the coat and lack of cuts in the dress – a configuration that the Crown was never able to address adequately.

The time had come to distill the years of detective work and re-evaluation of evidence into a concise and persuasive appeal to the justice minister for a reopening of the case. The application was completed and forwarded in December 1988.

The first element of the appeal was a commentary on the facts of the case. Wolch and Asper realized it was pointless to re-argue the facts, since the justice minister was unlikely to interfere with a jury's verdict merely on the basis of a different interpretation. Nevertheless, they considered it important to review some of the aspects of the case so that their viewpoint would be known if a new trial were ever to be ordered.

"[T]he time sequence simply does not fit," the application argued. "The evidence was that Milgaard was out of his car from approximately 6:30 to 6:45 a.m. Gail Miller did not usually leave for work until approximately 7:00 a.m. and was seen alive at home sometime between 6:35 and 6:45 a.m. From 6:45 on Milgaard was always in the company of another individual. Obviously the jury must have found that people were wrong about the times. Even if we accept this evidence, the 'window of opportunity' for Milgaard was no more than about ten minutes. Moreover, the evidence of attending police officers was unequivocal that there was no evidence of a car having been stuck anywhere in the area surrounding the crime scene, including the adjacent residential streets."

The strongest pieces of evidence tying Milgaard to the offence, the application argued, were the combined testimonies of Lapchuk and Melnyk, and the forensic evidence that purportedly linked Milgaard to the crime. The minister was therefore urged to reopen the case on the basis that:

"1. Debra [sic] Hall, who was not called at trial, has provided an affidavit contradicting the evidence of Melnyk and Lapchuk.

"2. Advances in scientific technology have allowed the applicant to discredit the forensic evidence called at his trial and to provide evidence that exculpates him as the perpetrator of the crime."

Attached were summations of Hall's statement and Ferris's report, along with the actual documents. The minister was being asked to order a new trial, or to refer the matter to a Court of Appeal or the Supreme Court for a further judicial review.

For the time being, Wolch and Asper considered they had done as much as they could. The matter was now in the minister's hands. But it was not to be the last of their presentations to the minister. Over the next two years, far more evidence would be put forward to buttress the case that David Milgaard was wrongly convicted. Much of that evidence would not surface until after the twentieth anniversary of Milgaard's conviction for murder.

15

The Other Victims

By the beginning of 1990, Milgaard's hopes of winning his freedom were no further ahead. A year had passed since the application was filed with Justice, and there was still no hint that a decision would be made soon. The process had begun with a glimmer of hope that the Justice Department would render a speedy decision on the application to reopen the matter. On February 16, 1989, Justice Minister Doug Lewis asked for copies of all the original trial transcripts and factums filed in the appeal. He also wanted any laboratory reports the lawyers had in their possession and further details on Nichol John's statement to police that implicated Milgaard in the killing.

It was a signal the department was taking the application seriously and was launching its own investigation. But it was also the beginning of a frustrating series of delays and episodes of bureaucratic intransigence which led the Milgaard family to the brink of despair.

In June 1989, the department notified Wolch and Asper that the application was still being assessed. A few months later, the two lawyers asked for a report on the status of the department's investigation. It was still being investigated, came the reply. In the meantime, the lawyers demanded that any information the department gleaned from the original prosecution file be disclosed to them. The department did not agree to such disclosure, except for the occasional release of selected material.

Joyce Milgaard managed to get the media interested in running a handful of stories about the Justice Department's review. In October 1989 the publicity encouraged a member of the original jury at Milgaard's trial to step forward and claim he had been mentally unfit to serve on the panel. Fernley Cooney, a part-time janitor in Saskatoon, revealed that he had suffered a mental breakdown in 1962 and was in and out of hospital until 1969, when he was chosen to sit on the jury. He claimed he originally thought Milgaard was innocent, and was the last holdout in the jury room before finally caving into pressure from the other jurors.

The bizarre revelation did the cause no good. It was of no value to have someone who insisted he was mentally unstable to say David Milgaard was innocent. As to Cooney's ability to serve on the jury in the first place, why did he take twenty years to make his concerns public? There is no indication the Justice Department paid any attention to Cooney's revelation. Even if it did, it was highly unlikely that a mistrial would be declared twenty years after the fact. After a brief period of media excitement, his statements were forgotten.

In early January 1990, the Justice Department announced it had completed the fact-gathering aspects of the Milgaard application. It set a two-week deadline for any further submissions by his lawyers. All this time, Asper and Wolch had been stymied in their efforts to get funding so that further investigations could be initiated. Their renewed efforts to secure legal aid in Manitoba and Saskatchewan were denied, as was a special request to the Justice Department itself. More money, they argued, could help them conduct a video re-enactment of the crime, and perhaps hire an investigator to look into other aspects of the case. A frustrated Asper fired off an angry letter to Ottawa, charging: "It is virtually impossible to know what might be uncovered had we been provided with funds that would have enabled us to broaden the scope of our investigation to date."

While Joyce spared no expense in fighting for her son's release, she was in no position to bankroll an expensive legal campaign. Joyce had quit her job as a property manager in 1985 to devote more time to her son's case, and her savings gradually eroded as the fight wore on. After leaving her job, she recognized a spiritual void in her life. Though she was christened an Anglican, Joyce had become interested in Christian Science twenty years earlier. Her beliefs grew stronger over the years, and in 1985 she decided to devote more time to them. She enrolled in a Christian Scientist nursing program in New Jersey. For the next five years, she shuttled between New Jersey and Winnipeg, spending a month at her studies and the next month trying to free her son. In her mind, both pursuits were linked – both involved a search for the truth.

On a Monday, the last week of February 1990, a call came into the law office of Wolch, Pinx, Tapper, and Scurfield from a man with some information about the David Milgaard case. David Asper was on holiday in Florida. The caller was put through to Hersh Wolch.

"Would you like to know who really killed Gail Miller?" the anonymous caller asked.

"Sure," replied a sceptical Wolch.

"Why don't you check out a guy called Larry Fisher? He lived in the basement suite of the Cadrain house. He's serving time in Prince Albert right now for a bunch of rapes. If you can find his wife, she'll tell you that he came home on the morning of the murder covered in blood."

The call seemed too specific to be a prank. But could it be true? A man who lived in Cadrain's house, now in jail for a series of rapes, had come home covered in blood on the day of Miller's murder? After nearly four years of working on the case, Wolch thought he might finally have found the smoking gun that would set his client free. He contacted Asper in Florida and told him about the call.

In an instant, the Larry Fisher tip revitalized Asper's efforts at uncovering new evidence. Once back in Winnipeg, it didn't take long for him to confirm that a Larry Earl Fisher of Saskatoon was indeed serving time in Prince Albert for a string of rape convictions in Saskatchewan and Winnipeg. He quickly contacted Joyce and told her about the call. Asper was amazed once more at Joyce's encyclopedic knowledge of the case. She said she remembered the name Larry Fisher. She recalled that years earlier she and Carlyle-Gordge – the journalist who helped her track down witnesses in the early eighties – had gleaned some information about Fisher from the original police investigation. In the days following the murder, officers had interviewed people in the neighbour-hood, asking if they had any information. One of the people they had spoken to was Larry Fisher. He was approached while waiting for a bus on Saskatoon's 20th Street just before 7:00 a.m. – the same bus stop Gail Miller normally used. Joyce remembered that Fisher told police he had taken the bus to work as usual on January 31, but knew nothing about the murder. It had been a routine police interview, one of dozens they conducted with people in the neighbourhood. Fisher was never taken in for further questioning and was never considered a suspect.

Asper notified the Justice Department within days of the anonymous phone call. But he and Joyce realized the urgency of investigating the tip independently. The anonymous caller said Fisher's wife would be able to confirm his guilt. It was imperative that she be found and interviewed as soon as possible.

Joyce decided to turn to a friend for help, a friend who would be immediately sympathetic to her predicament. She called Jim McCloskey in New Jersey, head of Centurion Ministries Inc. McCloskey was a naval officer-turned-businessman-turned-seminary student, who had earned his Master of Divinity degree a decade earlier and founded Centurion – a non-profit organization whose sole purpose was to overturn wrongful criminal convictions. Since 1983, McCloskey and his staff had helped prove the innocence of a dozen convicts.

Eight of them had been serving life sentences. Four had been on death row.

McCloskey had been a successful businessman for an international management consulting firm in Philadelphia when he decided he needed some meaningful work injected into his life. At age thirty-seven, he made a radical decision. He quit his job and enrolled in a three-year program at Princeton Theological Seminary. Part of his field work requirement took him to Trent State prison, where he spent two days a week as the chaplain.

Although McCloskey had forty inmates assigned to him, his attention was quickly focused on just one, George De Los Santos, who had been sentenced to life in prison for the murder of a Newark used-car salesman. De Los Santos proclaimed his innocence, and in a provocative way he challenged McCloskey to look into the facts.

Although he had no previous experience with the criminal justice system, McCloskey got hold of the trial transcripts and immersed himself in the case. He gradually became convinced that the convict's story was true.

McCloskey devoted his full attention to the case, taking one full year off from his studies. Finally, in July 1983, De Los Santos was freed after a judge found that the key witness had committed perjury.

While visiting De Los Santos in prison, McCloskey met two other convicts who also proclaimed their innocence. After researching their stories, he undertook to argue their cases as well, and set them free. McCloskey realized he had found his life's calling.

Joyce first met McCloskey in the summer of 1989, when she was attending a Christian Science retreat in Princeton, New Jersey. She had heard about Centurion's work, and decided to pay him a visit. She found a vibrant staff committed to seeking justice for innocent people in prison. Centurion workers weren't naïve enough to believe that every inmate who wrote to them was innocent. They did an exhaustive study of each case before deciding whether to take it on. But once they were convinced of the inmate's innocence, they spared no effort in clearing his name.

Joyce learned about Nathaniel Walker, convicted in 1975 for raping a New Jersey woman and sentenced to life plus fifty years. He spent eight years in prison and three as a fugitive before being exonerated in 1986. McCloskey had uncovered medical specimens never checked by either prosecution or defence that proved Walker was not the rapist.

She learned about Rene Santana, convicted in 1976 and sentenced to life in prison for murdering a Newark building superintendent. He served ten years in prison before Centurion showed that the state's star witness had a secret deal with prosecutors to have his own charges dropped in exchange for false eyewitness testimony.

She learned about Damaso Vega, convicted in 1982 and sentenced to life in prison for the strangulation murder of a sixteen-year-old New Jersey girl. After a five-year investigation, Centurion talked to the three main prosecution witnesses, who all admitted lying on the urging of a police officer. Vega was freed in 1989.

She learned about Clarence Brandley, sentenced to death for the 1980 rape and murder of a sixteen-year-old student at a high school north of Houston. Days before his scheduled execution, Centurion produced an eyewitness to the crime who named the real killers and cleared Brandley. He was finally freed after spending a decade on death row in Texas.

Joyce was mesmerized. Here was an agency going up against the mighty justice system and proving that it was putting innocent people in prison. This is exactly what was needed for her son, she thought. Joyce decided she would stay in New Jersey and do some volunteer work for Centurion. She was put to work screening calls and letters from inmates who claimed they were wrongly convicted and needed help. She got a sense of how the system worked and gathered as much information on each case as she could. Between phone calls, she would talk to McCloskey about her son and the situation he faced.

McCloskey was sympathetic. He believed David Milgaard

was innocent, but he wouldn't get involved. Centurion was busy with too many cases already, and a new and expensive project in Canada seemed beyond its means, he said.

That was several months before. Now, in early 1990, Joyce faced the urgent need to track down information that could lead to Gail Miller's real killer. It was important to act before Justice Department officials closed the book on the case. Once they did, it might be impossible to get them to reopen it, no matter how compelling the evidence.

McCloskey agreed that something had to be done quickly. He said he was too busy to get directly involved, but he knew someone else who would, a private investigator in Seattle named Paul Henderson. He's good, McCloskey said, but he's expensive. Centurion agreed to pay his fee.

"Thank God for the mothers of the world," McCloskey said afterwards. "They hang in there with their sons and daughters much longer than the fathers, the husbands, the siblings, or anyone else. It's the mothers of the world who stay with their unjustly convicted offspring."

Like McCloskey, Paul Henderson had also heard his share of mothers insisting that their sons weren't murderers. He knew better than most that it takes more than a mother's plea to prove a case. Fifteen years earlier he had listened to Ted Bundy's mother argue that her son was innocent. That was before Bundy confessed to a killing spree that spread across the western United States. As a reporter with the *Seattle Times*, Henderson had covered the murders of eight Bundy victims who were killed in Washington state. A police tip then took Henderson to Colorado, where he discovered that Bundy had used a Chevron gas credit card on the same day and in the same location as another murder. That evidence had helped to prove Bundy's guilt.

The Bundy story was out of character for Henderson. His preference was for cases where he could prove someone's innocence. In 1981, he was able to do just that in the case of thirty-year-old Steve Titus. Titus had been convicted of rape and was facing a fifteen-year prison sentence. Henderson wrote a series of stories highlighting the discrepancies in the case and pointing the finger at another suspect who had a long string of similar crimes. The stories helped set Titus free, and Henderson was awarded the Pulitzer Prize for investigative reporting.

Crusading journalism appealed to Henderson, but stories that cry out for major investigations don't come along every day. At age forty-six, he was getting tired of the day-to-day grind of police reporting. After twenty-two years as a newspaper reporter, Henderson opted for a career change. He became a private investigator, specializing in criminal justice.

Since changing jobs, Henderson has helped overturn eight convictions. He has pinpointed everything from police misconduct to attorney malpractice to new evidence. David Milgaard was Henderson's second case on behalf of Centurion Ministries. His first involved two men who were serving life sentences for the 1975 murder of a Los Angeles police officer. Henderson found the witnesses whose testimony had helped convict the men. He got the witnesses to admit they had been pressured and threatened by police to say what they had on the stand. Over the course of his two careers, he has seen countless cases of police misconduct and shoddy investigative work. He has long since stopped being shocked at the many different ways things can go wrong in the justice system. What still upsets him, though, is what happens when those errors are brought to light.

"Mistakes are made in anything in life," he says. "And certainly the criminal justice system is an example of that. But in the criminal justice system when a mistake is made there are dire consequences on a human life. And my God, they ought to be able to admit that they're only human. They ought to be able to admit that these mistakes are made and rectify the error when it's painfully obvious to everyone."

Within days of getting the call from Centurion, Henderson was on a plane to Saskatoon. He had arranged to meet Joyce there. She had tracked Linda Fisher to Cando, a small town northwest of Saskatoon. The plan was to arrive on her doorstep unannounced and persuade her to give them a sworn statement.

The temperature was hovering around the freezing point when Henderson arrived in Saskatoon in early March. He was surprised. It was his first working experience in Canada, and somehow he expected it to be colder. He was also surprised at Joyce Milgaard's cool composure. She seemed able to separate her emotions from the facts of the case, he thought. On the three-hour drive from Saskatoon to Cando, Joyce told Henderson the history of her son's conviction and the evidence that had come to light since. It took little argument to convince him that David was innocent, and he pledged to do everything he could to help overturn the conviction.

With more than a bit of trepidation, Henderson and Joyce knocked on Linda Fisher's door. Her teenage son answered. Linda wasn't home, he said, but they were more than welcome to come inside and wait. She was attending a class in school and would be home soon. They waited for more than an hour, chatting idly. Finally, Linda arrived back home.

"Hello, I'm Joyce Milgaard," Joyce said, extending her hand.

Linda had been waiting for this day for ten years. Her surprise at seeing Joyce in her home was eclipsed by the shock of finding out that the Milgaard family had never been told about her statement a decade earlier. That statement, which pointed to her husband as a likely suspect in the Miller murder, had been prompted by Joyce's reward poster in December 1980. Linda assumed the police would have notified the family as part of their investigation into Larry's activities on the day of the murder.

"I've been working on behalf of my son for twenty years," Joyce said. "He didn't kill Gail Miller; I'm trying to prove that. You're a mother, too, you can probably understand why I'm doing this."

Linda needed very little prompting to start talking. She began telling the story of the conversation she had with Larry on the day of the murder, and the strange behaviour he exhibited. She recounted all the details she had given to police.

Henderson could sense that she, like many people he had met through the years, felt uncomfortable that someone was in prison for a crime he didn't commit.

Yet Linda was not unaware of the consequences that could flow from her actions. Her daughter, Tammy, still visited Larry in prison, and she worried about jeopardizing Tammy's safety. She also realized that Larry was due to be released in 1994. With his history of violence, she feared what he might do to her in the future. As she learned later, Larry told Tammy that her mother "signed his death warrant" by speaking out.

Despite the dangers, Linda felt she was doing the right thing, and she had the support of everyone around her. "Tammy thinks it's wrong for Milgaard to be in jail if he didn't do it," she says. "Larry's mother thinks that, too. Everybody thinks if David's in there innocently he shouldn't be in there. . . . I don't know who killed Gail Miller, but I don't think David did. The evidence, to me, points more to Larry with his record."

Linda agreed to meet with Joyce and Henderson the next day, March 11, in Saskatoon. They spent four hours going over an official statement that would form part of David Milgaard's appeal to the justice minister. Henderson realized that Linda might be accused of having come forward ten years earlier only because of the reward. The Justice Department would surely challenge her credibility, possibly suggesting that she was trying to get back at an estranged husband who had abused her. They made it clear to Linda that the reward money that was offered in 1980 was no longer available. They wanted to be certain she was giving the statement with no ulterior motives and with no illusions that there was some hidden promise of benefit.

At the end, Linda signed the statement, but not before some last minute hesitation.

"She made it clear to us that she was signing the statement with some concern about possible repercussions on herself and her daughter," Henderson says. "In short, she is afraid of her ex-husband, but she signed the statement, and I have absolutely no doubt in my mind that Linda Fisher was telling us the truth. I found her to be extremely credible. Linda had nothing to gain personally from this except, I think, that it was important to her conscience that she tell us the truth."

Four days after Linda Fisher's statement was signed, Asper sent a copy to the Justice Department. The statement, he said, was self-explanatory. At the same time, he didn't want to leave any room for doubt that Larry Fisher should now be considered the prime suspect in Gail Miller's murder. "There was evidence that the slash wounds inflicted on the neck of the deceased would most likely have been caused by a right-handed person," he wrote. "David Milgaard is left-handed, and we understand from Linda Fisher that Larry Fisher is right-handed."

The first phase of Paul Henderson's job was complete. He knew from his experience in other cases, however, that it was crucial to interview all the witnesses that had helped the prosecution's case. Joyce had attempted to do so a decade earlier, with limited success. Perhaps they had been reluctant to open up to the mother of the man they had helped put in prison. If any of them had guilty consciences about their testimony, that guilt would only have been stoked in recent months because of the publicity surrounding the case.

Henderson doesn't do the nitty-gritty work of tracing; he leaves that to local investigators and detectives. So Joyce hired Robinson Agencies in Saskatoon to find the address and phone numbers of Ron Wilson, Albert Cadrain, and Nichol John. Late in May 1990, Joyce had the information in hand. All three were living in British Columbia. It was fortuitous; Henderson could drive up from Seattle to complete his work on the case.

His first task was to visit Albert "Shorty" Cadrain, the happy-go-lucky kid from the sixties who had been the prosecution's key witness. Henderson knew that Cadrain had ultimately picked up the $2,000 reward for his information. He also knew that Cadrain had earlier told police he knew nothing about the murder. Why had Cadrain's story changed? Was the reward a factor, or was there something else?

His gut feeling was that Cadrain had been lying. If he had actually seen blood on Milgaard's clothes as he had claimed –

if any of his travelling companions had seen the blood – why wouldn't they have confronted him with it? Wouldn't their curiosity at least have been piqued enough to ask him why he had blood splattered on his clothes? Instead, the jury was asked to believe that the witnesses had seen blood on Milgaard, but had said nothing to him at the time, only to remember it later in court. To Henderson it was pathetically transparent; but to the jury, it had been crucial evidence in finding Milgaard guilty.

Henderson found Cadrain living in Port Coquitlam, near Vancouver. His head was shaved bald – an attempt, Henderson was told, to make his hair thicker so that when it grew back it would cover his bald spot. Dark circles underneath his eyes gave them a haunting look. Henderson learned that Cadrain did not sleep well. For the last twenty years, his nights had been filled with memories, and fear. "Would you sleep at night knowing you've been through all this stuff?" Albert asked. "No. You'd never sleep at night."

Cadrain was now a troubled man, his personality permanently scarred by the events of 1969 and 1970. Henderson learned that Cadrain had been married once, but he and his wife had separated after a violent fight, in which she grabbed a knife and cut off the tip of his nose. He has no permanent home. More often than not, he stays with his younger brother, Dennis, sleeping in a treehouse in Dennis's backyard.

Albert was nervous about talking to Henderson and didn't want to cooperate. The two exchanged a few words, but Albert made it clear he had no interest in giving him a statement. The police had a job to do, Albert said, and they did it. He didn't want to get involved any further.

Henderson recognized that Cadrain's state of mind, before his incriminating statement to police and after, was an important consideration in assessing his credibility. The jury had seen Cadrain as a young man who, though lacking in education and sophistication, clung to his story. They would have had no reason to question his mental state. If Henderson could bring new facts to light about that mental state, it would have an important bearing on the appeal.

He was able to learn a great deal about Albert from his brother. Dennis told Henderson that the police had put tremendous pressure on Albert after he had gone to them with the story of seeing blood on Milgaard's clothes. Officers would pick him up in the morning, keep him for questioning all day, and drop him back home in the evening. This went on for what seemed like weeks.

"I'd ask him what happened, and he told me that the police thought he had done it," Dennis said. "He told me they had a good guy, bad guy routine, where one guy would give him a smoke and then half an hour later would be screaming his head off at him, and then the other guy would be good to him. He couldn't figure out why they were being so hard on him because he went in there of his own volition with something that he saw, and it seemed like they were turning on him. I guess they were trying to rule him out, I don't know. But he couldn't understand it."

As the questioning had progressed, everything that had happened on the trip with Milgaard had started to take on greater significance for Albert. He had begun talking about the Mafia, about suitcases full of drugs that were passed to anonymous truck drivers in the night, and other fanciful tales. He had related a story about how Milgaard had asked him to shoot Ron Wilson and Nichol John. Dennis had seen the intense police questioning change his brother's personality and affect his mental state.

After police had elicited as much from him as they could, they had told him to be careful and keep a low profile until the preliminary hearing began, as he was the key witness. This admonition had only increased Cadrain's fears. He had left Saskatoon for a farm in the Jackfish Lake area, where he had driven a tractor all day. He had developed serious ulcer problems, and had been spitting up a great deal of blood. But it was more than his physical health that had been deteriorating as the date for the preliminary inquiry had approached.

Dennis recalled the time Albert came back from the farm and told him about a vision he had concerning Milgaard. "He was standing on the highway to come back into town, and he looked up in the sky and he saw a vision. He saw a cloud and a snake, and the Virgin Mary up there, stamping on the snake. And David was the snake."

At the trial, the jury had heard nothing about these visions, nothing about Cadrain's stories concerning Milgaard's Mafia connections. Nor would the jury have had any way of knowing that before long, this key witness would commit himself to a psychiatric institution, where he would receive extensive drug and shock treatment and be diagnosed as a paranoid schizophrenic.

To this day, Dennis said, Albert harbours a morbid fear of the police. In the winter of 1989, Albert was a passenger in a car his brother was driving. It was raining heavily and the car went through a stop sign. The car was hit broadside by another vehicle, and Albert's head smashed into the windshield. The driver of the other car suggested the police be called. Albert, in need of immediate medical attention, had done nothing wrong, but was terrified at the thought of police becoming involved. He turned and ran away in the pouring rain.

Dennis agreed to put his recollections in the form of a statement for Henderson. It, too, would become part of the formal appeal to the justice minister on behalf of David Milgaard. In the statement, Dennis Cadrain defends his brother's good intentions, but issues a warning to anyone who thinks Albert's testimony is an important part of the case against Milgaard.

"I am certain that he [Albert] would not intentionally lie about anything," the statement says. "But I also know that he is prone to exaggeration and suggestion, and that he could easily be coerced and manipulated by police. If ideas were planted in Albert's mind it is quite possible that he would come to accept them as the truth. Frankly, I would not consider my brother to be a reliable witness at that time, and for this reason I have concerns that David Milgaard may not have received a fair trial."

Henderson returned to Seattle with mixed emotions. He had a powerful statement from Dennis Cadrain which cast doubt on the reliability of his brother's testimony. But he was unable to get Albert himself to talk.

* * *

His next challenge was Ron Wilson, who had delivered the greatest quantity of damning testimony at the trial. At age thirty-nine, Wilson had finally turned his life turned around, but it had been a long struggle. He was a Grade 10 dropout who had openly admitted he spent all his time stealing, selling drugs, and getting himself in trouble. While still in his teens, he had built up a criminal record of more than half a dozen charges, ranging from break and enter and theft to uttering. He had used every conceivable kind of drug available, graduating from soft drugs to narcotics. Sometime after Milgaard's preliminary hearing, he had joined the Apollos motorcycle gang and had ridden with them off and on for a decade.

Soon after Milgaard had been sentenced to life in prison, Wilson had moved to Vancouver. Fresh from a sentence of two years' probation on his latest charge, he had needed a change in scenery. He had landed a job with the Department of Public Works, but had continued to sell drugs on the side. Over the next few years he had drifted across Western Canada, selling drugs and moving from job to job.

In 1980, Wilson had kicked his addiction to narcotics and had begun to straighten out his life. He left behind his biker friends and brushes with the law, finally settling down in a secure job with a tire company in Nakusp, about fifty miles south of Revelstoke in the interior of British Columbia. Friends now called him by his middle name, Dale, and his involvement in a murder trial was unknown to the people of Nakusp. This is where Paul Henderson headed in early June.

Henderson arrived in Nakusp on the evening of June 3 and booked into the Gooseneck Lodge. Early the next morning, he called Wilson. It was a Monday, a day Henderson knew was one of Wilson's regular days off.

Wilson was startled. He had been following developments in the Milgaard case through the media, but the last thing he expected was someone to show up in Nakusp unannounced and ask to interview him. His mind flashed back to the days when Joyce Milgaard was chasing after him and asking to go over all the details. He had no interest in reopening the case.

"I told him about the developments, about the new suspect emerging," Henderson said. "I told him some of the things about Cadrain that we had learned. I could tell he was very upset that I was there. But I said, 'Look, I've driven five hundred miles from Seattle to see you, and all I'm asking you to do is hear me out.'"

Wilson finally agreed. He came to the hotel, still suspicious and nervous. Gradually, Henderson says, he began opening up.

"We talked over coffee for an hour, and I think he started feeling comfortable with me. He agreed that he wanted to tell me some things. We went into the room and started taping. I spent a full eight hours with him, from nine o'clock until five. At the end of the day the poor guy was in tears, just unloading these things. Around noon I said to him, 'Do you want some lunch?' And he said, 'No man, I just want a beer.' We went in and we sat in there and he ventilated all afternoon."

Henderson sat in amazement as Ron Wilson recanted every single element of incriminating evidence he had offered at Milgaard's trial. It had all been lies, he said, concocted to relieve the pressure of police questioning and badgering. "I began to implicate Milgaard in the murder, telling police the things they wanted to hear," Wilson said. "I was manipulated by police into lying and later giving false testimony against Milgaard."

At the trial, Wilson said he saw blood on Milgaard's pants. He told Henderson this wasn't true. "In truth, I have no recollection of seeing the blood on his pants. I believe that the police somehow convinced me that I had to have seen the blood because Cadrain had."

At the trial, Wilson had said he saw Milgaard in possession of a maroon-handled paring knife. He told Henderson this wasn't true. He recalled David did have a wide-bladed hunting knife. The only paring knife he remembered was one that David bought later in the trip, after they had already left Saskatoon, which they used to cut the meat and cheese they ate along the way.

At the trial, Wilson had testified his car got stuck adjacent to the alley where Gail Miller's body was later found. He told Henderson he really had no idea where the car became stuck, but agreed with the police suggestion that it must have been in that location.

At the trial, Wilson had said he was gone from the stuck car for fifteen minutes looking for help, and Milgaard was gone even longer. He told Henderson that he was gone for about two minutes at most, with Milgaard returning about thirty seconds to a minute afterwards.

At the trial, Wilson had said Nichol John was hysterical when he got back in the car. He told Henderson he had made this up to coincide with Nichol's story that she witnessed Milgaard grabbing the girl.

At the trial, Wilson had said he saw Milgaard throw a cosmetics' case from the car. He told Henderson he had no independent recollection of such a thing ever happening.

Most critical of all, Wilson maintained that the conversation he said he had had with Milgaard in the Calgary bus depot, in which Milgaard told him he had "hit a girl" and disposed of her purse, was a complete fabrication. "I was telling police what they wanted to hear," he said. "It was all bullshit."

Wilson said police had been playing a game with him, and he had gone along with it. He had realized they'd wanted him to implicate Milgaard as specifically as he could, and they'd provided all the information he would need. For instance, when he'd been brought to Saskatoon in May 1969 for intensive questioning, they had driven him to the murder scene and pointed out all the key locations. They'd showed him where Gail Miller's purse had been found. Later, Wilson had incorporated that information into his story about Milgaard's confession in Calgary.

Police had also shown Wilson five different knives and had asked him to confirm which one Milgaard had owned. "It was a shell game," he said. "It always seemed to come back to the one they wanted me to pick out. That's the one they pointed at the most, and that's the one I picked out.

"I think I was scared that if they weren't going to charge David with this they were going to charge me with it."

Wilson then told Henderson something that provided insight into the pressure Nichol John must also have been feeling at the time. He recalled that police had brought her into the Cavalier Motel in Saskatoon for questioning at the same time he was undergoing a lie detector test there. It was the first time he had seen her since returning from the trip in February.

"It was the day of the polygraph when Nicky and I were together in the hallway of the hotel. We were left alone and we started discussing things, that she was scared, I was scared, and I just told her, 'Well, let's give them what they want. Let's sink him.'"

In fact, what Wilson told Henderson was largely a reiteration of the very first statement he had given police when confronted in March 1969. In that statement, which was not seen by Milgaard or any of his lawyers until 1990, Wilson denies all knowledge of the murder and makes it clear that Milgaard was never out of his sight for more than a few moments on January 31, 1969.

"I have been haunted through all these years by my role in helping convict David," Wilson said. "Although he has suffered the most, I feel that I was also a victim of this case."

Henderson could not have dreamed his trip to Nakusp would have been so successful. He had persuaded a reluctant man, troubled by more than two decades of guilt, to tell the truth. It was a difficult thing for Wilson to do. Not only was he risking charges of perjury for lying at the trial, but he was disturbing the tranquil life he had finally built for himself. Henderson felt happy that Milgaard was finally benefitting from his friend's desire to set the record straight, and he felt the confession would ultimately be good for Wilson as well.

"It was amazing after all these years this guy had kept all this torment and turmoil and guilt inside him," Henderson said. "I think it was really beneficial for Ron Wilson to get this out after twenty years. It made him feel much better about himself.

"The last thing he said before I left that evening was, 'Is there any chance I could talk to David and apologize for what I did?'"

The following day, Milgaard phoned Ron Wilson from Stony Mountain penitentiary. He accepted Wilson's apology. What happened twenty years ago gave rise to many victims, Milgaard said. "Thanks very much, Dave," Ron Wilson told him. "I'm glad there aren't any hard feelings."

Robinson Agencies had only managed to come up with a phone number for Nichol John. She lived in British Columbia, and the number was for her parents' home in Penticton. Of all the witnesses Joyce Milgaard had tracked down a decade earlier, Nichol was the most elusive. She had maintained that she could remember little about the original incident. Her constantly changing stories had presented a problem to both Crown and defence attorneys at the trial. In the end, the jury may have been influenced most by the statement that Nichol had later rejected, the statement that alleged she saw David Milgaard grab and stab Gail Miller.

Nichol's mother answered the phone when Henderson called. Henderson introduced himself and indicated that he wanted to get in touch with Nichol. It was important for him to reach all of the key witnesses and confirm the accuracy of what they had said at the trial, he said. He gave the background of Milgaard's appeal to the justice minister, and said there might never be another chance for Nichol to speak about the case if she didn't come forward now.

Fresh from his success in Nakusp, Henderson had checked into a motel in Penticton, hopeful of being able to set up an interview with Nichol. He was at his persuasive best with her mother, but he didn't seem to be making any progress. Finally, Nichol's father came on the line, and Henderson realized that his luck had run out.

Nichol was tired of being hounded and harassed, her father said. As far as he was concerned, the right man was behind bars. The police had done nothing wrong in their treatment of

Nichol. In his view, all of the stories regarding Milgaard's innocence were just media hype.

Undeterred, Henderson tried calling back later in the day and reasoning once more with Nichol's mother. He told her about some of the evidence he had uncovered, about the forensic assessments that tended to exonerate Milgaard. He appealed to her sense of logic and fair-mindedness. At one point he felt they might actually put him in touch with her, but it never happened. Instead, Nichol's parents called the RCMP and complained that Henderson was harassing them. He was forced to check out of his motel room to elude the RCMP's grasp. He realized it was a lost cause and returned to Seattle.

Henderson knew his work was still not complete, especially as it concerned Albert Cadrain. Unlike Nichol John, there were no overprotective family members trying to build a wall around Cadrain. On the contrary, Dennis Cadrain had been most helpful in shedding light on his brother's original testimony. Henderson had to try once again to get Albert talking.

Later in the month, he drove to Port Coquitlam once more. He invited Cadrain to a restaurant, where they talked over coffee. Cadrain was in a more talkative mood this time. Several days earlier, he had agreed to an interview with a CBC television documentary crew from Winnipeg. During the interview, he told journalist Sharon Basaraba about the stress he endured as a result of the police interrogation. He also revealed some of his paranoia about his role in the affair, saying that "when he [Milgaard] gets out then it's going to bother me because I know he's going to be after me."

Cadrain agreed to give Henderson a sworn statement this time. He stuck to his story about seeing blood on David Milgaard's clothes. But his other comments, dealing with the nature of the police investigation, painted a picture of incessant pressure consistent with the one Ron Wilson had described.

"I remember two detectives in particular working me over," Cadrain said. "They worked like a tag team: one would be the bad guy and the other would act like he was my friend. The bad guy would scream at me, and the other would offer me coffee and cigarettes. Then they would switch roles.

"They asked me the same questions repeatedly, time after time, until I was exhausted and couldn't take it anymore. This went on for months, continuing through the preliminary hearing. They put me through hell and mental torture. It finally reached the point where I couldn't stand the constant pressure, threats, and bullying any more. I was scared. The police told me to go back on the farm and hide away from the Mafia."

Cadrain confirmed that the whole experience had driven him to commit himself later to a psychiatric institution. He has nightmares about that experience as well, and attributes it all to the pressure put on him by police.

"I was drugged twenty-four hours a day and subjected to repeated shock treatment. The experience was hell on earth. A person would be better off dead than going through what I did in that hospital. I came out of the hospital like a walking zombie, and it took many years for my memory to come back."

Before leaving British Columbia, Henderson had one last witness to try. Joyce Milgaard had provided him a phone number for George Lapchuk, one of the eleventh-hour witnesses who claimed to have seen David re-enact the murder in the hotel room. Deborah Hall already disputed the truth of that testimony, but if Henderson could get Lapchuk to recant, it would be one more point in Milgaard's favour. Henderson dialled the number and a man answered.

"Is this George Lapchuk?"

"Yes," the man said.

After explaining who he was and what he wanted, Henderson was interrupted. "You've got the wrong George Lapchuk. I don't know what you're talking about."

Henderson wasn't about to be conned. He had the right George Lapchuk, and he knew it. Lapchuk changed tactics. "I've got a naked woman right here next to me waiting to rock and roll, so whatever you want to say to me, just say it and get off the line."

Henderson did not get his interview, but the phone call gave him some idea of the calibre of witness the Crown had relied on to convict David Milgaard.

Back in Winnipeg, Joyce Milgaard and David Asper followed Henderson's activities with impatient interest. As soon as Henderson obtained a statement, he faxed it to Winnipeg, from where it was subsequently sent on to Ottawa. They also realized the media potential these revelations had.

After Ron Wilson had told his story to Henderson in early June, he was asked if he would agree to tell the same thing to the media. It was one thing to get his statement on the record as part of the appeal to the justice minister, but media exposure of a witness who admitted to perjury might help speed the minister's decision along.

A reluctant Wilson agreed to do one media interview only. He had no interest in becoming a media personality, and wanted to do everything possible to keep the news quiet in Nakusp. He would talk to one reporter, as long as that reporter agreed to keep his location a secret.

Joyce and Asper approached a reporter at the *Winnipeg Free Press*, who honoured the condition. The result was a front page story on June 7, quoting Wilson as saying that threats and manipulation by Saskatoon police had led him to lie in court in 1969.

Two weeks later, CBC television revealed Larry Fisher's name for the first time. In a report from Saskatoon, Sharon Basaraba detailed Fisher's history of rapes and sexual assaults. The report showed that Fisher used a similar *modus operandi* in many of his assaults, using a knife and following his victims from bus stops. It stressed that four of Fisher's sexual assaults occurred in Saskatoon, three of them shortly before Gail Miller's murder and one a year after. That was news to Asper and Joyce, who until then believed that Fisher's earliest Saskatchewan assaults had been committed in Regina. It only bolstered their argument that Fisher had to be seriously investigated as a suspect in the Gail Miller murder.

There was a further revelation in that television report, which Milgaard's lawyers considered the most damaging piece of evidence yet against Fisher. At least two of his Saskatoon victims lived in the same neighbourhood as Miller did; both could well have taken the 20th Street bus downtown every day, just as Miller and Larry Fisher had.

If a series of sexual assaults had indeed taken place in Saskatoon within months of the Miller rape and murder – and if some had been in the same neighbourhood – the jury should have been made aware of it, according to Asper and Wolch. They contacted Milgaard's original trial lawyer, Cal Tallis, to see if he knew about these incidents at the time. Tallis, now a judge with Saskatchewan's Court of Appeal, said he wasn't aware of them. That prompted a further letter from Wolch to the Justice Department:

"At the very least, the undisputed fact that a serial rapist was operating in Saskatoon at the time of the Gail Miller murder, and that this rapist had attacked at least two women who resided in the neighborhood where Gail Miller was murdered, would have been very relevant at the trial. We have communicated with Mr. Justice Tallis, and he advises that he was never made aware of the fact that these rapes were occurring in such short proximity before the Gail Miller murder. The jury was never given the opportunity to consider that Milgaard might not be guilty because another person who had committed two rapes and an indecent assault was on the loose in Saskatoon and that this person might be responsible."

Albert Cadrain's statement later in the month was also the occasion for some shrewd publicity by Joyce and Asper. They called a press conference to release the contents of his statement and to point to the inaction on the part of the Justice Department, which had been sitting on the appeal since December 1988.

It all added up to a blitz of media attention. By the beginning of July, many people in Winnipeg were beginning to wonder why David Milgaard was still in jail.

Paul Henderson headed home to Seattle, satisfied that he had made a contribution to the eventual reversal of another injustice. In the Milgaard case, he says, he saw an all too familiar story. "I think that the Milgaard case, like a lot of them down here, has the same ingredients: bad police work; zealous police trying to solve a crime, going after someone with tunnel vision; abuse of authority in the way that they dealt with the witnesses; taking vulnerable kids and manipulating them into being witnesses for the Crown. It happens the same way up there as down here."

What was especially gratifying for Henderson, though, was that he felt his intervention made a difference not just for Milgaard, but for the other people who were victimized by the events of 1969.

"I feel I really helped these witnesses – I mean these people who had been haunted all these years – helped them to finally come out with the truth. As far as I'm concerned, and I think most people would agree, they're also victims in the Milgaard case."

16

Conflicting Opinions

By the summer of 1990, the media no longer needed prompting from the Milgaard family. David Milgaard's story was major news, and the public's appetite for every bit of fresh evidence was voracious. No longer was the story confined to Manitoba and Saskatchewan. The national media, sensing another scandal of Donald Marshall proportions, began running with the story.

Donald Marshall, the Nova Scotia Micmac Indian who spent eleven years in prison for a murder he didn't commit, has become the most celebrated example in the country of gross miscarriage of justice. Jailed at the age of seventeen, he languished in prison while police ignored eyewitness testimony that identified the real killer. Not only was Marshall unjustly imprisoned, but efforts were made at the highest levels to cover up his wrongful conviction. Then, when the cover-up began to unravel, the Supreme Court of Nova Scotia accused Marshall himself of being partly to blame for his misfortune. For critics of the Canadian justice system, Marshall typifies everything that's wrong with the current regime: racism, prejudice against the poor and the young, excessive police powers, and a judicial system that's weighted in favour of the prosecution.

The more reporters and editorialists wrote about the Milgaard case, the more the similarities to Donald Marshall's became clearer.

Early in July, CBC Winnipeg aired its full-length documentary on the Milgaard case, putting together all the elements that were known at the time. Later in the week a version of the same documentary ran across the network on CBC's "Saturday Report." There were articles in *Maclean's*, the *Globe and Mail* and the *Toronto Star*. The *Winnipeg Free Press*, in an editorial entitled "Justice too long delayed," blasted Justice Department officials for their hesitation in dealing with Milgaard's appeal. "They should focus on the strength of the evidence, the demands of justice and the possibility that every passing day inflicts another 24 hours of unjust imprisonment on David Milgaard," the newspaper said.

By August, the story had spread even further. A crew from the U.S. network show "A Current Affair" came north to do a piece on Milgaard. It was seen by some 25 million viewers in the U.S.A., and across Europe on Rupert Murdoch's SKY channel. Soon after, the CBC's "the fifth estate" opened its 1990 season with the Milgaard story. It was a story the program had years earlier chosen to shelve because of what it considered inconclusive evidence.

All the publicity resulted in even more evidence coming to the fore. In Regina, a man was casually watching the CBC documentary when the picture of Larry Fisher came on the screen. He sat bolt upright in his chair, remembering an incident he thought might prove important to the case. He phoned the CBC in Winnipeg and dropped a bombshell. He had served time with Fisher in Prince Albert penitentiary, and Fisher had made comments that all but amounted to a confession that he had murdered someone. The man would tell his story, but he insisted on anonymity. He had left the world of crime behind him long ago, and didn't want his neighbours or friends to know he was a former inmate.

The CBC arranged to meet with him. After assessing his credibility and verifying the authenticity of his claim that he had served time with Fisher, an interview was conducted. It was broadcast the same day, with the man's identity protected.

"During a hockey game," the man said, "in the winter of '77-'78, he slashed me. Of course I slashed him back. We grabbed each other and rassled around a bit. Some other inmates came and pulled us apart. At that time Larry said to me, 'I'll shank you and I'll stick you in a snowbank, the guards will find you in the spring.' And I laughed and said, 'You and whose army?' He says, 'Listen, I've done it before, I got no problem doing it again.' I said, 'Ya, right, Fisher, when did this happen? You're not doing time for murder or manslaughter, so when did this happen?' He says, 'Wouldn't you like to know?'"

Fisher had a chance to defend himself when "the fifth estate" aired its documentary on Milgaard. For the first time, he agreed to a media interview, with reporter Gillian Findlay. Throughout the interview, Fisher emphatically denied any involvement in the Gail Miller murder. Yet his answers revealed a selective memory. He maintained that he was at work on January 31, 1969, even though he could remember nothing else about that day. The work records have since been destroyed, so it is impossible to verify Fisher's claim. Early in the interview, he insisted that he only heard of Miller's murder within the last year. But when confronted with the fact that police had interviewed him at the bus stop several days after the murder, he admitted that he had known about the case in 1969.

Fisher also said during the interview that he usually had a hunting knife with him in his vehicle. He admitted to using knives in several of his assaults, and a paring knife in particular in one of his Winnipeg crimes. But he was certain that he didn't take a paring knife from their Saskatoon home in 1969, as his former wife had said.

There was another interesting admission on Fisher's part. He said he occasionally met women on buses and later invited them to have coffee with him. But he said this wasn't a tactic for choosing any of his victims. Rather, his victims were women he encountered randomly, he said.

Findlay confronted Fisher with the evidence directly:

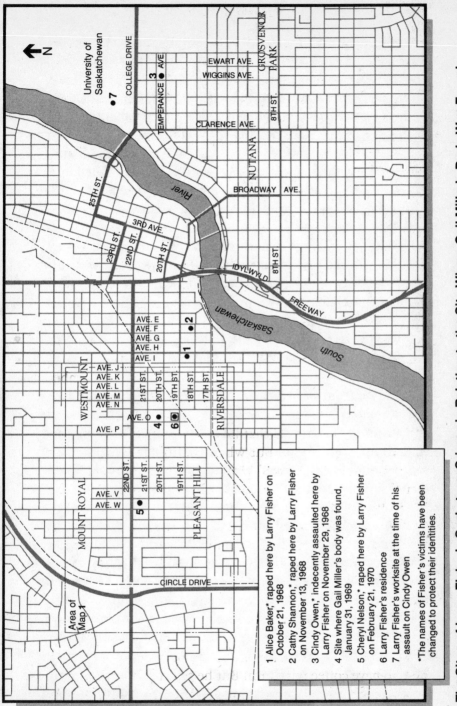

N

University of
Saskatchewan
• 7

COLLEGE DRIVE

GROSVENOR
PARK

EWART AVE.
WIGGINS AVE.

TEMPERANCE ● AVE

3

CLARENCE AVE.

8TH ST.

NUTANA

25TH ST.

River

3RD AVE.

BROADWAY AVE.

23RD ST.
22ND ST.
20TH ST.

IDYLWYLD

8TH ST.

FREEWAY

Saskatchewan

South

AVE. E
AVE. F
AVE. G
AVE. H
AVE. I

2

1

WESTMOUNT

AVE. J
AVE. K
AVE. L
AVE. M
AVE. N

21ST ST.
20TH ST.
19TH ST.
18TH ST.
17TH ST.

RIVERSIDE

AVE. O

4

6

AVE. P

22ND ST.

MOUNT ROYAL

AVE. V
AVE. W

21ST ST.
20TH ST.
19TH ST.

PLEASANT HILL

5

CIRCLE DRIVE

Area of
Map 1

1 Alice Baker,* raped here by Larry Fisher on
   October 21, 1968

2 Cathy Shannon,* raped here by Larry Fisher
   on November 13, 1968

3 Cindy Owen,* indecently assaulted here by
   Larry Fisher on November 29, 1968

4 Site where Gail Miller's body was found,
   January 31, 1969

5 Cheryl Nelson,* raped here by Larry Fisher
   on February 21, 1970

6 Larry Fisher's residence

7 Larry Fisher's worksite at the time of his
   assault on Cindy Owen

*The names of Fisher's victims have been
 changed to protect their identities.

The Sites of Larry Fisher's Saskatoon Crimes in Relation to the Site Where Gail Miller's Body Was Found

Findlay: Did you kill Gail Miller?
Fisher: No, I did not. Had nothing to do with that
           death . . .
Findlay: There are certain facts here, and if you list them
           together it can add up to a pretty damning pic-
           ture. Here you are, you're a man with a history of
           brutal rapes, you're living a block and a half away
           from the place that Gail Miller was killed. You
           had a history at least on one other occasion of
           using knives to threaten women. It's logical
           you'd be a suspect, don't you think?
Fisher: I fully agree with you. But the cops have already
           had my name for twenty-one years. Now if they
           had some concrete evidence, why didn't they
           charge me twenty-one years ago?

It was the last media interview Fisher agreed to do.

The momentum was shifting in favour of David Milgaard and
his supporters. After years of measured, incremental advances, the evidence was now mushrooming. There were too
many elements for the Justice Department to ignore. No
longer could the arguments be dismissed as the hopeful ram-
blings of a mother who wanted her son free.

Yet there was a feeling that even more was needed, something substantial and irrefutable. Dr. Ferris had provided just
such an element, with his incisive examination of the physical
evidence. Amazingly, however, the Justice Department still
hadn't seen fit to interview him about his findings. His creden-
tials were impeccable, his reputation solid. Could the Justice
Department have some confidential evidence that challenged
the credibility of Ferris or his findings? That lingering doubt
was one of the factors that prompted David Asper to approach
Peter Markesteyn, Manitoba's chief medical examiner.

Markesteyn agreed to offer a second opinion on the physical
evidence. The fifty-eight-year-old native of the Netherlands
was an ideal choice. In the course of thirty years, he had

practised forensic pathology across Canada and was familiar with contemporary techniques in various provinces. Markesteyn had followed Milgaard's case in the media and saw the necessity of a speedy review. He was given Ferris's report along with all the original documentation Ferris had used to arrive at his decision.

It was a calculated risk for Asper to take. Expert testimony is a fragile commodity. Anyone who has ever sat through a trial knows that no two experts are likely to agree on every point. In many cases, the Crown and defence each rely on their own experts to provide conflicting accounts. A negative report from Markesteyn, or even a non-committal one, could deal a fatal blow to Milgaard's application.

Within a month, Markesteyn prepared his written report. He supported Ferris in every critical area. Asper's confidence in the innocence of his client had paid off.

"I agree with Dr. Ferris that the serological evidence presented at the trial failed to link David Milgaard with the semen retrieved from vagina, snowbank and crotch of panties," Markesteyn wrote.

When it came to the yellowish lumps of snow that Lieutenant Penkala had retrieved four days after the murder, Markesteyn was equally unconvinced. He echoed Ferris's scepticism about the integrity of the sample. He went even further, suggesting another possible explanation for why the yellowish stains were in the snow.

"Human semen does not freeze into a yellowish stain at -40 degrees Fahrenheit. In fact, it is white and difficult to spot in snow other than through special techniques such as ultraviolet light exposure," he said. "Yellowish stains in snowbanks most commonly find their origin, not in human ejaculates, but in urine, most commonly of canine origin. I have been informed that male dog urine often contains semen. Unused semen in dogs is not reabsorbed but is secreted in the urine."

Even if it could be proved to everyone's satisfaction that the yellow lumps of snow contained human semen, he said, the evidence strongly suggested that the semen could not have come from Milgaard.

The stains had become important at Milgaard's trial only after it had been revealed that the semen contained A antigens. Although Milgaard was not a secretor of such antigens, the Crown had suggested that he might have had a genital infection or injury which released some of his type A blood into the sample. Markesteyn disputed that evidence, taking issue with the testimony that had been provided by coroner Harry Emson.

"I disagree with Dr. Emson's testimony that shedding blood in semen is quite a 'common occurrence' as a result of inflammation to penis, urethra, prostate and/or bladder. I disagree with Dr. Emson's thought expressed at that time that it was 'accepted medical knowledge that small amounts of blood commonly find their way into seminal fluid of males of any age beyond puberty.' I have been informed that the forensic laboratory in Winnipeg has never seen such a case. Other investigators also have failed to confirm this impression of Dr. Emson's."

Markesteyn was not even convinced the Crown had proved the existence of blood in the semen sample. Evidence at the trial suggested that the Hemostix test was used to prove the presence of blood in the semen. Markesteyn noted this would have been contrary to the manufacturer's instructions for the application of the test, which specifically limit its use to a screening test for blood in urine, not semen. The soil from shovels, or any number of other things, might have provided a false reading with the Hemostix test, he said.

Asper had asked Markesteyn to comment on the Crown's theory that a sufficient "window of opportunity" existed for Milgaard to have committed the murder. Ferris had offered his opinion about the unlikelihood of Milgaard having had sufficient time. But Markesteyn said the lack of scale drawings, photos, and maps of the scene made it impossible for him to give any assessment on that point.

It would have been useful to have a second pathologist question this aspect of the Crown's theory, but Asper wasn't about to complain. Markesteyn's summation of the physical evidence that the Crown had assembled was enough of an indictment.

"In my opinion," Markesteyn concluded, "the serological evidence presented at the trial was on very shaky scientific grounds to a degree that it may very well have been erroneous. I do not know what effect, if any, this evidence had on the jury in order to reach a verdict in Mr. Milgaard's trial. Unless another trial were held, we will never know if another jury, properly instructed on the scientific merits of the these forensic tests, would draw another inference."

Markesteyn's report was followed by yet another round of media attention, this time focusing on the physical evidence. The growing body of evidence that suggested errors in the interpretation of evidence, as well as mistreatment of witnesses at the hands of Saskatoon police, cried out for a response. Reporters from around the country tried getting a reaction from the department, only to be told that no one was willing to comment. They were especially curious to know what Chief Joe Penkala had to say. After all, it was his work in the identification section that played a key role in convicting Milgaard.

With the public release of Ron Wilson's statement, in which he describes police coercion, Penkala finally felt obliged to comment. He called reporters together at a press conference where he read a brief statement. Instead of dealing with the allegations that had been levelled against the department, however, he expressed disappointment with the publicity the Milgaard story had generated.

"My disappointment lies with the fact of the insensitivity of the media for the victims of a very heinous crime that occurred in 1969," he said. "I'm not prepared to defend or comment on any matters relating to the media's Milgaard controversy. If there is an established need for a judicial review, I will be available at such a call."

The only officer involved in the original investigation who agreed to speak in detail was Eddie Karst, who had already retired from the force. Karst emphatically denied any mistreatment of Cadrain, Wilson, or any other witness. He thinks Wilson is simply lying today, but he isn't so sure about the man who collected the reward.

"I can't understand why Cadrain is saying what he is today. It is not true that he got a working over by police. We didn't go out and hustle this guy in. He comes in and tells us his story. There was no pressure there. There was certainly no pressure by me or anybody I worked with. It just doesn't make sense that he'd make these comments now."

As far as Cadrain's testimony was concerned, Karst said it was credible. There was never any question about his mental state. "He didn't seem messed up to me. Not at that time. I understood from his parents that later on he had a problem."

Karst is the first to admit that the case against Milgaard was circumstantial. But he says that is common with most murder cases, and there were too many elements in the Milgaard prosecution for any reasonable doubt to exist. Karst still firmly believes Milgaard is guilty. He puts no stock in any of the new evidence or reinterpretation of the old. "I was convinced then and still am that we had the proper person. Everything that's come out hasn't changed my mind one iota. I'd have to see some more compelling evidence to change my mind. What I've seen so far are just a bunch of stories."

How does he explain what Wilson and Cadrain are saying about their treatment at the hands of police? And how does he explain why Nichol John gave police an eyewitness account of the murder, only to refuse to confirm it on the stand?

"I have my own theory about that," he says. "They're scared. All these witnesses, like Nichol, Cadrain, and Wilson, all said at that time that they were afraid of Milgaard. They are still scared."

17

Tangled in Bureaucracy

It's an established cliché in Hollywood movies. The condemned inmate is on death row, marching towards the electric chair with a guard on one side and a chaplain on the other. As he is strapped into the chair, newspaper reporters peer through the glass partition and scribble notes. The second hand on the clock sweeps forward relentlessly. Moments before the switch is thrown, the telephone rings. It's the governor. The death sentence is commuted. The inmate's life is spared.

The idea that an elected politician can interfere in the decision of a court seems foreign in Canada. Political scientists place great emphasis on the absolute separation of powers between the judicial, executive, and legislative arms of government. In theory, this is what provides the system with its checks and balances. But this theory is somewhat lacking when it comes to practice. It is the politicians, after all, who appoint the judges in the first place. And when a judicial decision becomes controversial in Canada, it is the politicians who inevitably come under fire to do something about it.

Politicians have been known to change the law when a court decision has not been to their liking. That happens most often in civil matters. In criminal cases as well, the hand of a partisan politician can often be detected. The attorney general, for

instance, has the power to send a case to trial directly, bypass-
ing the normal preliminary hearing stage. And it is ultimately
the attorney general or justice minister, both provincially and
federally, who decides whether a charge will be pressed or an
appeal launched.

Once the judicial process has begun, however, it is more
difficult for politicians to exercise a direct influence. There
have been cases of ministerial telephone calls to judges, an
impropriety that can cost the politician his job. But these are
the exception rather than the rule. It is even rarer for a judicial
verdict to be disturbed when a jury has been involved.

That is the situation the Milgaard family faced when it
confronted the task of overturning a conviction that had been
upheld throughout the judicial process. Every avenue had
been exhausted, except for one. That was the rarely used section of the Criminal Code that allows a politician to refer a
case back to the courts – even a case that has already been
considered by every level of court.

In 1988, Section 617 of the Code (now called Section 690)
provided that:

"The Minister of Justice may upon an application for the
mercy of the Crown by or on behalf of a person who has been
convicted in proceedings by indictment or who has been sentenced to preventative detention under Part XXIV:

"a) direct, by order in writing, a new trial, or in the case of a
person under sentence of preventative detention, a new
hearing, before any Court that he thinks proper, if after
enquiry, he is satisfied that in the circumstances a new
trial or hearing, as the case may be, should be directed;
or,

"b) refer the matter at any time to the Court of Appeal for
hearing and determination by that Court as if it were an
appeal by the convicted person under sentence of preventative detention, as the case may be; or,

"c) refer to the Court of Appeal at any time for its opinion,
any question on which he desires the assistance of that
Court, and the Court shall furnish its opinion accord-
ingly."

When Milgaard first made his application under this section, Joe Clark occupied the justice minister's post. It then passed to Doug Lewis, and on to Kim Campbell. But it would be a long time before any elected official would judge the substance of the application. The minister is not expected to wade through the details of each application under the section. That task falls to officials in the Justice Department, who first assess the facts and decide if further investigation is necessary.

More than a year passed while the bureaucrats studied the Milgaard application. Asper and Wolch couldn't understand why the process was taking so long. The original application had just two central elements: Ferris's report and Deborah Hall's statement. Justice officials didn't even bother contacting Ferris, and it took them more than nine months to take a statement from Hall. No sense of urgency seemed to accompany their work.

As 1990 began with no indication of how much longer the process would take, Joyce Milgaard decided it was time to initiate some political pressure on the minister. She approached her member of Parliament, John Harvard, and briefed him about the case. Harvard is a Liberal MP and former CBC broadcaster who is never reluctant to raise a commotion in the House. Before running for office, he had built a reputation as a feisty television interviewer who enjoyed pillorying his guests. If anyone could make some noise about the David Milgaard case in Ottawa, it was Harvard.

While he recognized the potential publicity benefit of championing Milgaard's cause, Harvard was also careful not to jump on a bandwagon before he knew all the facts. He listened to what Joyce had to say, then investigated for himself.

"She spoke with determination and conviction that her son was innocent," he said. "She laid out the facts of the case and explained to me what she had done. She felt it was time to start raising it in Parliament. She did a good job on behalf of her son. I'm not a politician who will say, 'Yes, he's innocent.' That's not my job. I just think the evidence is so overwhelming, casting doubt on his conviction."

After meeting with Joyce, Harvard got in touch with Asper and read the file. On March 16, he questioned Campbell in the House of Commons about the case for the first time. The minister seemed prepared. "The case is under investigation by the Department of Justice," she replied curtly. "It is not ready for presentation to me, and when it is and I am in a position to make a decision, I will advise the House." She would provide no further details.

In May, following release of Markesteyn's report, Harvard became more insistent. At a Justice Department estimates committee, Harvard accused Campbell of foot-dragging. "Madam Minister, I feel just incredulous. I just cannot believe that after fifteen months a matter as serious as this has not yet reached your personal attention. What is the hold-up?"

Once again, Campbell was prepared. Estimates committee was not the place to discuss the status of Milgaard's application, but the minister provided a reply which would become the rationale for repeated Justice Department delays stretching into 1991.

"The hold-up is a result of new witnesses being identified by the applicant," she said. "The original submission that was made was under investigation by the department, but recently the applicant identified new witnesses he thought would assist his case. That required the department to prolong its investigation in order to look at those areas of evidence. So it is not delay in the department that has resulted in that time frame, but rather the applicant's identification of new witnesses he felt could assist his case."

Simply put, the minister was blaming David Milgaard for prolonging the investigation by constantly coming up with new evidence. It would be the same argument she would use over and over again during the next few months, much to Harvard's frustration. The following exchange in the House of Commons in December was typical of the animosity that arose between the two.

Harvard: This case has been dragging on and on and on. People are frustrated, nerves are on edge. I do not know whether the minister is aware of it, but Milgaard himself is taking it very hard. He has spent many days in recent weeks in prison hospital. Is the minister aware of this? Is she aware of the frustration? I want to know whether the Minister of Justice can give us a report today.

Campbell: Madam Speaker, no I cannot.

Harvard: Madam Speaker, I am very disappointed. It is typical of this minister's stonewalling. I want to make it very clear to this House. This minister has said over and over that if the Milgaard family would only stop giving new information and new arguments, her department could come to a decision. She knows very well that the Milgaard family has not provided any new information, any new arguments since summer. She does not have an excuse. It is time for her to make a decision. I want to know from this minister. Give us a commitment, give us a promise as to when she is going to face her responsibility and make a decision.

Campbell: Madam Speaker, it is regrettably the case that when the honourable member rises in this House he creates no traffic jam on the high road . . .

Harvard: You are the minister of excuses . . .

Campbell: The case is complex, and the advisory process is continuing. When it is complete, I will exercise my very serious responsibility under section 690 of the Criminal Code and make a decision based on the highest principles of justice and fairness.

Joyce Milgaard was no more successful in her attempts to put direct pressure on the minister. On May 14, Campbell came to Winnipeg to address a luncheon on the Meech Lake constitutional accord. Joyce and her daughter Maureen were waiting for her outside the meeting room. When Joyce tried handing Campbell a copy of Ferris's report, the minister abruptly rushed past her and into the room.

Media reports of the encounter show a startled Campbell trying to avoid any contact with Joyce. "I'm sorry," she told her, "but if you want your son to have a fair hearing, don't approach me personally." Campbell somehow took the view that a personal plea to the minister would not be appropriate, even though the entire application process amounted to a such a plea. She consistently held on to this view, right up to the time her decision was announced.

Even the John Howard Society was unable to get the minister to move more quickly in considering Milgaard's application. In May, the society called on Campbell to wind up the investigation as soon as possible and make a determination about Milgaard's status. Society staff had worked with Milgaard ever since he had come to Stony Mountain and knew his case intimately. They were careful not to express an opinion about his claims for innocence, merely asking for a quick resolution to the case.

The following month, however, the society took an unprecedented step. It set up a support fund for Milgaard and pledged to publicize his case. It was an unusual move for the society, which normally shies away from advocacy. More than anything else, it showed how persuasive Milgaard and his supporters had become in arguing their case. At the society's annual meeting, all ten provincial federations endorsed the move.

18

A Partial Investigation

When Justice Minister Jean Chretien referred Donald Marshall's case back to the courts in 1982, he sent out a signal to every inmate who considered himself wrongly convicted. It didn't matter that the weight of evidence and public opinion in the Marshall case was so overwhelming as to force Chretien's hand. For desperate inmates who had exhausted all legal appeals, there was now renewed hope that a politician could intervene and set things right. The prospect of a lucrative compensation package for unjust imprisonment made the idea of appealing even more enticing.

By the time David Milgaard's application for ministerial review arrived in Ottawa in December 1988, Justice Department bureaucrats had been exposed to all manner of arguments from Canadian convicts and their lawyers. Between 1985 and 1989, there were more than a hundred requests from across the country. Of those, only three were considered worthy enough to reopen. The civil servants who reviewed the applications approached each with more than a healthy dose of scepticism. For them even to consider interfering with a judge or jury's verdict, some new and spectacular evidence had to be uncovered. In each case, they asked the question: Is a miscarriage of justice likely to have occurred here? If no such miscarriage could be proven, the application was rejected.

The department assigned Eugene Williams to handle Milgaard's case. After nearly a decade with the department, the methodical and soft-spoken lawyer was no stranger to pleas of wrongful conviction. He had been involved in more than a dozen similar applications, but none had consumed as much time or garnered so much publicity as this one would.

Williams was called to the Ontario bar in 1976, and his entire working career was spent as a prosecutor and functionary with federal agencies. Like all prosecutors, his skills lay in identifying evidence that tended to implicate people in crimes. And he was also adept at cross-examining potential witnesses to see if their stories could withstand thorough scrutiny. It was a talent he would employ many times when grilling some of the principals in the Milgaard case.

Milgaard's application seemed to get mired in the Justice Department's bureaucracy for the first few months of 1989. Whether through wilful neglect or a backlog of other work, officials did not pay much attention to the application at first. In the summer and early fall of 1989, the first newspaper stories began appearing about David Milgaard and his renewed bid to overturn his conviction. The media activity seemed to jolt the Justice officials out of their deep sleep. In October, Williams made arrangements to travel to Regina for an interview with Deborah Hall. It would be the first in a series of interrogations that would later lead the Milgaard family to accuse Justice Department officials of being prejudiced against the application.

Hall remembers feeling intimidated when Williams arrived. He had a tape recorder, court stenographer, and bundles of documents in tow, and the first order of business was to have her swear an oath. Williams would later admit that the swearing-in of people he interviewed was a selective process. In the end, most of the witnesses who offered evidence favourable to Milgaard's application were sworn, while the original police investigators and others were not.

The interview was far from what Hall imagined it would be

like when she first gave David Asper her statement nearly three years before. Instead of a friendly exploration into what Hall might offer as new evidence, the session made her very tense.

"He didn't make me feel like I had any credibility at all," she said of Williams. I felt like I was being cross-examined. I thought this has got to be the closest to what it would be like to be grilled up on the stand."

Hall felt she was at a disadvantage. She was trying to remember events that had occurred twenty years earlier, and didn't have the luxury of having reviewed the trial transcripts. Williams, on the other hand, was well-versed in the transcripts and made Hall feel uncomfortable by asking if she could remember small details. What was David wearing that day? Are you positive that George Lapchuk didn't take you home that night? Is it possible your thinking was impaired because of drugs?

"By the time I left there I couldn't even think straight," she said. "He had me doubting myself."

Immediately after the interview, Hall called Asper and described the process. Asper was outraged. It was the first real sign of how the Justice Department viewed Milgaard's application, and it confirmed his worst fears. In Asper's mind, the application was not being taken seriously, and efforts were being made to discredit the new evidence that had emerged.

There were other indications that the bureaucrats assigned to review the case did not think much of Milgaard's claims. Bill Corbett, senior counsel for the department's criminal prosecutions branch, dropped hints several times in interviews with reporters that the weight of opinion was not in Milgaard's favour. On one occasion, when discussing the campaign that was being mounted by Milgaard's supporters, Corbett told a *Globe and Mail* reporter, "Seventeen per cent of people still believe Elvis Presley is alive."

There's little doubt Justice Department officials were annoyed at the political and media attention surrounding the whole process. Accustomed to working in secrecy and at their own speed, the bureaucrats felt pressured by the constant telephone calls and media reports.

"This application was unique in the media attention it attracted," Williams said. "It made the task more difficult in respect to my time that was taken up responding to media requests. It was more challenging because in a number of instances the applicant and his counsel chose to divulge the information he obtained before we received it – before he brought it to our attention. It makes the task more challenging because if you have an entirely brand new subject of inquiry that's being advanced first publicly, before you get on it, a reporter will call and say: 'What about this?' And you'll say, 'What about it?' "

Deborah Hall wasn't the only witness to feel frustration and anger after being interviewed by Williams. When Dennis Cadrain tried explaining the doubts he harboured about his brother's credibility, Williams didn't seem to put much stock in his opinion. To Dennis, it seemed the Justice Department had a vested interest in defending the integrity of Albert's original testimony.

"If Williams has his way he won't do anything, guaranteed," Dennis commented after being interviewed by him. "Every time I said something it would be, like, so what? Like he doesn't want to hear about it."

It might be argued that the adversarial approach Williams adopted in his interrogations was important to test the accuracy of witness statements, some of which were in direct contradiction to sworn testimony given twenty years earlier. That argument might make sense if the questioning had been done in public with counsel for all sides present. In many cases, the people offering important evidence – such as Deborah Hall and Dennis Cadrain – never considered having their own lawyer present to balance the prosecutorial tone of the questioning. Nor was counsel for David Milgaard allowed to be present at any of the sessions. The resulting, arguably one-sided, transcripts formed the official record of the Justice Department investigation, the record which would ultimately be seen by the justice minister. It's as if an Appeal

Court were asked to rule on a case by reviewing only the prosecution's questioning of witnesses, without seeing how the defence had attempted to handle the same witnesses.

In the eyes of the Milgaard family, the Justice Department investigation fell short of the mark in almost every respect. It was never a full review of the case, only a reaction to the evidence the family itself unearthed. Instead of reviewing all relevant files and statements relating to the original trial, the department restricted itself to the points raised in the application. Similarly, when Larry Fisher's name surfaced, the department seconded an RCMP officer in Saskatoon to see if Fisher would be willing to be interviewed. An independent review of the police files would have raised questions about Fisher's involvement, but the department didn't do that; it only reacted when asked to do so by Milgaard's family. There is no indication it seriously attempted to gather any evidence that might point to Fisher's guilt.

What really outraged the Milgaard family was the department's use of Bobs Caldwell to assist in their investigation. Asper complained more than once that it was a blatant conflict of interest to use the man who had prosecuted Milgaard in the first place as a resource person in the investigation. Even after the trial was finished, Caldwell had not suddenly become a disinterested observer. He continued to monitor Milgaard's parole applications, personally making sure the parole board remembered the brutality of Gail Miller's murder.

But for Williams, it was only logical to rely on someone who had intimate knowledge of the case to provide assistance. Williams adamantly rejects any charge of bias in any of the Justice Department procedures: "We have no axe to grind. An application is brought, and it's our job to look at it and to do so as objectively and impartially as possible. Now this is the same basic philosophy that was used in the case of Donald Marshall. My colleague handled that case. That matter was referred back to a court of appeal and the rest is history. That is the approach that we have taken. When a minister is called upon to reverse the decision of the highest courts, that's not something to be taken lightly. Consequently, for the proper exercise of that discretion, all of the facts that are relevant should be examined in as full and complete an examination that is required. Where allegations of fact are made, those are examined. They are not done with the premise of defeating it. It's done in order to assure that the factual basis upon which the recommendation is made is an accurate one."

Williams personally handled about twenty of the three dozen witnesses interviewed for the investigation. He dismisses the notion that the presence of defence counsel at an interview is a major issue: "If a person wants defence counsel there during the interview, that's their option," he says. "It doesn't matter if counsel is present. If a witness wants that, I have no problem with that." As for the selectivity exercised by the department in swearing-in witnesses, Williams is unrepentant: "Whether or not the witness is sworn depends on the circumstances. Sometimes it's better. The nature of the evidence will have a large bearing on whether it's taken under oath or not."

The most crucial witness Williams had to interview was Ron Wilson, particularly after Wilson's sworn statement to Paul Henderson that he had lied at Milgaard's trial. Unlike some of the other witnesses, Wilson only agreed to be interviewed in the presence of his lawyer. Using trial transcripts and original police statements, Williams tried to find contradictions in Wilson's story, but after extensive interrogation, Wilson stuck to his contention that he had wrongly implicated Milgaard in the murder.

Wilson's statement posed a difficult problem for the government investigators. His original trial testimony had played a critical part in convincing the jury to convict Milgaard. At the time, portions of Wilson's story were tested by a police lie detector test – the results of which have never been made public. But now Wilson was recanting that testimony completely, for no other apparent motive than to clear his guilty conscience. If Wilson was a credible witness in 1970, why should his statement of 1990 be any less credible?

In an effort to solve the problem, Williams contacted

Wilson's lawyer soon after the interview to see if Wilson would agree to another lie detector test. What followed was a series of letters between the two sides on the nature of the test and who should conduct it. Wilson never ruled out taking the test, but he wanted the results of his 1969 polygraph made available to whomever performed the new test.

Finally, in a letter to Wilson's lawyer dated September 6, 1990, Williams put an end to the negotiations. "After further consideration of all the circumstances and following a review of the materials obtained to date," he said, "it appears that there may be limited value in performing a polygraph test on your client at this time. Consequently this avenue of investigation will not be pursued further."

As would become evident some months later, officials in the department felt there was little value in a polygraph examination of Wilson because they were already forming the conclusion that Wilson was not to be believed.

For David Asper and the Milgaard family, the Justice Department investigation lacked all semblance of justice. Like Donald Marshall, the inmate was being partially blamed for his own misfortune. In Milgaard's case, the repeated delays in determining the validity of the application were attributed to the family's incessant addition of more and more evidence. But unlike the Marshall case, Milgaard lacked the one irrefutable bit of evidence that would force the government's hand.

No longer did Milgaard have the luxury of presenting a reasonable doubt about his guilt. That's the test which normally suffices for a jury. But something far more convincing was now being demanded. He was being asked to prove that he hadn't committed the crime.

By September of 1990, Asper had run out of new evidence to provide. Nearly two years after it began, the Justice Department prepared to put the final touches to its investigation.

19

At Loggerheads with Justice

David Milgaard followed the Justice Department's progress from inside his small cell at Stony Mountain institution. He was buoyed by the new evidence that was coming to the surface after so many years. At the same time, he found it hard to concentrate on the complex nature of the process in which he was the central figure. The mind-numbing routine of the federal penitentiary, which dictates when inmates can eat, sleep, work, and even think, had taken its toll on one of Canada's longest serving prisoners.

Every inmate entering Stony Mountain for the first time is given a seventy-eight-page handbook – a detailed list of rules and regulations that explains how life is regimented within the institution. Inmate responsibilities are clearly defined, as is the punishment to be meted out if they are ignored. Each prisoner is confined to one of three ranges – narrow, multi-level cell-block corridors that jut out from the institution's central dome. Inmates who want to move from one area to another must have a pass and a valid reason for doing so. Nothing inside Stony takes place without a reason and without permission. The handbook makes it clear that "all activities, including conversations and telephone communications, are subject to monitoring."

David Milgaard and his mother, Joyce, during a visit in jail in the seventies.

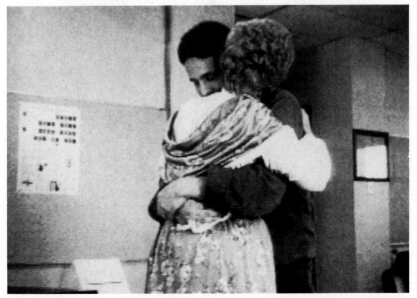

David and Joyce embrace after a visit in Stony Mountain prison in 1985.

The RCMP escort David Milgaard back to jail following his escape from Dorchester penitentiary in March 1973. (Arnold Clow, New Brunswick Provincial Archives)

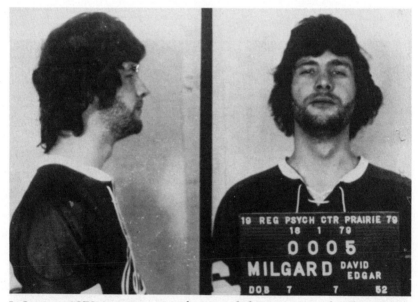

In January 1979, in preparation for a parole hearing, David Milgaard was sent to the Regional Psychiatric Centre in Saskatoon for a month-long assessment. (Courtesy Saskatoon *Star-Phoenix*)

David and his mother during one of her visits to Stony Mountain in 1985.

David Milgaard in his cell at Stony Mountain, 1990.

Paul Henderson, private investigator, talked to Ron Wilson in 1990. Wilson told him his testimony at the trial had been all lies.

Joyce Milgaard in 1991. She never believed her son was a murderer and since 1980 has worked tirelessly for his release. *(The Winnipeg Sun)*

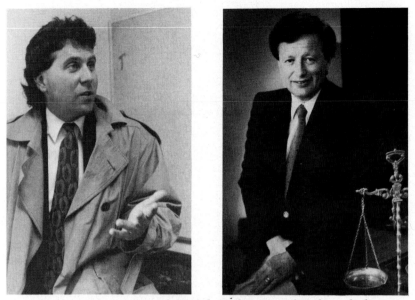

David Asper (left) and Hersh Wolch (right), David Milgaard's lawyers since 1986. (Both photos: *The Winnipeg Sun*)

In 1988 Dr. James Ferris re-examined the contentious semen samples presented at the trial. He concluded that the evidence did not implicate David Milgaard.

Albert "Shorty" Cadrain in 1990. Cadrain became convinced of David Milgaard's guilt after seeing a vision of the Virgin Mary stepping on a snake that had David's face.

Deborah Hall demonstrates how David reacted when he saw the TV news item on Gail Miller's murder. She denies he re-enacted the murder, but she was never called to testify at the trial.

Linda Fisher. She believes her former husband, Larry, may have murdered Gail Miller.

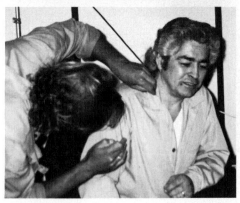

Larry Fisher being fitted with a microphone before his interview on "the fifth estate" in 1990. (Morris Karp)

"My fight and my family's struggle for my freedom is not over." David and his sister Maureen at the press conference at Stony Mountain on March 12, 1991. *(The Winnipeg Sun)*

Prime Minister Brian Mulroney complimented Joyce Milgaard on her courage during a visit to Winnipeg on September 6, 1991. *(The Winnipeg Sun)*

David Milgaard, still in jail more than twenty years after being convicted of a murder he did not commit. *(The Winnipeg Sun)*

Every day the inmate routine repeats itself, with no variation: 0730 hours: Breakfast, and return to cells for inmate count. 0830 hours: Inmates proceed to designated work areas; 1130 hours: Return from work areas to cells, and inmate count; 1200 hours: Noon meal, and return to cells for count; 1300 hours: Proceed to designated work area; 1630 hours: Return from work areas to cells and inmate count; 1700 hours: Evening meal, and return to cells for inmate count; 1845 hours: Inmates proceed to programs or exercise; 2110 hours: Programs terminate; 2220 hours: Exercise ends, library, recreation hall, canteen closes; 2240 hours: Lock up, inmate count, and lights out.

Inmates who choose to work earn between $5.25 and $6.90 a day. Those who choose not to are locked in their cells all day. Meagre as it is, the money that inmates earn can be spent inside, but only in certain ways. Items can be purchased from approved prison sources for use within the cells, but only if they are below a prescribed value. No inmate is allowed more than $1,500 worth of possessions in his cell. For the vast majority of inmates, money earned on the job is quickly converted to tokens for the purchase of cigarettes in the prison canteen.

Although guards carry no guns inside the medium-security institution, an atmosphere of quiet repression permeates the ranges. All key areas are compartmentalized, with monitors trained on each door. Guards spin massive wheels to open and close the cell doors. And on each level of the central dome, an austere, semi-circular post with rifle ports serves as a reminder that inmates will not get far if they try to cause a disturbance inside.

Outside the imposing stone structure, huge fences topped with razor wire discourage any attempts at escape. Those who still think they can make it over the fence must contend with armed guards in watchtowers. The only escape in recent years came after an inmate drove a souped-up four-by-four from the automotive shop through the fence. He was recaptured a few miles up the road.

Despite the stern admonitions of the handbook, inmates at

Stony routinely run afoul of the institution's rules. Whether they are caught using drugs, drinking home-brew, threatening other inmates, or in possession of contraband, they risk being thrown into the hole – or punitive dissociation, as it is more politely called. There, only the essentials of survival are provided, as inmates spend twenty three and a half hours a day in their individual cells – coming out only for a brief period of exercise and a shower.

Although he has never been a serious troublemaker, Milgaard is disliked by many of the corrections staff. Some see him as a manipulator, a devious character who wins people over so he can use them to his advantage; others chafe at his popularity with the media.

"He doesn't have a lot of friends," one guard claimed. "Most of the population ignores him and lets him do his own thing. Half the time that he's walking around he looks like he's bombed. You look at this guy and you think, Oh God, he's really flying high. I don't know if he's heavy into drugs or not. You just assume inside that place that anybody who wants to be is."

Most prison guards and employees, even those who have never met him, don't have much sympathy for Milgaard's claims of innocence. They go by the premise that inmates wouldn't be in jail in the first place if they were innocent. Every bit of publicity surrounding the case only serves to stoke their anger further.

One of those employees was Ben Dozenko, who served as Milgaard's living unit officer at Stony Mountain from 1976 to 1980. The living unit officers were a cross between guards and social workers, plainclothes employees who had their offices inside the institution so that they had immediate access to the inmates. Dozenko built up a good relationship with Milgaard over the years, helping him with his education and ensuring that he adjusted to the medium security environment of Stony Mountain after six years in tougher federal penitentiaries. Five years older than Milgaard, he considered him a regular guy, someone who might even be a personal friend under other circumstances. He didn't even hold a grudge against Milgaard for his 1980 escape, when he betrayed Dozenko's trust and slipped away during an escorted absence. As a result of that escape, Dozenko was reprimanded and suspended for two days.

Like many of his colleagues in the prison system, Dozenko also believes Milgaard belongs in jail. But unlike the others, his belief isn't based on vague impressions. Nor is it based on Milgaard's behaviour in prison – Dozenko says he never exhibited any violent tendencies. Dozenko says adamantly that Milgaard admitted his guilt to him three or four times during conversations inside the prison, between 1977 and 1980.

"David lived on M-5 at the time," Dozenko recalls. "He was always honest with me. He would come and tell me things in confidence. I would be sitting in my office and he would come and sit on the outside. We would talk about all kinds of things." Dozenko claims the admission of guilt didn't come until about a year after he first started working with him.

Over the last twenty-one years, Dozenko is the only person to have claimed that Milgaard admitted responsibility for Gail Miller's death. But is he telling the truth?

Prison officials who worked with Dozenko say he was a reliable and honest employee during his stay at Stony. Although he was criticized for allowing Milgaard to escape in 1980, there is no evidence he bore a grudge. In fact, Dozenko says today that he does not harbour any ill feelings toward Milgaard.

Dozenko left Stony Mountain in 1982 when his marriage began to break up. At that time, he admits he was "starting to hit the bottle pretty heavily." Since then, he has held a number of security-related jobs. But he admits that alcohol is a major problem for him, and he goes on periodic binges. One recent three-week drinking binge was so severe that he was admitted to hospital for extended treatment.

Every time Milgaard made his admission to him, Dozenko claims he recorded it in his written reports. He also says his superiors would have had access to those reports. But there is no evidence that anyone else inside the prison system knew anything about a confession by Milgaard in any of Dozenko's reports. If Dozenko was actually recording such conversations, no one else was aware of it. Prison and parole officials said they would have expected any admissions of guilt to be brought to their attention, yet they said none were. In fact, the parole board had numerous reports indicating that Milgaard was always insistent on proclaiming his innocence. A claim to the contrary, if it was officially recorded, would have become widely known.

When asked about the allegations, Milgaard called Dozenko a liar. Yet it's unclear what motives Dozenko would have for lying. He has never approached the media or the Justice Department with his story, so it's unlikely he is motivated by the desire for publicity. Given the apparent lack of written documentation, however, Dozenko's assertions are impossible to verify. And in light of the overwhelming evidence from everyone else in the prison and parole system, who claim that Milgaard never confessed to the crime, it is difficult to believe that he would have done so to Ben Dozenko.

Prison is a highly artificial environment, and a potentially explosive one. In the early eighties, Stony Mountain's population was growing at a pace that the staff and facilities couldn't accommodate. More than five hundred inmates were crammed into the aging facility. The practice of double-bunking in the tiny cells was expanded, and tensions simmered. Finally, in 1984, the boiling point was reached. Inmates rioted, taking a number of guards hostage and issuing demands for improved conditions. Two guards were killed in the dome before authorities restored order. The warden instituted a lockdown that was lifted reluctantly and incrementally as the months passed. But the institution learned its lesson. Double-bunking, though still a legal measure, is no longer in use, and the prison population is kept below the capacity of 465.

Milgaard played no active role in the 1984 riot. He was lost in his own world, worried more about his fight for exoneration than the concerns of the wider prison population.

Several years after the Stony riot, Milgaard underwent a qualitative change in his thinking. He started developing an interest in social issues, not just as they affected the prison population, but society in general. In many ways it was a return to the values he once held as a teenager, when he sold the *Canadian Free Press* at the Sparks Street mall in Ottawa.

Milgaard started meeting with a group of like-minded inmates inside the institution to discuss the issue of prisoners' rights. They assembled information about correctional concerns and found that Canada's rate of imprisonment is second highest in the world. Eventually they founded an organization called the Justice Group, and Milgaard became its coordinator. The group talked about prisons and the conditions inmates had to face; about Indian and Métis inmates and aboriginal concerns in general, an important issue at Stony Mountain, where 41 per cent of the population is Native; about women's issues and violence against women; about the cycle of poverty in Canada and how society has failed the poor and the oppressed.

In a Justice Group newsletter, Milgaard offered the following message: "These are hard times for everyone. We do not know what your situation is, but we do know our situation deserves your consideration. Our situation is still one of suppression. Correctional Services of Canada are responsible for a resistance to our ideas and needs as prisoners trying to do well for ourselves and others. We simply want to open people to the truth about each other in these troubled times. We need you to stand with us so we may learn to care more about others by sharing the social justice needs of people."

The group invites speakers from outside the institution to give lectures, and it has also established relations with other prisoners' rights groups across North America. A support group in Winnipeg assists the inmates in developing some of their programs.

The Justice Group has become an important aspect of Milgaard's prison life – and marks a big change from his early years in jail. He says, "For me it's been a growing experience. It's given me a chance to take a bit more seriously other people, rather than just trying to do things for myself. Before the group, I wasn't too concerned or involved in issues. That's one thing more and more people should get into – trying to be concerned about others rather than themselves."

At no time did Milgaard's involvement with social issues distract him from the matter still closest to his heart – justice for himself. By the summer and early fall of 1990, media interest in his case was at its highest. No longer was there any pressure on his family and lawyers to provide further evidence to prove his innocence. They had made their final submissions, and now the pressure shifted to the Justice Minister for a decision.

Before the minister would even look at the application, however, the bureaucracy inside the department had to develop its recommendations. That meant a series of internal reports and memos, starting with Eugene Williams's analysis of his interviews with all the key players in the case.

An official in the Justice Department, responding to a reporter's question on when the matter would be decided, said it wouldn't be until the summer ended. That comment fuelled speculation that the minister would wait until Parliament resumed in the fall to make the announcement. To the most optimistic of Milgaard's supporters, it made sense. If the justice minister was to release a man who had been unjustly imprisoned for twenty-one years, she surely wouldn't do it when half the Ottawa press gallery was away on holidays. The announcement would have to be made in Parliament, with a press conference to follow.

This made sense to Milgaard as well. He was sure his long years of waiting would soon be over.

On September 24, Milgaard remained in his cell during the day. The fall session of the House of Commons was set to resume, and he wanted to see for himself what would happen. His family and lawyers had warned him not to get his hopes up, but the level of excitement was too high for him to pay any attention. He tuned into the Parliamentary channel and anxiously sat through the formalities, waiting for Kim Campbell to rise from her chair and make an announcement.

But the summer had seen many controversial issues nationally and internationally, and there were a multitude of questions that opposition members wanted to pose. A stormy exchange erupted over Canada's response to Iraq's invasion of Kuwait. Another matter that generated heated debate was the Mohawk occupation in Oka, Quebec. Milgaard watched intently. They were all issues he was interested in, issues of importance. But he couldn't hear what was being said. On that day, everything was a blur except the imminent announcement that would set him free.

Finally, Kim Campbell stood up to speak. Milgaard braced himself. But her remarks had nothing to do with David Milgaard. They involved the government's stand on the situation in Oka. Then she sat down again. Milgaard continued to watch, but there was no mention of his case. By the end of the afternoon, he was crushed. When interviewed about his feelings, he exploded in anger. "If I could talk to the Minister of Justice face to face, with the material that she's been given, I would ask her if she's read that. And if she has read that, why hasn't she gotten off her ass and done something with it? Because I have done nothing!"

With no date for the decision in sight, Milgaard sank into a deep depression. He checked into the prison's psychiatric ward where he was given medication for his condition. Attempts by his family and friends to console him were rebuffed. He argued and fought with his mother. He fired his lawyers, only to rehire them a short time later. In the end, he decided that he didn't want a new trial after all. He simply wanted to be set free.

"I've been screwed. They're screwing me now, that's how I feel. A new trial is the same thing. If they have all the evidence in front of them, why delay justice even more? That's a further injustice as far as I'm concerned."

Unknown to Milgaard, the report on his application hadn't even reached the minister's desk by the opening of Parliament. It was still in the process of being drafted by Eugene Williams, the chief investigator. Even after all the evidence was in, it was taking an unusually long time for the bureaucracy within the department to decide whether Milgaard deserved a new trial.

On September 10, David Asper received an unusual call from Ottawa. On the other end was Williams, asking that Asper summarize his position on the Milgaard case. "It was just unbelievable," Asper said. "We were baffled by it. We were starting to get frustrated, because we see the thing so clearly and we can't understand what the problem is."

As soon as Asper got off the phone he dictated a two-page letter to Williams, summarizing the case. The process had begun with an application containing Dr. Ferris's forensic report and the evidence of Deborah Hall. Then there had been Ron Wilson's retraction of his incriminating testimony; the discrediting of Albert Cadrain's testimony because of his mental state; the discrediting of the original forensic evidence by Dr. Markesteyn; the revelations about serial rapist Larry Fisher, and how he might be connected to Gail Miller's murder; the sheer implausibility of Milgaard having committed the crime, given the facts of the case itself.

There was an abrupt, impatient tone to the letter. "We have provided your office with additional evidence that overwhelmingly establishes the innocence of David Milgaard," Asper wrote. He sent the letter to Williams by fax the same day. There was no response.

Over the next few days, Asper and Wolch began to wonder just how much impact their arguments were having on the Justice Department officials reviewing the matter. All along they had felt that a face-to-face meeting would be useful, and now they insisted. The department agreed, and asked the two lawyers to appear in their Ottawa offices on October 1.

Wolch is no stranger to the Justice Department. Over his twenty-five-year career, he has attended many meetings with officials at all levels; he had even worked for the department for two years in the early 1970s. But for Asper, this meeting assumed special significance. It was the culmination of a four-year effort on behalf of Milgaard, the final chapter in the biggest case of his young career. And it was the opportunity to see the people he was trying to convince.

Heading into the meeting, Asper was excited. He came armed with a stack of "Free David Milgaard" bumper stickers and pens bearing the inscription of Wolch's law firm. As the two lawyers walked through the Justice building's fourth floor, they bumped into a number of former Winnipeggers now working with the department in Ottawa. Like a kid at a sports card convention, Asper brandished his bumper stickers and pens, chatting with everyone about the Blue Bombers and their chances for the Grey Cup.

The kibitzing came to an end when Wolch and Asper began their formal meeting with the departmental officials. Present were Eugene Williams, Bill Corbett, and Bruce MacFarlane, the assistant deputy minister. Undeterred by the sombre looks that greeted them when they walked through the door, Asper introduced himself and gave Corbett and Williams each a bumper sticker and a pen. Williams was deadpan, and didn't say a word. Corbett, meanwhile, who had spent the last few months trading verbal barbs with Asper through the media, pushed the items away. Asper's blood pressure started to rise. The fight was on.

"Very early on in the conversation we got to a very intense level, and kept it at an intense level for about five straight hours," Asper said.

Every major aspect of the case was canvassed, with the Justice officials raising their concerns and offering their interpretations. It became instantly clear to Milgaard's lawyers that the Justice officials were inclined to discount any evidence that favoured their client. They were quick to see interpretations that discredited the application and upheld the original verdict. It was, as Wolch would later indicate, a kind of inherent bias that some prosecutors have – a firm belief in everyone's guilt unless the facts of innocence are clearly demonstrated in irrefutable terms.

"They started out believing in guilt very strongly, because to admit to innocence is to admit what would be the greatest legal mistake in Canadian history," Wolch said. "Once they'd taken that mindset, as they got more information, the inclination was: No, it can't be right, or let's pooh-pooh it.

They built themselves a trench and never really dug themselves out."

The first argument to erupt centred on Deborah Hall's affidavit. The department took the position that she actually corroborated Lapchuk and Melnyk's description of how Milgaard acted in the Park Lane Motel. At one point, a department official said the issue could come down to semantics. Asper was livid. "I sprung out of my chair," Asper recalls, "and said, 'My friend, we are not talking about an issue of semantics, we are talking about a huge physical difference in what you say she says and in what she, in fact, says.'"

MacFarlane tried to calm down the atmosphere, but Wolch picked up where his partner had left off. When Milgaard's lawyers had both finished, the Justice officials did not respond. They took careful notes.

The government investigators also intimated that they didn't put too much stock in Ron Wilson's story, as they believed he had something to gain by recanting his original testimony. They suspected Wilson may have feared Milgaard, once released, would come after him for providing the damning testimony at the trial. As for the forensic evidence, they were also sceptical, arguing that the forensic testimony didn't play a large role at the trial, so that any new interpretation of what it meant wasn't very important. Asper and Wolch countered with a summary showing the many pages of trial transcripts devoted to the forensic evidence, and the emphasis the Crown had placed on it during his opening and closing addresses.

Towards the end, Wolch expressed his incredulity that there were so many questions still remaining in what seemed a straightforward case. "You give me every judge on the Supreme Court and I guarantee you that I don't get a dissent," he told them.

The meeting ended abruptly at 5:00 p.m. Williams and Corbett left, leaving MacFarlane – another former Winnipegger and acquaintance of Wolch's – to chat with Milgaard's lawyers for a few minutes. MacFarlane indicated that Williams would be working on the report over the Thanksgiving Day weekend. The minister would likely see it within a couple of weeks, and a very speedy decision would follow.

The meeting didn't bode well for the outcome of the case. All Wolch and Asper could hope for was an honest presentation of all the facts to the minister, and an open mind on her part. At the same time, they realized that the recommendation of the Justice officials would be crucial in swaying Kim Campbell one way or another. And they could not forget that one of those same officials had compared Milgaard's supporters to fanatics who believe Elvis Presley is still alive.

20

Justice Delayed

If the long wait for justice was painful for Milgaard's lawyers, it was doubly so for Joyce Milgaard. Her crusade was reaching its culmination, and she could have been forgiven if she had sat back and patiently awaited the Justice Minister's decision. But patience was never one of her virtues, and inactivity would have been tantamount to abandoning the cause. Even though the lawyers declared that the case was complete and all the evidence was in, she was determined to carry on.

Joyce is the first to admit that her devotion to her son's cause is obsessive. She meticulously tape-records all her telephone conversations dealing with the case, and maintains a small library of tapes and transcripts. "At night I'll be in my room, going through the tapes, cataloguing them and getting them in order." She even tapes conversations with her son, for what she claims is his own good.

"David and I have running battles at times," she said. "He wants to do a certain thing and I want to do a certain thing, and I'll say to him, 'David, you told me this.' And he'll say, 'No, I didn't say that.' And I'll say, 'You be careful, I've got it on tape.'"

Throughout 1990, Joyce's routine was every bit as ordered as her son's. She got up early every morning and spent an hour reading. Then she would begin her daily tasks of phone calls, letter-writing, and organizing. Together with her daughters, Susan and Maureen, she set up booths around Winnipeg to publicize her son's case and encourage people to sign a petition demanding his freedom. They put all the relevant clippings and material on display, speaking to anyone who would listen about David's case. Supporters were asked to buy bumper stickers and badges that promoted the cause.

Letters were written everywhere to drum up support. Joyce felt every avenue should be explored, even the most remote. She wrote to the Queen twice, and took pride in a response that indicated the information was being passed along to the Governor General. "I may be naïve," she told a reporter, "but it gave me hope. Definitely, the Queen has seen what we sent and feels there's merit. She is taking it seriously and asking someone to look into it."

Joyce was never unaware of the wider implications of her fight for justice. Her main objective was freedom for David, but she knew her cause would appeal to all those who distrusted or hated the system of justice in Canada. That group was a large one, consisting generally of the poor, Native people, the youth, and those who felt dispossessed. Canada's jails and prisons are mostly populated with members of those strata of society; they, their friends, and families had a natural tendency to be sympathetic to the Milgaard cause.

Joyce's attempt to win wide support among these groups was not entirely pragmatic. She wanted them to press for the freedom of her son, but she also sympathized with their desire to see a change in how society treated them. "I feel the more people that are aware this injustice is taking place, and that the system should be changed, the better it is. Ideally, I'm fighting for David. That's the main thrust of this, to get David out of prison. But the byproduct of that has got to be that this system has got to change. Because it's a wrong system, and I can't as a citizen support a system that is so totally wrong."

In her quest for publicity, Joyce wasn't afraid to open herself up to potential ridicule. In July, she penned a song that was addressed to Campbell. The manager of Winnipeg's West End

Cultural Centre, a Milgaard supporter, offered the building's space and equipment for Joyce to record her song. Some volunteer musicians were recruited, and the session was quickly arranged. With the media again in attendance, Joyce belted out the tune:

Please, madam minister, listen to me.
Please, madam minister, set David free.
He is not guilty, you have the proof.
How can you stand there, so cold and aloof?

Copies of the recording were sent to radio stations across the country. When the recording session was over, Joyce admitted to reporters that she was a neophyte when it came to music, adding, "I don't ever want to do that again."

Yet she did do it again. A month later she had composed another tune, and this time persuaded the El Mocambo night club in Toronto to let her record it there. It was another personal plea.

It's been a long time since this struggle began.
I've watched as my boy has turned into a man,
Inside of a jail cell, away from us all.
Oh why don't they listen to this mother's call?

Her obsession took other forms. When Asper and his wife had a baby, Joyce noticed he was spending more time than usual with his family and less on the case. She offered to look after the baby so he could start devoting all his waking hours to the job. It was a suggestion that Asper's wife didn't appreciate.

Ruth Asper has perhaps been in the best position to observe how much energy the Milgaard family demanded from those working with them. It has led to some strained situations with her husband. "At the time when Daniel was about to be born, I was wondering where he [her husband] would be at the time. With me, or with David, or Joyce, or one of the sisters. But it worked out well," she says. Still, there were times when her husband's preoccupation took its toll. "He's not completely focussed on our family life," she said. "There are times when we go out for walks, or drives with the baby, or just on our own, and he's got the phone with him. And all he does is talk on the phone. That's how I get updated on the case, but it doesn't give me a chance to communicate with him about other things."

As the year wore on, Joyce felt a sense of urgency that something should happen before Christmas. Christmas has always been an important deadline for her; it had been two days before Christmas in 1980 when Joyce distributed the reward leaflet all over Saskatoon – the real starting point for her crusade to free David.

"Do you know how hard it is to buy a Christmas card for someone in prison?" Joyce asks.

Her hopes of a decision by Christmas 1990 were dampened when Kim Campbell passed through Winnipeg in late November. Inevitably, although she was in town for other business, the question of Milgaard's case arose. She told a television reporter that the case was being delayed by Milgaard's lawyers.

"Where does the Justice Minister get this stuff?" asked John Harvard in the House of Commons when he heard of Campbell's comments. "She is dead wrong. . . . The minister had better get a grip on her department. Someone is feeding her a line. It puts justice under a cloud and makes her look like a fool."

Joyce felt it was important to make one last public relations push, a final act that would force the national media and federal politicians to put the case on the agenda for speedy resolution. She booked a flight to Ottawa and made plans to visit Parliament Hill on December 14, just before the House broke for Christmas. She came armed with copies of the Centurion Ministries' report, which summarized the evidence the Milgaards had submitted to Ottawa.

Every member of Parliament received the report that day, together with a personal plea from Joyce. "I know you're all probably going home soon to spend time with your families for Christmas," her letter said. "The Milgaard family would also like to be together."

MPs who read the Centurion report found an unequivocal exoneration. "When one considers the new evidence in light of the undisputed facts at the trial, one is led to the inescapable conclusion that David Milgaard is absolutely innocent," the report says. "The time has long since passed for the Minister of Justice to intervene and take all steps necessary to see that justice is done. David Milgaard and his family have waited two years for an answer to their application, and the toll is incalculable. Justice delayed is justice denied."

The report unquestionably made an impact on those members who had only a vague idea of the David Milgaard case. For some of the Winnipeg members of Parliament, it prompted them to speak out. As Joyce sat in the visitor's gallery, Liberal MP Lloyd Axworthy made an impassioned plea for her son:

Madam Speaker, I wish to speak of a travesty of justice. I speak of the plight of David Milgaard who has spent the last twenty-one years of his life in prison for a crime he did not commit. Yet for the last two years the Department of Justice has been sitting on an application to reopen his case.

The facts are overwhelming. One of the main witnesses now admits he had lied at the trial. Dr. Ferris, a well-known forensic pathologist, has stated: "I have no reasonable doubt that the evidence presented at the trial failed to link David Milgaard with the offence and that in fact could be reasonably considered to exclude him from being the perpetrator of the murder." Investigators have also identified the person who is most likely the true killer.

But rather than review these conclusive reports, rather than appreciate the agony and trauma of the Milgaard family, the Minister of Justice has refused to act.

I am sure the House will join me in asking the minister to reopen the case. Too many years have been wasted and a human life irreparably affected. The time to act is now.

During Question Period, John Harvard hammered away at the minister so intently that he had to be called to order by the speaker. Campbell was unmoved by the oratory of the Opposition members. She stood her ground, defending her decision to consider the case carefully before making a judgement. "I believe that is what I owe to all parties concerned, and most particularly to the system of justice in Canada," she said.

As Joyce left Ottawa, she realized her hopes of seeing a decision by Christmas would not be fulfilled. Despite the giant advances that had been made in 1990, the year would close with still no end in sight. While her cause had been well-publicized all year, she also knew that the media are fickle and could not be relied on to carry the struggle indefinitely. Stories that deserve front-page treatment one day are all but forgotten the next, as new issues come to the fore. With the furore over the Goods and Services Tax still raging, and war imminent in the Persian Gulf, it would not take long for the media once again to ignore the plight of a man who was trying to convince the world he was innocent.

21

Justice Denied

"Hey, Milgaard, you've got a visitor."

David Milgaard sat up in his cell, startled. It wasn't even noon yet, and someone was here to see him. Clearly this was not going to be an ordinary visit.

It was February 27, 1991, and Milgaard was in the hole at Stony Mountain. He had asked to be removed from the general prison population. The tension of waiting for the decision on his fate was overwhelming, and Milgaard needed some quiet time away from fellow inmates. There was no room in the prison hospital, so he was put in the area usually reserved for punitive dissociation.

Milgaard was led down the corridor to a small room where Stony holds its disciplinary court. The room had a raised platform where the tribunal normally sits, with a desk in front of it. He turned and saw that his visitor was David Asper.

"Here's the decision," Asper said, as he threw the file on the desk. "She turned us down."

Milgaard's eyes glazed. It was as if he wasn't listening to the words being spoken, but gauging what was happening by Asper's movements.

"I don't remember much else of what was said," Asper recalled. "I was apologizing to him. I was pacing the room, but

I don't remember what I was saying. My impression was that it didn't really sink in."

Once Milgaard realized what was happening, he reacted serenely. "He was consoling me!" Asper said. "He was saying it's okay, don't worry. He said, 'I'm as innocent today as I was yesterday, and somewhere in this system is justice, and we will find it.'"

After a few minutes, Asper left and Milgaard was led back to his cell. Twenty-six months after appealing his case to the minister of justice, Milgaard had his answer. He had refused to take a copy of the decision from Asper. The first paragraph of the press release was all he needed to hear.

"The Honourable Kim Campbell, Minister of Justice, today announced that she will not intervene in the conviction of David Milgaard for the murder in 1969 of Gail Miller, a Saskatoon nursing assistant."

It took two weeks for Milgaard to react publicly to the decision. When he did, there was a subdued anger in his tone. "I couldn't believe the news," he said. "It's hard to explain, I just couldn't believe it. I just felt sick inside. It's so sad."

Asper strode out of the prison where David's sister Susan was waiting for him. They had driven to Stony together, but prison regulations didn't allow her to see her brother in the hole. As they began the drive back to Winnipeg, Asper finally felt the impact of what had happened that day. "I felt like a horrible failure," he said. "I didn't succeed. Maybe I did something wrong; maybe things that weren't done should have been done; maybe we should have gone further out on a limb moneywise; maybe we should have insisted on being with Wilson when he was interviewed; maybe we should have done this or that. I don't know. So I felt a big sense of failure."

By the time Asper got back to the city, the Justice Department had made its decision public. Officials wanted to wait until Milgaard himself had been notified before telling the press.

The timing of the announcement seemed carefully calculated to draw the least possible reaction. The press release was distributed on the same day the Gulf War was coming to its conclusion – virtually guaranteeing that the news of Milgaard's plight would be lost in the sea of headlines about the war. Although the House of Commons was in session, the news was released outside the chamber while Question Period was in progress. That meant many reporters were caught off guard by the release; and it also insulated Campbell from being grilled by the Opposition in the House the same day.

Joyce Milgaard was in New Jersey that day, and Asper had the painful duty of informing her as well. She was devastated by the news. But she was quick to put it into perspective. For her, it didn't represent a final defeat, only a setback in the long struggle that had become the central focus of her life. A struggle that would continue with undiminished force.

Joyce made immediate plans to return to Winnipeg that evening, and when reporters met her at the airport there was no hint of defeatism in her voice. "We're going to come out fighting, that's all we can do," she told a reporter. "We'll just start all over again if that's what it takes to prove David is innocent. We're not down, and we're certainly not going to give up."

The next day, there was an emotional family reunion at Stony Mountain. A news conference to respond formally to the decision was called for the afternoon, only to be abruptly cancelled. The family decided to allow for a breathing space so everyone could put the events of the last twenty-four hours into perspective. It would also allow a thorough review by Asper and Wolch of the twelve-page judgement that Campbell had rendered.

. The Justice Department had provided only a brief communiqué and background note to the media regarding its decision. In the communiqué, Campbell noted that the opinion of an eminent specialist in criminal law – former Supreme Court Justice William McIntyre – was sought before she reached her conclusion.

"There has been a thorough and diligent review of every piece of evidence submitted. I have concluded that there is no reason to believe that a miscarriage of justice is likely to have occurred in this case," Campbell said.

Campbell provided a more detailed judgement to Hersh Wolch. It explained how the department viewed each piece of evidence the lawyers had submitted.

On Deborah Hall's affidavit, the minister states that Hall confirmed the testimony heard at trial about Milgaard's reenactment of the murder in a Regina motel room in May 1969. The only difference in her testimony, she says, is Hall's interpretation that she felt Milgaard was making a "sick" comment and was not serious.

Interpretation, however, is the key aspect of the testimony; otherwise, anyone who ever made a joke about a crime would be considered a suspect. The minister doesn't address the Crown's decision to call Lapchuk and Melnyk, two witnesses of questionable character who had charges pending against them at the time, while making no effort to locate Hall. Of the three, Hall is by far the most credible. But Campbell wasn't impressed. "Whether her opinion of Milgaard's sincerity would have been shared by the jury is, at best, debatable. . . . The information provided by Deborah Hall does not detract from the evidence led at trial."

On the forensic evidence: In discussing the reports by Dr. James Ferris and Dr. Peter Markesteyn, Campbell points out that neither study actually exonerates Milgaard. She notes that the forensic evidence presented at the trial was all based on samples found days after the murder – samples that in all likelihood were contaminated.

"In the final analysis, the forensic evidence presented at trial proved nothing. With the benefit of hindsight, it may have been preferable had the evidence simply not been tendered. Nevertheless, the case against Milgaard was a strong one. The suggestion that the forensic evidence exonerates Milgaard mis-states the value of that evidence. The forensic evidence tendered at trial, when elevated to its highest probative value, is neutral, establishing neither guilt nor innocence. The recent opinions do not establish that the evidence should now be viewed any differently."

Campbell does not address why the Crown spent hours at the original trial eliciting evidence that was merely neutral.

Of the two likely conclusions offered by the new forensic reports – that the samples were either contaminated, or that they exonerated Milgaard – she chooses the former, without offering any compelling reason.

On the new evidence from Ron Wilson, Campbell simply states that she doesn't believe Wilson is now telling the truth when he says he lied on the stand because of police pressure. She notes a number of inconsistencies when comparing the stories he told police and the jury, and his statement of 1990. Most importantly, she says, Wilson alleged he was coerced into implicating Milgaard after he was brought to Saskatoon for a "sweat session" by police in May 1969. She notes that his previous testimony and statements show that he first implicated Milgaard several days earlier, while still in Regina.

"On the whole of the evidence available to me, I can find no basis for confidence in Mr. Wilson's allegations that his statement incriminating Milgaard was obtained by the manipulation or coercion of police investigators. The current retraction by Mr. Wilson of much of his trial evidence is unconvincing."

Once again, the minister picks the interpretation most unfavourable to Milgaard's case. If Wilson is an unreliable person and someone prone to lying, as Campbell herself says, what value should be placed on his original trial testimony? If Campbell's arguments about the reliability of Wilson had been presented to the original jury, would they have believed the Crown's key witness?

On the suggestion that Albert Cadrain's mental condition made his testimony unreliable, Campbell says, "Little if any weight can be given to suggestions that Albert Cadrain's trial testimony was unreliable. While Mr. Cadrain experienced personal and emotional difficulties *after* the trial, his trial evidence was confirmed by other witnesses and has since been confirmed by inquiries conducted during this application. It should be noted that he withstood a vigorous cross-examination by experienced counsel. Mr. Cadrain's personal difficulties since the trial do not detract from the credibility of the evidence he provided during the trial."

Yet again, the minister seems to ignore facts that have come to light since the trial: Cadrain's fanciful tales about the Mafia, his intense paranoia, his pre-trial visions of snakes and the Virgin Mary, his receipt of the reward for implicating Milgaard. To suggest that his trial testimony was confirmed by "other witnesses," principally by Wilson, doesn't lend much credibility to his story.

On the possibility that Larry Fisher may be the real killer: Campbell devotes a single paragraph to the matter, noting that all of Linda Fisher's assertions were investigated. She says the paring knife Linda Fisher reported missing was different in colour and type from the one found at the murder scene.

The minister didn't seem convinced that evidence about a serial rapist who had attacked women in the same neighbourhood, who had a similar *modus operandi* to the Miller murderer, who apparently took the same bus to work every morning as Miller, and who lived in the Cadrain house would have had any impact on the jury's decision that Milgaard was the real killer.

"However serious Mr. Fisher's criminal record may be, the entire record at trial and in this application reveals no evidence to connect him with the killing of Gail Miller. Although it was, as you have conceded, quite coincidental that Mr. Fisher resided at the Cadrain residence during Mr. Milgaard's visit, no guilt or suspicion of guilt can be attributed to Fisher in the absence of some form of evidence linking him to the crime."

On the suggestion that the physical evidence and timing of events was not consistent with Milgaard having committed the crime, she states: "The submissions concerning the location of the offence and Mr. Milgaard's opportunity to commit the offence were fully canvassed by trial counsel and by the judge who properly charged them on that point. . . . There is no new evidence to suggest that their conclusion was probably wrong."

Wolch was astonished by the decision. Not only did it contain factual errors (Cadrain, for instance, said he had experienced mental anguish and saw visions *before* his testimony, not after), it deliberately highlighted some minor aspects while leaving other crucial evidence out altogether.

"It didn't strike me as being a judicious decision," Wolch said. "It struck me that this was the argument being advanced by the prosecution, saying here's why you should decide the following as opposed to weighing both sides. All the strong arguments were just passed by. It was picking and choosing whatever they wanted to pick and choose, believing people in certain situations and not in others."

Wolch denounced the department's tactic of only putting those witnesses it wanted to attack under oath. Not only did this standard not apply to others, such as the police officers involved in the case, but the police were also allowed to refresh their memories by examining original notes and statements. Wilson, meanwhile, was expected to remember everything he had said twenty years earlier, and when discrepancies arose, they were used to discredit him.

"I find it so bewildering, and that's why it's so frustrating not to be able to argue with them. I would love to sit down and debate it in front of any tribunal anywhere," Wolch said.

Wolch was not the only one to express outrage. Politicians, social workers, lawyers, and others joined in the chorus. The decision, however, was not up for debate. It was final.

On March 12, Stony Mountain penitentiary was invaded by a small army of reporters, photographers and television cameramen as the Milgaard family convened a press conference. It was the first time since the decision was announced that David Milgaard agreed to comment publicly. Flanked by his parents and two sisters, Milgaard opened the news conference with an emotional statement:

First of all I would like to thank all of you for being here. In terms of the decision I guess the best thing is just to say how I feel. I feel kind of swollen up emotionally right now, and I'm nervous, but I've written this down and I'll do the best I can.

My fight and my family's struggle for my freedom is not over. There is no honest explanation for the Justice Department's failure to add up all the facts correctly. I feel that's the truth in my heart. These facts speak for themselves and prove that I'm an innocent man. The case has been gone over, reviewed, and analyzed many times. How is it possible for these facts to be ignored?

I now challenge the Justice Department and Kim Campbell, the Minister of Justice, to come out from behind their closed doors. We challenge them to show the country how it was possible for me to commit the crime at all. Kim Campbell and her department are not worthy. And her integrity is in question.

There are so many people in the community, groups and organizations, still behind my family and me. We thank you all from the bottom of our hearts. Our next campaign will be to have the government simply face the facts. It isn't just a matter of me. The system is failing. It's a matter of justice for everyone.

There were more speeches and comments. The family pledged to fight on, appealing to the Federal Court and the Saskatchewan Court of Appeal for justice. Political pressure would be escalated, new evidence would be found.

When it was all over, after the reporters had rushed out to file their stories, David Milgaard was led back to his cell to continue serving his sentence for life imprisonment.

The next day, Milgaard appeared before the National Parole Board for a routine hearing. He had asked permission to be enrolled in a program of unescorted temporary absences. According to criteria set by the board, one of the cardinal requirements for any inmate seeking parole is: "You must show that you understand what you did and how you hurt someone else."

David Milgaard has never been able to show that he understands what he did and how he hurt someone else.

His application was turned down.

22

Final Judgement

David's disappointment quickly turned to despair inside Stony Mountain penitentiary. Despite the brave words at his press conference, he realized the campaign to set him free had failed. With nothing more to look forward to, he settled back into the prison routine. But many of the inmates, as well as some staff, were not so eager to forget the past. They resented all the media attention that had been focused on one of their own. Now it was their turn to gloat. David became the butt of ridicule and derision.

He sought refuge from the general prison population, first in the hospital wing and then, when it was full, in solitary confinement. He sank deeper and deeper into depression, refusing to see anyone. Requests for a transfer to other institutions were denied. Family members began to fear for his sanity.

Like his client, David Asper also craved solitude in the days following the justice minister's decision. He took a week off work, and spent most of his time at home, reluctant to venture out socially. "Everywhere I go people ask me about it. I knew I would see people who'd say, 'How about that Milgaard case?' And I didn't want to deal with that."

Back at work, Asper tried to catch up on his other cases. He won an acquittal for a client after a two-day trial, but the sense of satisfaction was weak. He couldn't get his mind off the Milgaard case, even though all appeals, and now the final plea for mercy, had been rejected. Asper consulted Wolch about the next move, and asked for feedback from other lawyers in the firm. There was talk of approaching the Saskatchewan Court of Appeal with the fresh evidence and asking for a new hearing – until a spokesman for the Saskatchewan Attorney General said the court wouldn't get involved unless the federal Justice Department asked it to. A constitutional law professor in Ottawa was contacted, and Asper began formulating strategy for an action in federal court. Still, he realized the chances were slim. Overturning the justice minister's decision would be a monumental and unprecedented task.

Joyce Milgaard wasn't content to rely solely on the legal avenues. She realized there was more investigative work to be done, especially when it came to Larry Fisher. There was no indication Kim Campbell had given any serious credence to the possibility that Fisher was the real killer. Campbell had not even bothered interviewing Fisher's victims to determine if the *modus operandi* was similar to the one used by Gail Miller's murderer. Joyce knew what had to be done. If Campbell was unwilling to interview the victims, someone else would have to do the job for her.

Joyce realized she would need help. Once again she contacted Jim McCloskey of Centurion Ministries, who in turn phoned Paul Henderson and offered to pay his fee. Henderson, who was outraged by Campbell's decision to deny the application, was happy to get involved in the case once more. But he was hesitant about the particular assignment.

"I told Jim, to begin with, I did not feel comfortable about my chances of looking up brutalized rape victims twenty years later and rekindling the horror of what they went through by myself. I said I think Joyce has to be with me. And that was certainly the right call, because in each of the cases Joyce was the one who would speak first, and it worked out fine."

A skip-tracing firm tracked down all of Fisher's victims, and by late April Henderson and Joyce Milgaard began the unsavoury task of getting them to relive that horrific period of their lives. Over the next two weeks, they made contact with all of them, persuading them to share their memories of the attacks. Some of the victims were reluctant. In one case, they conducted the interview in the victim's car with her two-year-old son strapped in the back seat. Other women were happy to talk about their experiences, inviting Joyce and Henderson into their homes. Some took them to the scene of the attacks, pointing out in detail where everything had taken place.

Joyce was astounded to learn from Fisher's four Saskatoon victims that police had never notified them about Fisher's arrest and confessions. One of the women said she has lived in fear for the last twenty years that her attacker might return one day. She keeps the doors to her house locked day and night – far from the norm in rural Saskatchewan, where she lives. Life for her would have been very different if she had known that Fisher had been safely behind bars all these years. For Joyce, the failure by Saskatoon police to notify victims of the arrest was one more indication that they were reluctant to publicize Larry Fisher's crimes, for fear of casting doubt on David Milgaard's conviction.

Fisher's four victims in Saskatoon and two in Winnipeg all painted the same picture of an attacker who grabbed them from behind and dragged them to an alley or secluded spot before raping them. In some cases, he rifled through their purses after the assault. Three of the Saskatoon incidents took place within blocks of the Miller murder. And all his victims were young women, most in their late teens, who routinely took the bus to work or school. In almost all the attacks he was armed with a knife, and all the victims felt lucky to have escaped with their lives. The similarities to Gail Miller's rape and murder were too numerous to ignore.

Henderson, who reported back to McCloskey every day on the results of their interviews, was amazed at the cooperation they received from Fisher's victims. He took no personal credit. "The success of this particular trip went far beyond anybody's expectations, thanks to the gentle, persuasive manner of Joyce," he said. "We were six for six on Fisher's 1968-1970 victims, and we walked in on [Ellen Samuelson]. Her nightmare was probably the most traumatic of all. This was the one interview we particularly dreaded."

Samuelson had been savagely raped by Fisher a block from her North Battleford, Saskatchewan home in March 1980, shortly after Fisher had been paroled for his previous offences. She was fifty-six years old at the time. Following the rape, with no provocation, Fisher had slashed her throat and stabbed her in the chest. He had tied her hands and legs and left her for dead.

"Of all of Fisher's victims, we expected to find this woman still terrified and most resistant to recounting the horror she'd been through," Henderson wrote in his report of the interview. "Instead, she was courageous and totally cooperative. We didn't have to convince [Ellen] that Gail Miller was murdered by Fisher. She has suspected this ever since Fisher's name surfaced a year ago in the Milgaard case. This is not to say that [Ellen] is no longer traumatized. While relating her ordeal, she started shaking and sobbing and almost became hysterical. But what frightens her the most is the prospect of Fisher being released this year."

Here was a crime that was almost identical to the Miller murder – a rape followed by a senseless stabbing. But Samuelson provided an even closer link. During his attack on her, Fisher claimed to have done this to a woman before, adding that he had "slit her throat." For Joyce and Henderson, that was as good as a confession to the Miller murder.

Back in Winnipeg, Joyce, David Asper, and Paul Henderson excitedly compiled their findings into a thick blue binder. At the back, they included a map which showed the location of Fisher's Saskatoon offences in relation to the Miller murder. It was a compelling and damning document. No direct link was established between Fisher and Gail Miller, but the circumstantial evidence of similar offences at roughly the same time and place was immediately obvious.

In August, the binder was released to the press. The reaction was overwhelming. Once again the Milgaard case was in the news, and this time the focus was on Larry Fisher as the likely killer. The *Toronto Star* carried extensive coverage of the latest findings, encouraging the *Globe and Mail* to follow suit soon afterwards. People across the country who had only vaguely heard of David Milgaard were now being bombarded with information about the case. Editorial writers jumped on the bandwagon, with the *Globe and Mail* writing, for instance, that "in the interest of justice, we believe Ms. Campbell should reverse her decision and order a new trial for Mr. Milgaard to confirm or reject the original verdict."

Reporters tried to scoop their colleagues with new revelations about the Milgaard case. One report claimed that police files relating to Larry Fisher's Saskatoon rapes were mysteriously missing. Another said the original polygraph tests given to Ron Wilson in 1969 had also gone astray. Whether all this was a result of tampering on someone's part, bungling, or routine destruction of outdated files, no one knew for sure. The Saskatoon police department was refusing to make any comment.

Just when the Milgaard camp felt they had learned as much as they possibly could about the freezing morning of January 31, 1969, in Saskatoon, there was another revelation. A woman in Toronto, reading about Larry Fisher's string of crimes in her old hometown, came forward to say that she too had been attacked on January 31, 1969, by a man who bore a strong resemblance to Fisher. In a sworn affidavit, she said she had been on her way to the university at about eight in the morning when a man emerged from a back lane across the street and began walking towards her. She had been on Avenue H near 20th Street, some half dozen blocks from the spot where Gail Miller's body lay. The man had shoved her a couple of times and grabbed her between the legs. The woman had dropped her school books and screamed, and the assailant had run off.

It was a strange story to emerge nearly twenty-three years after the fact, but the woman was not making it up. She had proof that she reported it to Saskatoon police at the time. Again, the police could offer no explanation as to why this attack was never publicized at the time.

In the midst of all the media excitement, Asper bundled the blue binder off to Ottawa with a covering letter. It was a second application to the justice minister under Section 690 of the Criminal Code. On the basis of the new evidence, he was asking her once more to order a new hearing for David Milgaard. This time, Asper had a powerful ally in the application. During the summer, with Jim McCloskey's assistance, Gail Miller's family was persuaded to join in the campaign to give Milgaard another hearing. The family issued a statement saying that the new evidence gave them reason to feel "there is reasonable doubt as to the guilt of David Edgar Milgaard."

Once again, David Milgaard's fate was in the hands of the minister of justice. But his mother wasn't content to sit back and wait quietly for a decision. Joyce took advantage of every opportunity to mobilize public opinion for the cause. And a big opportunity was on the way. In early September, Prime Minister Brian Mulroney planned to visit Winnipeg for the first time in three years. As soon as Joyce heard about the visit, she knew she had to be there.

Mulroney arrived in Winnipeg on September 5, and was immediately besieged by striking postal workers and public servants. The television cameras rolled as angry workers pounded on his limousine and hurled abuse. Joyce knew she couldn't compete with the fury of the workers, who were denouncing the government's attempts to freeze their wages and endanger job security. Nor did she want a confrontation with the prime minister. She approached one of Mulroney's aides and said she would like an opportunity to speak to him. She was startled when the aide said that the prime minister had every intention of doing just that.

The next day, Joyce and about thirty supporters gathered outside a hotel where Mulroney was to address a gathering of Conservative Party faithful. They held a banner and placards calling for David Milgaard to be freed. The group lit twenty-two candles, one for every year of David's imprisonment, and said a prayer. Joyce told a reporter the demonstration was a peaceful way of bringing the issue to Mulroney's attention. "I don't want to bother him or go up to him or do anything. I don't want to be put into a position to look like I'm chasing someone down a hallway," she said. Try as she might, though, she couldn't erase the image of her pursuit of Kim Campbell a year earlier, when Campbell had rushed past her and refused to discuss anything. This time the media was out in full force, anticipating some sort of repetition of that confrontation.

Suddenly, a blue sedan pulled in front of the hotel. Mulroney emerged from the back seat, and an aide led him directly to Joyce.

"This is Mrs. Milgaard right here," the aide said. Mulroney walked up to Joyce and shook her hand. Surrounded by reporters, Joyce seized the opportunity. "Thank you, I've been trying to see you just to ask you, anything that you could do to help towards getting him transferred would be so helpful."

The prime minister listened intently as Joyce spoke about David's health, and her urgent desire for a quick resolution to the appeal. Mulroney was clearly well-briefed before the exchange. He was intent on not repeating Kim Campbell's performance of a year earlier, when the image of an uncaring minister rushing past a distraught mother had been conveyed to television viewers across Canada.

"I've just checked in Ottawa," Mulroney said, "and I gather that information is either *en route* or has just been received down there, so they'll be taking a close look at it very soon . . . . Miss Campbell is going to take a look at the new information that has come in. And I'm sure that the minister of justice will be back to the attorney general and so on, but – "

"A speedy review?" Joyce asked.

"Well, I can't speak for her but I'll be talking to her when I get back."

"Thank you."

"But I'm happy to see you," Mulroney said, extending his hand again. "I hope you're well."

"I'm trying my very best."

"I know you are. You're working very hard. You're very courageous."

After a few more words, Mulroney turned to leave. "I suppose we know where we can reach you?" he said.

"You certainly do," Joyce replied, and they shook hands a third time before Mulroney was ushered into the hotel by his aides.

The entire exchange lasted just under three minutes, but for Joyce Milgaard it seemed like a turning point. The prime minister himself was aware of her son's plight, and had promised to intervene directly. Surely justice would now prevail.

Hopes were high that some good news would emerge from the new Parliamentary session that opened ten days later. But there was no announcement, or even a hint of one. The euphoria that spread through the Milgaard camp following Mulroney's conversation with Joyce began to evaporate when Kim Campbell was asked for her interpretation of the prime minister's intervention.

"The prime minister would never, ever interfere with the exercise of discretion of the [justice minister] on an important question like this," she told reporters outside the House of Commons. "The prime minister is too good a lawyer to make that kind of a statement." Instead, Campbell said, Mulroney had expressed concern over Milgaard's health. That's what he meant when he said he would "look into it right away," she said, adding that he had already raised the issue with her. "I think that was a very humane and humanitarian concern on the part of the prime minister."

Once again, David Milgaard could do nothing else but wait in his prison cell. His fate was still in the hands of the Canadian justice system – a system that had convicted him and confined him to prison for most of his life. A system that had failed him since the moment he was arrested in 1969.

Last Words

"Mercy as set out in Section 690 means a royal prerogative of mercy, and is not the subject of legal rights. It begins where legal rights end."
— Snow's Annotated Criminal Code of Canada

As this book goes to press in early November 1991, David Milgaard is still waiting to hear if Justice Minister Kim Campbell will set him free. His legal rights ended more than twenty years ago, when he exhausted all avenues of appeal. No matter how powerful the evidence in his favour, his only hope for freedom is the royal prerogative of mercy – a prerogative no longer exercised in Canada by the Queen, but by the elected minister of justice. Even if mercy is extended to him, his ordeal is far from over. It will undoubtedly take years for him to clear his name conclusively, win adequate compensation, and reintegrate into society after such a long absence.

Section 690 of the Criminal Code allows for a number of different responses by the justice minister. The simplest course, and the one followed in the vast majority of cases, is for the minister to deny the application. No reasons need be given for the decision, and there is no requirement that the outcome be made public. The minister's judgement, like the investigative process itself, can remain shrouded in secrecy forever.

The section also allows the minister to order a new trial or hearing for the applicant. In this case, the Crown would have to reintroduce all the relevant evidence against the accused in an effort to convince a judge or jury to reconvict. The minister is also empowered to refer any question relating to the case to an appeal court for its opinion. A more usual course of events

258

would be for the minister to refer the entire case to a court of appeal, normally in the jurisdiction where the original offence occurred. The court would then decide whether to call witnesses or simply hear arguments as to why the applicant should have his conviction overturned. In Milgaard's case, a reference to the Saskatchewan Court of Appeal would pose some problems. Calvin Tallis, his original defence counsel, is now a member of that court.

There is also the possibility that the minister would recommend the applicant be given a pardon. The Criminal Code allows the government to issue pardons in exceptional circumstances, even when all levels of courts have determined that an accused is guilty.

No matter which option Kim Campbell chooses in the case of David Milgaard, the Justice Department and the entire system of justice in Canada will remain under a cloud. The minister will have to explain why she and her department did not adequately investigate the first Milgaard application before rejecting it in February 1991. She will have to explain why it fell to the Milgaard family to uncover evidence about Larry Fisher and his victims – evidence that was readily available to the department if it had the will to pursue it. She will have to explain why an independent review mechanism to deal with allegations of wrongful conviction has never been instituted, even though this was strongly recommended two years ago by the Hickman Royal Commission on the Donald Marshall prosecution.

Anyone reading this book who is familiar with Donald Marshall's ordeal will undoubtedly experience a sense of *déjà vu*. In almost every key respect, there are echoes of Marshall's case in the Milgaard story. Both were sentenced to life imprisonment at the age of seventeen for murders they did not commit. Both were victims of overzealous police departments that pressured young and impressionable witnesses into changing their original stories. Both were unjustifiably deemed troublemakers and dangerous characters by investigating officers. And both were kept incarcerated even when convincing evidence of another suspect surfaced.

The Hickman Royal Commission, after an exhaustive investigation into the Marshall case, found fault with virtually every facet of the justice system, including the police, the Crown, Marshall's own defence counsel, the trial judge, the RCMP, and the courts. It mercilessly exposed the hypocrisy of the justice system for trying to blame Marshall himself for his plight, and for attempting to cover up the blatant injustice of the original conviction. Even after Marshall's conviction was overturned, the Nova Scotia Court of Appeal declared that "any miscarriage of justice is more apparent than real" and that "Donald Marshall's untruthfulness through this whole affair contributed in large measure to his conviction." The Royal Commission denounced those sentiments, stating that "for any citizen to spend eleven years in a federal penitentiary for a crime he did not commit constitutes – even in the narrowest sense – a miscarriage of justice in the extreme."

Another important parallel in the two cases is the manner in which both Marshall and Milgaard were treated by prison staff and the parole system. The Hickman commission notes, "Corrections personnel, not surprisingly, act on the assumption that people incarcerated are guilty of the offences for which they have been found guilty. If an inmate persists in claiming innocence, this would be regarded as a negative indication that the inmate has not come to terms with his or her guilt." This conclusion was drawn, in part, from the testimony provided by Diahann McConkey, Marshall's former parole officer and a member of the National Parole Board. The following exchange comes from McConkey's testimony to the royal commission:

> Q. . . . if a man is in jail and has been found guilty of an offence, then you have to assume that he is guilty of the offence. But there is just that small possibility that he may not be guilty of the offence, yet during the entire length of his stay in jail, you have to presume that he is guilty and accordingly get him to come to terms with the factors that led to that offence. You've got to act that way.

A. To a certain extent, yes. And if he does not ever acknowledge his guilt, it may well be seen as one negative factor, but by no means an overriding factor, ever at any time.

Q. But surely, Ms. McConkey, the effect of this approach is that for the prisoner claiming innocence, he has a harder time getting released.

A. I would think so, yes.

Chief Justice Alexander Hickman concluded that the criminal justice system failed Donald Marshall at virtually every turn, from his arrest and conviction in 1971 up to and beyond his acquittal in 1983. He insisted that this miscarriage of justice could have and should have been prevented. Hickman offered eighty-two specific recommendations for ensuring that future travesties do not occur.

The scathing nature of Hickman's findings explains, in part, the federal government's reluctance to reopen the Milgaard case. The government is not eager to have the most basic tenets of its justice system called into question yet again. After all, the Marshall affair can no longer be deemed an unfortunate and rare occurrence when a similar case surfaces so soon afterwards. Any admission that a miscarriage of justice might have taken place in the Milgaard case would almost certainly necessitate another royal commission or public inquiry. Everyone involved in the original investigation and prosecution would be called upon to explain what happened. It might prove embarrassing for many people, including those who occupy positions of authority and prestige in Saskatchewan today.

Whatever the outcome, there is little doubt that the public's faith in Canada's justice system has been severely shaken. And public confidence sinks even lower when the elected official who acts as the court of last resort insists on conducting business behind the cloak of bureaucratic secrecy.

No one can reasonably demand that a system of justice, in whatever country, be perfect. But as a minimum, it must discharge its obligations with the highest ideals in mind. And it must never shrink from admitting that a miscarriage of justice has occurred, when the evidence so warrants. The British Section of the International Commission of Jurists, in its report on miscarriages of justice in 1989, summed up the situation aptly when it said, "The manner in which a society concerns itself with persons who may have been wrongly convicted and imprisoned must be one of the yardsticks by which civilization is measured."